Beyond the Barricades

The Sixties Generation Grows Up

Beyond the Barricades

The Sixties Generation Grows Up

JACK WHALEN AND RICHARD FLACKS

 Temple University Press · Philadelphia

Temple University Press, Philadelphia 19122
Copyright © 1989 by Temple University. All rights reserved
Published 1989
Printed in the United States of America

The paper used in this publication meets the minimum
requirements of American National Standard for Information
Sciences—Permanence of Paper for Printed Library Materials,
ANSI Z39.48-1984

Library of Congress Cataloging-in-Publication Data

Whalen, Jack
    Beyond the barricades : the sixties generation grows up / Jack
Whalen and Richard Flacks.
      p. cm.
    Bibliography: p.
    Includes index.
    ISBN 0-87722-606-7
    1. Student movements—California—Longitudinal studies.
2. College students—California—Political activity—Longitudinal
studies. I. Flacks, Richard. II. Title.
LA243.5.W48 1989
378'.198'1—dc 19   88-39172
                                        CIP

Contents

Acknowledgments

First and foremost, we want to give our heartfelt thanks to the men and women whose life stories form the basis of this book. Because we promised to protect their identities, we cannot name them, but these thirty-four people are the real authors of the stories we tell. Indeed, they gave so much of themselves to us that no thanks can ever be adequate. All we can hope is that we have been true to some of the meanings and textures of the lives they are trying to live.

The study on which this book is based had its beginnings in discussions during a seminar on political consciousness that Dick Flacks organized for graduate students in sociology at the University of California, Santa Barbara. Rob Rosenthal, Craig Reinarman, and David Keown were among the members of that group, and all provided important ideas and much-appreciated social support as Jack Whalen shaped the proposed study into a doctoral dissertation. Jack's office mate, Douglas Maynard, also spent many hours discussing the project with him, contributing valuable suggestions and earnest (but always gentle) criticisms.

Other colleagues at Santa Barbara also deserve thanks. Sarah Fenstermaker, Don Zimmerman, and Richard Appelbaum served as members of Whalen's dissertation committee and provided much help in organizing the work and supplying needed encouragement. Kim de Cunha and Jannalee Smithey served as staff on the project from 1980 to 1983, transcribing many of the interview sessions and doing a variety of other tasks that were indispensable and thankless.

We benefited from reactions to earlier reports of this research by others doing similar studies, particularly Doug McAdam and Richard Braungart. Other colleagues and friends whose criticisms and suggestions were valuable include Mary Freifeld, Dave Goldberg, Mimi and Paul Goldman, and the late Al Szymanski.

Steve Cavrak read the entire manuscript and offered editorial and substantive comments that were especially helpful in the final stages of the project. Carl Boggs evaluated the manuscript at various stages; his thoughtful comments suggested that he understood the book better than we did.

Marilyn Whalen read each and every word we wrote on this material and literally lived with all of it as well. She has been a tireless and wonderfully caring critic. All of us—Jack and Marilyn Whalen, Dick and Mickey Flacks—were ourselves participants in the movements of the sixties. Inevitably, and we think fruitfully, the family lives we have constructed since provide an important part of the context for what is written here.

Financial assistance from both the Academic Senate and the Graduate Division of the University of California, Santa Barbara, and from the grants-in-aid program of the Society for the Psychological Study of Social Issues was crucial for the completion of the project. Early reports on the study were published in *Sociological Focus* (Whalen and Flacks, 1980), the *Journal of Political and Military Sociology* (Whalen and Flacks, 1984), and *Radical Teacher* (Whalen and Flacks, 1982). The *Utne Reader* reprinted material from all these reports in their October/November 1986 issue (no. 18, pp. 51–58). Jack Whalen's doctoral dissertation (Whalen, 1984) is the foundation for this work.

Finally, we owe special thanks to the people at Temple University Press who brought this book into being. Janet Francendese provided detailed comments that greatly improved the work in both stylistic and substantive ways; it was, we feel, something of a privilege to have had her as our editor. Thanks also for the patience and enthusiasm of Jane Barry, Steve Wallace, and Richard Gilbertie.

Eugene, Oregon and Santa Barbara, California
February 1989

Beyond the Barricades

The Sixties Generation Grows Up

1

The Fate of Sixties Activism: An Introduction

What happens to youthful idealism as people leave their youth behind? Can an identity centered on active dissent be sustained over the long haul? Where do young revolutionaries go when the revolution doesn't happen? These perennial questions in our culture are usually raised most forcefully by those most dubious about the possibility of transforming either individuals or the world for the better. In every generation, voices of "realism" and "maturity" say to those who are questioning established ways: "Wait till you grow up. You will inevitably come to accept things the way they are." In such dialogue, the fact that youths ask questions and challenge authority may be tolerated and even welcomed, but it is assumed that "radical" protest and "idealistic" commitment are developmental phases that precede adulthood. In this view, the mental soundness or patriotism of older radical activists is questioned, since they are perceived as adopting a stance inappropriate for their age and station. Oddly enough, a very elderly radical whose moral consistency has been sustained over a lifetime typically is relabeled. Yesterday's "crazy" might be regarded as a saint if he or she lives long enough. Saints, however, are also deviant. If saints are the only people who can remain principled throughout life, then the notion that youthful idealism is normally abandoned is not challenged.

Such beliefs about the ephemerality of idealism have gained force since the end of the 1960s, when young people led a wide-ranging revolt against established authority and conventional culture. Defined in large measure as a generational rebellion, this revolt differed significantly from those in previous periods, since, for the most part, earlier protest movements were based in classes (farmers, industrial workers) or in other social groups and were not sharply age-graded. During such upheavals, youth added much spark and fervor and young intellectuals and artists vigorously criticized established ways, but even in the period of bohemian protest prior to World War I, few young participants defined their stance in terms of their youthfulness or their generational membership. The sheer number of youths who participated in the sixties' rebellions therefore makes the "fate of youthful idealism" a central issue for social understanding.

Even more important were the reasons for these rebellions. The sixties youth revolt was in part about the possibility of redefining "adulthood" in our society. If a single theme united the otherwise disparate forms of political and cultural protest that characterized the period, it was the romantic belief that the young could make themselves into new persons, that they need not follow in their parents' footsteps, that they could build lives in which they could exercise a degree of self-mastery not given by the established structures of role, relationship, and routine. In a sense, what was being sought—and what many believed possible—was a life in which one remained a youth. That is, if adulthood involves settling in to a particular identity, which is bounded by a particular set of roles and relationships, and if youth is, instead, a time in which one is free to continuously reformulate one's identity, the attempt to sustain that freedom forever can be construed as an attempt to reject adulthood.

From another angle, the great personal hope of the sixties was that one would be able to live a life of ongoing self-examination, a life of scrutinizing the moral content of one's actions, a life grounded in principle and social responsibility, a life of service, care, and commitment to justice and social betterment. Such visions and hopes can be read in the rhetoric of movement leaders and in the arguments of interpreters and ideologues of the New Left and the counterculture (see, for example, Roszak 1969 and Reich 1970). Such sentiments could also be read in the dress and demeanor of the era, for the most evident meaning of long hair and blue jeans was that one was deliberately trying to look like anything but a conventional adult. And there was the music, which not only expressed teenage hostility to adult authority, but seemed, both explicitly and implicitly, to advocate a different "style of being" from that which was programed in established rules and institutions.

To a great extent, then, the meaning of the movements of the sixties cannot be discerned without understanding how these visions and hopes affected the developing lives of those who held them. Obviously, one interprets the long-term social meaning of the New Left, the counter-culture, and the civil rights, black power, and women's movements according to one's assessment of the ways such movements affected social structure, public policy, power relations, and institutional arrangements. But because these movements also said they were about the changing of people, their full historical meaning cannot be known without an effort to understand the nature and extent of their impact on individual lives.

Such an inquiry can also help illuminate the organization of the life course in contemporary society. The experiences of people who have consciously sought to avoid the established patterns of personal development can reveal much about the tenuous balance between freedom and constraint that presently characterizes adult life in our culture. The character, timing, and duration of the roles, relationships, and events that constitute the adult life course are all subjects of considerable analysis and debate. Investigations into such matters can provide individuals with a sense of what is possible for them while challenging institutionalized assumptions about what society's members are like (see especially Dannefer 1984).

Conventional wisdom calls idealism into question by making it appear to be the province of the naive young. This notion undermines the potential for commitment to social responsibility, not only among adults but among the young as well. In the cynical climate of post-sixties America, young people seemed to be asking: "Why bother being a youthful idealist if your principles don't survive into adulthood?" The prevailing popular understanding of the sixties rebels—promulgated by many in the mass media—is that they "sold out," "gave up," or "settled down."[1] Such images have become key elements in pervasive cynicism, depoliticization, and privatism. Images of sustained commitment, of persistent principle, of adult idealism, rarely enter popular discourse, and the processes by which people struggle to sustain and fulfill their aspirations for autonomous and socially responsible lives are rarely studied.

These thoughts about the social meaning of youthful idealism and rebellion stimulated the development of the project described in this book. The project was simply to identify a group of people who had, in their youth, been strongly committed to the student movement and to see what had happened to them as they moved on in life. When we began to plan this study in the late seventies, a handful of similar efforts had been undertaken. In the years since then, a few additional studies have been published. Taken together, these studies of former civil rights workers (Demerath, Marwell, and Aiken 1971; Fendrich and Tarleau 1973; Fendrich 1974, 1976, 1977; Fendrich and Lovoy 1988; Marwell, Aiken, and Demerath 1987); Free Speech Movement participants (Nassi and Abramowitz 1979; Nassi 1981); University of Michigan student radicals (Hoge and Ankney 1982); activist leaders from the various movements of the sixties (Braungart and Braungart 1980); and protesters from a broad range of campuses (Jennings 1987) lend little support to the view that student rebels abandoned their convictions after they left the university and ventured into the adult world. In fact, they support the opposite conclusion: even though the level of political involvement of former student radicals has decreased considerably over the intervening years —concomitant with the decline of the mass movements of the sixties— their current political, vocational, and moral commitments exhibit many continuities with their movement past.[2]

Our own investigation also found plotlines defined by terms like "selling out" quite inappropriate for understanding the post-movement lives of sixties activists. But we wanted to go beyond this rudimentary issue, and our research thus took an approach very different in method and focus from other studies. Although earlier studies challenge conventional wisdom about the fate of youthful idealism, the information they provide about the post-sixties political attitudes and activities of former student protesters is limited in several ways. Because they are based on survey data—almost invariably generated by mail questionnaires—their findings are presented largely in statistical terms and focus on documenting general patterns of continuity in youthful commitment. This methodology could not trace the routes activists followed as they made their way from the sixties to the eighties, nor capture processes of reflection and choice or the details of personal style and daily routine. Neither could it record activists' struggles to reconcile principle and pressure, nor recount their interpretations of such struggles. In order to address these critical issues, we elected to treat previous research as a point of departure for a qualitative life-history project. In our view, the survey research points to an underlying reality that needs to be explored in terms of individual experience.[3]

HOW THIS STUDY WAS DONE

We decided to work with a group of people small enough to permit close contact and detailed interviews over a period of years. This approach sacrificed our ability to develop statistical results that could be persuasively generalized. We would not be able to tell what proportion of the sixties generation was left or right, or to determine the average income or occupational distribution of the broader cohort. The survey studies cited above had already addressed many of those questions, however. Our work could learn something about patterns of persistence and change, dilemmas of personal choice and their resolution, and people's reasons for being the way they were. Based on these life-history case studies, our generalizations might provide plausible rather than definitive insights, which might then serve as hypotheses for further statistical testing by social scientists and as material for reflection and debate. In short, our intention was to produce an empirically warranted, theoretically relevant description (compare Weider and Zimmerman 1976).

Richard Flacks came to the University of California at Santa Barbara in 1969. In February 1970 the student community of Isla Vista, adjacent to UCSB, was engulfed in militant protest that resulted, among other things, in the burning of the local Bank of America. The object of worldwide media attention, this event represented only one moment out of several months of very considerable turmoil, during which one student was killed and hundreds were arrested. Flacks, who had been a leader in the early New Left, had done extensive research on the sources of student protest, was well known to student activists as a sympathizer, and had become acquainted with many of the activist leaders during his first year at the university.

In the winter and spring of 1970, two major groups of indictments were handed down relating to campus and Isla Vista protest, indictments that included most of the active core of the Radical Union, the key organization in 1969 and 1970 for white campus activists. We decided to define our target population as all those who had been indicted in either of two major cases: the "Santa Barbara 19" and the group brought to trial for setting fire to the bank. None, incidentally, served time for burning the bank, although some were jailed on various misdemeanor offenses associated with protest. These twenty-five individuals (some had been arrested on both sets of charges) constituted our potential sample. Because we had no systematic data about these people in 1970, the fact of their indictment provided a rough "baseline" indication of their political commitment at the time. All of these people were, at least in the eyes of the police, committed radicals; all but two were, in fact, visible members of the Radical Union. Because Flacks had known many of these people as students, we also had some well-formed impressions of what they were about in those years.

As a graduate student in the UCSB sociology department in the late seventies, Jack Whalen was interested in the fate of New Left radicalism as a result of his own participation in radical collectives and community organizing projects during the sixties and early seventies. It was he who would carry out the ongoing field work required by our approach. Whalen first contacted the former activists in 1979, interviewing eleven of them in an exploratory study (see Whalen and Flacks 1980 for a report of this phase of the project). After this exploratory phase, the study was extended in several ways. First, Whalen sought to reinterview the initial group of eleven and to add to their number as many others of the twenty-five indictees as could be contacted, as well as other Radical Union leaders. Second, both of us decided to identify a comparison group of people who had been students at UCSB during those years of protest but who were unlikely to have identified with the movement. We decided to select one fraternity and one sorority as a core framework (we will call the fraternity Delta Omega and the sorority Kappa Phi) for drawing such a sample. In addition, we added the names of some members of the football team during those years and those of several men who had received publicity for helping to defend a temporary bank building from attack in one of the Isla Vista riots, an incident during which one of the defenders was shot and killed by a police officer. We then tried to match the members of this nonactivist pool with the members of the activist sample by sex. The final samples selected for interviewing consisted of nineteen activists and sixteen nonactivists.

Whalen began the second round of interviews in 1980, ten years after the bank burning. Of the nineteen target activists, seventeen were interviewed—ten men and seven women. (One of the original eleven could not be located and another had left the country.) Of the sixteen targeted nonactivists, fifteen were finally interviewed (six fraternity, six sorority, two football players, and one bank defender). One of the sorority respondents, however, decided to withdraw soon after a very brief initial interview. A third round, in which most of these people were contacted by telephone, was carried out in 1982–83 (see Whalen and Flacks 1984 for a report on the research at this stage). Finally, in 1987 and 1988, as we began to develop this book, Whalen was able to contact most members of both groups for a last interview. These final encounters turned up important details about recent changes in careers and personal lives.

Whalen's interviews focused on the lives of respondents before they joined the movement, their experiences during their student years, and their lives in the years since. Primary themes were the respondents' own perceptions of persistence and change, and their own interpretations of their personal development. The interviews were relatively unstructured, but care was taken to ensure that each covered every question and issue listed in an interview guide Whalen had constructed. All were taped, with the respondents' permission. Most of the interviews were conducted face-to-face, but five of the nonactivists could be interviewed only by phone. The initial group of activists supplied the most material (an average of seven hours during the first two interview rounds); the other respondents—activist and nonactivist—supplied an average of five hours of material during the various interview phases. Moreover, we were able to obtain taped interviews/conversations conducted by one of the activists with several of the others in 1973. These tapes added considerably to our ability to reconstruct the early post-movement experience. Further, several respondents have sent us various things they have written, and both of us, through informal contacts with many of the respondents have made many observations that inevitably influenced the way we have interpreted the more formal interviews. Finally, Whalen sent a short, standardized questionnaire to the respondents in 1984. Data from these questionnaires allow comparisons between our respondents and the samples used in statistically based research on post-movement attitudes.[4] Brief biographies of all who were interviewed are given in the last section of this chapter.

THE DYNAMICS OF SIXTIES PROTEST

The Liberated Generation

In the mid-1960s, having been active in the launching and early development of Students for a Democratic Society, Flacks embarked on a systematic investigation of the personal roots of student protest. He interviewed a sample of student activists and their parents, comparing them with a sample of nonactivists and their parents, in an effort to explore the hypothesis that activist motivations were rooted in childhood socialization. Such a hypothesis seemed warranted in the early sixties; these activists were a small fraction of a generally apolitical student population. Why did they respond so passionately to the civil rights movement and the ban-the-bomb protests while most of their age-mates did not?

Flacks found that student activists in that period had parents who themselves were politically liberal (although not likely to be particularly active) and successful in professional careers. These families encouraged their offspring to be concerned about values, about ideas, and about the social relevance of their lives. They taught them that there are other things in life besides making money, while the material prosperity that they as parents had attained gave their offspring freedom to pursue non-monetary goals.

The title of the first report of this research, "The Liberated Generation" (Flacks 1967), was intended to convey the sense that life circumstances and upbringing had freed these young people from conventional concerns about material security and status. In short, one important source of sixties activism—especially germane to understanding those who had become active in the early days, when the movement was not at all popular—was a background of affluence coupled with a family tradition oriented toward social responsibility. Flacks argued in subsequent publications that such experience and such traditions were concentrated in families of what might be called the liberal intelligentsia: that is, the growing sector of society whose work involved research, teaching, and human services—work that had been encouraged by the expanding welfare state, but which tended to be in some conflict with the status quo. (See Flacks 1970 and, especially, 1971b for a detailed development of this argument.) The student movement, from this perspective, can be interpreted as an episode in the historical development of the intelligentsia as a class or sector of contemporary society, much as the trade union movement can be understood as a phase in the development of the industrial working class.

But, as we have already suggested, student protesters thought that they were making a sharp, permanent break with their parents' way of life, seeing it as rather hypocritical (a point with which many parents agreed) and ineffectual in terms of bringing about social change (again an argument that many parents themselves would have made). Accordingly, a potential value of the research on the fate of student activists is that it provides us with some understanding of how an important sector of society, the intelligentsia, continues to evolve.

Making History Versus Making Life

The New Left was not, however, simply a movement of and for the educated liberal middle class; it attempted to articulate a vision of social transformation best captured in the term "participatory democracy." It was a vision that addressed itself to a fundamental schism in American experience: the gap most people feel most of the time between their daily lives and history. The mainstream American definition of freedom emphasizes liberty as the ultimate value—the opportunity for each person to make his or her own life as freely as possible. Such a perspective says that the good society is one in which its members live largely removed from history, for history is an arena or realm in which decisions are made and actions taken that can powerfully influence and shape the conditions and terms of everyday life in society. Liberty imagines that history can be escaped—and that power to make it can be limited—so that the individual can make his or her own life.

The Left tradition, especially as expressed in the idea of participatory democracy, argues that liberty is not possible unless history-making is democratized. It seeks a social order in which history can be brought under the control of people in their daily lives. That requires the fundamental restructuring of institutions and the decentralization of economy and polity. It also requires psychological transformation. In order to be effective participants in self-government, people must develop both the capacity for resistance to authority and convention and an interest in issues beyond the private sphere. The New Left expressed the vision that the people should make their own history. It also embodied the belief that they could. One proof was the collective deliberation and action embodied in protest. If poor rural blacks in the South could meet and decide and act, it was evidence that all people could do so. A second source of evidence for New Leftists was their own lives. They were people who could passionately incorporate concern for social justice into their lives —why could not everyone?

Political activism, especially the leftwing kind, by its very nature calls on people to do what they generally avoid doing—namely, to pay active attention to history—while they are trying to live their everyday lives. Sometimes such calls succeed, because people discover that in order to live every day they will have to deal with history. But such involvements by large numbers are usually sporadic and spasmodic and tend to dissipate when daily living in relative freedom has been won.[5]

New Leftists envisioned a permanent fusion of the everyday and history. Because they were committed to activism, because they believed that their own self-fulfillment depended on implementing their social responsibility, they shared a strong sense that their own lives ought to somehow implement that fusion, that, as they came to put it, the "personal is political and vice versa." In the heat of sixties action, and, as we shall see, under the illusion of impending revolution, few gave serious thought, while they were students, to how such fusions might practically be accomplished for the long pull over the life course.

This book, then, is concerned with the stories of a group of people who in their youth committed themselves, to some degree, to finding a way to link their lives to history. The essential point we are looking for in these stories is how that commitment has fared, how it has been used, developed, reformulated, abandoned, revitalized.

Movement and Counterculture as Frameworks for Commitment

Understanding the fate of this commitment to link the personal with the political requires us to delve deeper into New Leftists' attempts to transform their lives and to remake their identities. From its beginnings in the early sixties, it was clear that the New Left was fueled by a discontent that some young people were feeling with their prospective lives. This alienation of privileged youths, whose family background and academic achievements provided them with keys to the best the society had to offer in the way of career and comfort, was puzzling to many. Why should so many youths with such advantages want to protest? Indeed, what made that protest particularly baffling was the fact that, to a great extent, the actions taken were explicitly and specifically directed against the very institutional arrangements and roles for which these young people were ostensibly being groomed.[6]

Thus, as the sixties opened, a small trickle of middle-class white students from elite universities began to drop out, or take leaves, or spend their summers working in poor black communities. Some joined the Student Non-Violent Coordinating Committee and other southern civil rights organizations in efforts to mobilize black voter registration and protest against segregation. Others were working in black ghetto neighborhoods, tutoring kids, setting up recreation programs, or otherwise trying to be of service. At their side were the sizable numbers of young people in the Peace Corps, established soon after John Kennedy took office in 1961, who quickly rallied to work with poor communities in developing countries rather than proceeding to law school or conventional careers. These volunteers were followed by dozens of students who were recruited by Students for a Democratic Society to work full time in urban slum neighborhoods as organizers of community unions, welfare rights organizations and the like.

By the mid-sixties a sizable fraction of the student body thought of themselves as rebels against the standard career programs defined by the universities and the professions, seeing themselves instead as committed to the well-being of the poor and contributing to social equality. Such identification was evident not only in these volunteer efforts, but also in the way increasing numbers of students were dressing and carrying themselves. The dress of campus intellectuals and activists combined residues of past bohemianism with a deliberate effort to be unpretentious, genteelly shabby, blue collar, or even rural. In a room of SDS activists in the mid-sixties, an uninitiated observer would no doubt have been shocked to learn that the very unassuming, and rather seedy, bunch before him was made up of the sons and daughters of elite families.

Parallel to the emerging New Left there was, of course, the emerging counterculture, a much larger number of youth who, while not necessarily interested in defining a political position, were self-consciously rebelling against a wide variety of norms and practices commonly called middle class. Hippie outfits expressed identification with all cultures that stood outside of or were being destroyed by western industrial society—from American to East Asian Indians, from cowboys to European peasants, from farm grandmothers to black slaves. Long hair, beads, painted faces, androgyny—all expressed not only a generalized desire to shock, but to shock in a particular way. For hippie styles all denied the superiority of conventional measures of status—the middle class, the adult, the male, the urban.

The use of illegal drugs, combined with explicit identification with the drug culture announced by one's appearance, inevitably got many white middle-class youths in trouble with the law. Such trouble reinforced fantasies of identification with the outlaw, which in turn further polarized "hippie" and "straight" sensibilities. To be seen as a hippie in the mid-sixties was, accordingly, not simply to be part of a new fashion trend; it was instead interpreted by many as a commitment to an alternative life course, a sign that one had made a break with the values and ways of life defined by one's parents, school, and community. "We are the people our parents warned us against," proudly declared a popular poster of the day.

At the risk of being excessively schematic, we want to identify two clusters of belief, value, and expectation that seemed to define the personal aspirations that underlay the behaviors and styles of the movement and the counterculture. As we have already suggested, in the movement members tended to believe that their life goals should entail a commitment to social responsibility, that one's life choices ought to be governed by a desire to make a contribution to social change and "making history." At its fullest, such a commitment would be represented by the full time activist or "organizer." Such a person would be working for a political organization at a grassroots level, providing the skills needed by relatively voiceless or powerless people to organize for voice and power. Obviously, such work would entail subsistence level livelihood; it would require the sacrifice of much in the way of personal free time or free choice (the responsible organizer being one who went where needed rather than where one most wanted to be), and the postponement or subordination of private relationships to the requirements of social need and political strategy. For many movement members, such an organizer represented the ideal in virtue and fulfillment.[7]

Few actually believed that they were destined to play such a role for more than a few months or years, given the obvious personal strains that would result from living the organizer's life. For a while, there was some effort to figure out how to live up to the movement's demand for commitment by finding some kind of vocational framework that could contribute significantly to social change. But the effort to link a career to movement commitment became harder to contemplate as the decade wore on. Careers, no matter how socially responsible, entailed training, preparation, discipline. How could one justify taking time out from the struggle while the war in Vietnam escalated? How could one carry on business as usual in school while increasingly tumultuous action was going on in the streets? Could one face the inevitable drudgery of training and the inevitable pressures to sell out? Was it really possible to be both inside and outside the "system"?

As the war escalated, the influence of the New Left on the consciousness of students grew. Questions that the activist core raised about the society—and about the personal futures available to them in that society —resonated with the alienation and ambivalence shared by many otherwise unpolitical youth. By the late years of the sixties, many who were not strongly politicized nevertheless felt some duty to think politically about career and lifestyle. In particular, many believed that they ought to avoid complicity with the "war machine" in their career decisions. By the late 1960s, a rather broadly accepted code of ethics was implicit on many campuses. This code included such tenets as:

—Don't work for a defense contractor, certainly not in anything having to do with weapons development.

—Don't work for a multinational corporation; not only will you find the bureaucracy stultifying, but you will inevitably be involved in the oppression of Third World people.

—Don't work in a context that supports environmental pollution or degradation; don't work for firms that rip people off. (Indeed, for many the very idea of working for a private profit-making firm was repugnant.)

—Organize your life so that you yourself are not part of the problem, and can be part of the solution. For example: use a bike, not a car; recycle waste; don't eat red meat; don't buy chemically processed foods.

—Don't cooperate with the draft; if you can't publicly resist, then try somehow to avoid it.

In short, if one was not prepared to commit one's life in a major way to social change, then one ought at the least to refuse to cooperate wherever possible with those institutions that were the enemies of positive change, especially those having to do with the Vietnam War and militarism. By the time our respondents were college seniors, such attitudes were pervasive among the student body.

Meanwhile, the counterculture was developing its own moral framework, one that emphasized personal rather than social change. In the code of the counterculture, what was valued was self-liberation—freeing impulse and emotion from social repression and psychic inhibition —and the fostering of persons aware of their needs and desires, and capable of expressing them. Such capability depended, it was believed, partly on inner transformation ("getting one's head together" using any means, including chemical ones, that helped) and partly on freeing oneself from dependency on the constraining institutions and relationships that blocked personal freedom. One point of contact between movement and counterculture was the anti-institutionalism of both. Both demanded that adherents avoid becoming cogs in the machinery of the established system. Both demanded an integrity that was inevitably threatened by joining the Establishment or "working for the man."

The models that nourished New Left identity were drawn from the revolutionary political traditions of the last 100 years. The counterculture as a framework of identity descended from romantic and bohemian artistic traditions. The apotheosis of New Left virtue was the selfless organizer of the dispossessed; by the second half of the decade, thousands of students wanted somehow to be like Che Guevara. Meanwhile, hundreds of thousands imagined that they could live as poets. To make one's life a work of art—in the manner of one's dress and carriage, in the ways one responded to nature and to other persons, and in the vocation one pursued—was a high goal. Such a goal demanded effort at refinement of awareness and expression; not, of course, through classical training and discipline, but through intense focus on one's inner life and on the processes of interaction. It demanded and fostered an openness to experience, meaning that one should not feel obligated or bound by roles, relationships, or expectations that set limits on possibilities for exploration, for new encounters, for new feelings. To "settle down" into career, marriage, family, neighborhood without having undertaken such exploration and without ensuring one's continuing freedom of movement would be profoundly wrong. One ought to remain free at least until one found a way to live and produce creatively, preferably as an artist or artisan.

We are suggesting, then, that the youth revolt of the sixties embodied two rather contradictory perspectives on self-development and transformation. The movement, by definition, demanded of its members active involvement in public events, continuous examination of one's duty to take action, an effort to stay aware of news and to deepen one's understanding of social processes and public events, constant self-scrutiny for signs of selfishness and self-indulgence, constant pressure on oneself to do more to end the war and to promote change, and pressure to be more effective in such efforts. Meanwhile, the counterculture at its heart expressed disgust with politics and with tedious talk and analysis about the public realm. It promoted a refusal of commitment where such commitment limited personal freedom of movement, or prevented people from doing their own thing in their own time. The counterculture reinforced the expressive rather than the instrumental, the personal rather than the political, retreatism rather than revolutionary action. It defined the good society as one in which liberty and autonomy rather than equality and democracy were primary values.

But in the late years of the sixties, these separate logics tended to produce similar conclusions about what people should actually do. For example, for the New Left, draft resistance was a refusal of complicity with the war machine and a strategy for opposing it. For the counterculture, the draft represented a fundamental, obvious threat to personal freedom and self-expression. Together, both movement and counterculture fostered opposition to the draft and efforts to reist or evade it. Similarly, for the New Left, refusal to orient toward conventional middle-class career and lifestyle was an effort to free one's energy and mind for an activist commitment felt to be threatened by "cooptation." For the counterculture, such refusal was necessitated by a desire to live more freely, expressively, and fully than was allowed in conventional social space. Together, both fostered increased questioning of conventional career aspirations; both reinforced and crystallized latent desires to refuse to become adult.

What neither movement nor counterculture provided was any concrete sense about what one ought to do with one's life once one had broken with conventional aspirations. Indeed, by the last years of the sixties questions about the future seemed impossible to answer credibly in the face of a growing belief, shared by many young people, that the entire social edifice was crumbling. In a climate poisoned by an escalating and vicious war, it seemed that movement and counterculture were inextricably interconnected expressions of youthful opposition to a dying order. Indeed, each symbiotically fed the other, with the antiwar movement providing concrete justification and reinforcement for the countercultural renunciation of established society, and the countercultural emphasis on personal liberation enabling otherwise apolitical young people to take action, such as opposing the draft or burning a bank, that had significant political meaning.

These convictions and their consequences, for the movement as a whole and for many of its individual participants, play a pivotal role in our story. What happened to movement and counterculture codes and principles, given this failure to prepare for or realistically confront the vicissitudes of adulthood? This issue is essential for understanding the fate of sixties activists.

HOW THE BOOK IS ORGANIZED

Organizing hours of interview materials into a form that is coherent and does justice to their richness is extremely difficult. We have tried to strike a balance between presenting miniature portraits and panorama. We wanted to provide enough detail so that the readers can independently analyze the material. We also wanted to point to some rather clearcut conclusions and have edited the interviews to emphasize them.

We could not present each person's story in full. Instead, we structured the book chronologically, as a series of phases, weaving together the accounts of our respondents and the historical events and processes that gave shape to their experiences. Individual cases are selected to exemplify the patterns we discern at each phase; thus, we propose that the narratives represent not only the attitudes of the individual telling the story, but those of other people as well.[8] Further, because the focus of this study is the fate of the young radicals of the sixties, we will be devoting much more space in the pages ahead to the stories of the activist members of our sample than to those of the nonactivists, whose accounts will be used primarily to emphasize points of comparison between their lives and the lives of the former Radical Union members.

The story begins in Isla Vista with the burning of the bank. Chapter 2 sets that scene and locates many of our respondents. Their recollections of events serve not as oral history but as indicators of their perspectives at the time. Any understanding of what has become of the young radicals of the sixties must start with what the experience of activism and protest was like, and with what individuals thought about who they were and what they were doing at the moment of intense movement involvement. For our respondents, that moment came in the tumult of the Isla Vista riots.

In the immediate aftermath of the bank burning, and for several months thereafter, most activists were convinced that apocalyptic events were imminent. Chapter 3 describes this mood and contrasts it with the mood of the nonactivists, who, rather than expecting the end of the world, were beginning a smooth entry into the life they had been preparing for. Many activists lived for a time as revolutionaries. Chapter 3 also shows that signs of individual disaffection were evident, beneath the totalistic revolutionary fervor expressed in movement collectives, and that some members began to move toward more individualized lives.

As the seventies wore on, more and more activists replaced apocalyptic revolutionary totalism with more balanced, long-term efforts to fuse commitment and survival. Chapter 4, based on reconstructions of experience in the middle to late seventies, focuses on what we call "experiments in daily living" as the characteristic pattern of that period for activists. At the end of the decade, reaching thirty years of age and just in time for Ronald Reagan's election, many activists were entering a new phase of more settled and more individualized lives. Chapter 4 also describes this transitional phase.

Chapter 5 begins with a collective portrait of the two groups in the present, delineating several different approaches to activist commitment. A close-up of representative individuals trying to discover how their current lives relate to their youthful selves occupies the remainder of Chapter 5 and all of Chapter 6, focusing on the possibilities for and barriers to everyday political involvement in the 1980s.

How well did the movement members' expectations about their own futures hold up? How would their youthful selves assess their present lives? Chapter 7 is an effort to see how various sorts of predictions about the fate of sixties commitment hold up in the light of what we now know. How well did various theories about what the sixties meant anticipate the outcomes we now see?

Problems of terminology plagued us during the writing. What do we call our two groups? We began with "activist and nonactivist samples." Concerned that the word "sample" implies a strict randomness of selection we did not use, we try to avoid using it. "Activist" is a reasonably accurate label for the Radical Union members as students; many, however, ceased to be activists as time went on. By the same token "former activist" would mislabel some who continue to be activist; "former radical" vs. "radical" presents similar difficulties; "former student radical or activist" becomes unwieldy. Of the many labels we use for the sake of variety, none is satisfactory but, we hope, none is misleading.

A similar problem pertains to finding appropriate labels for the collective experience of the sixties that serves as the historical context of this study. It is appropriate, as we have pointed out, to recognize two expressions of the youth revolt—the movement and the counterculture—and try to distinguish them. But, of course, they were also interpenetrating. The New Left was an organized, ideologically conscious component of the white movement, a term used to refer to all of the loosely connected protest activity aimed at governmental or institutional policies that captured the allegiance of students and other youth. The counterculture refers to the wide range of shared symbols and practices popular among youth during that period that projected and encouraged freedom of expression and feeling beyond limits set by dominant cultural institutions. Our discussion uses both terms together when we want to point to both political and cultural influences. More often we focus on the movement as the point of departure, because we chose our participants to reflect the experience of movement activists. The degree to which these people were imbued with countercultural perspectives is one of our topics for inquiry.

Our claims for this book are limited; we recognize its many holes, missing links, and unanswered questions. Moreover, at a time when interest in and discussion of these themes is widespread, we hope to provide sufficient empirical data, independent of our interpretations, to permit others to develop their own perspectives on these matters. We offer these stories in the same spirit that apparently guided our respondents: as contributions to the ongoing discourse on how we might live according to our dreams.

CAST OF CHARACTERS

The names we use for our respondents are fictional, and, because we promised them anonymity, we have changed some details of their biographies to protect their identities. The reader can get a quick sense of the plotline of this book—and can be helped in remembering the cast of characters—by consulting the following list of all those interviewed.

Activists

Sheila Barressi: Associate producer at a public television station in Northern California; earns about $25,000 a year; single; not active in politics at present but still defines herself as a radical.

David Carroll: Pastor of a Methodist church in Southern California; married, no children; left-liberal views, but minimal involvement in political activity; endorses "liberation theology"; income approximately $25,000 a year.

Kenneth Essian: Employed as a gardener and fruit-grove manager; income approximately $15,000; follower of Kirpal Singh, an Indian master of Sant Mat; met his wife through this religious group; one child, born in 1987.

Sarah Glenn: City editor for a statewide daily newspaper; salary approximately $35,000; recently married, no children; liberal views on social issues but takes conservative position on economic questions.

Ellen Hemmings: Nurse in a small community hospital in Oregon; earns close to $30,000; left-liberal views, not politically active; married, one child (a three-year-old); husband is a long-haul truck driver.

Martha Koch: Physician in charge of a statewide occupational health and safety program; salary $50,000; defines her politics as "progressive," generally takes a socialist perspective; very active in both local and state politics; married, two children; her husband is a city planner and also active in Left politics.

Terry Lennox: Teaches English in a black teacher-training college in South Africa; married to a white South African medical technician; his wife's salary provides almost all of their income; no children; left-liberal politics, very committed to bringing about majority rule and an end to apartheid in his new country.

Paul Little: When last contacted in 1983, was working as a musician and independent record producer; has also worked as a car salesman in recent years; separated from his wife and child; liberal politics, not active.

Bill McNaughton: Associate professor of chemistry at an Oklahoma university; salary about $35,000; communicates his love for science with great enthusiasm; left-liberal views, follows politics closely but is not active; single.

Warren Newhouser: Fled California after misdemeanor conviction in aftermath of Isla Vista riots; lives under an assumed identity in rural New England; holds radical political views; works as a traveling organizer for an environmental movement organization; also writes free-lance on ecology issues; average income about $5,000 a year; married, one child; committed to "trying to stay as self-sufficient as possible."

Ed Pines: Working as a substitute teacher in Northern California, hopes to find a full-time position; radical political views, very active in community and national projects; recently married, his wife (also a school teacher) has two boys, ages ten and fourteen.

Steve Rubin: Free-lance writer, concentrating on coastal fishing and environmental topics; income averages around $20,000; formerly worked as an independent commercial fisherman; defines his views as "libertarian," with strong commitment to individual freedom; recently divorced, no children.

Denise Saal: Law student; formerly member of a small collective of paralegal workers who assisted defense attorneys on capital punishment cases; socialist politics, very active in left-wing causes, a former national officer of a radical legal organization; single.

Cynthia Spivak: When last contacted in 1983, was a "full-time mother" of two young children, living in Northern California; husband is an auto mechanic; radical political views, but not involved in any organizations or movements.

Barney Thompson: Teaches in a ghetto school and in adult education classes in Los Angeles; also works in a bookstore owned by a Maoist political party, and is active in projects organized by the party; defines his politics as Marxist-Leninist, worked eight years as a postal clerk in Santa Barbara before move to Los Angeles; divorced, no children.

Kristen Van Duinen: Last contacted in 1983, when she was living in Greece and supporting herself as an English teacher; our most recent information is that her life is much the same today as it was then; liberal political views; single.

Roger Wade: Assistant professor of history at a large university; interested in social and labor history; salary approximately $32,000; describes himself as a "semi-passive radical," has had some recent involvement in community politics; married to a historian; no children.

Joyce Weston: Print production supervisor for a small advertising agency in Northern California; income about $30,000; liberal views, not politically active; has spent several months in the past few years traveling, and is currently saving money for a long visit to England; single.

Nonactivists

Mary Casey: Housewife, lives in Los Angeles area; husband is a lawyer with an annual income over $100,000; three children; describes herself as a liberal on social issues, but has somewhat more conservative views on economic questions; usually votes Democratic.

George Dawes: Bank executive, works in South American audit division and lives in Caracas, Venezuela; salary over $50,000; married to a native Venezuelan, two children; conservative Republican.

Larry Goodwin: Executive vice-president in charge of marketing for a multibillion-dollar conglomerate; income over $150,000 a year; has worked largely in advertising over the past two decades; married, one child; moderate to conservative politics, describes himself as an "independent" voter.

Bill James: Assistant football coach at one of the military academies; married, two children; generally conservative political views, but voted for Carter in 1976.

Clark Jeffries: Works as an independent salesman for several Southern California companies that manufacture packaging material; average income about $80,000; married, two children; very conservative political views, almost always votes Republican.

Charles Johnson: When last contacted in 1983, was living in Montana and working as a car salesman; studied history in graduate school after leaving UCSB, then taught high school– and college-level courses at California youth correctional facility before moving to Montana; single; generally conservative politics, particularly on foreign policy questions.

Lucy Lizotte: School teacher, lives in Santa Barbara; salary about $25,000; married, two children; husband works as administrator in county government; liberal political views, attributes her beliefs to her experiences at UCSB and during Isla Vista riots.

Melissa Meyers: Housewife, lives in Northern California; married to a businessman, annual family income close to $80,000; moderate to conservative politics.

Rhonda Miller: Executive secretary at a Southern California race track; salary about $22,000; divorced, no children; very conservative views, especially on racial problems and economic issues.

Frank Morrow: Executive in the steel industry; earns about $32,000; lives in Santa Barbara area; single; liberal on many social issues, generally moderate politics.

Ginny Phillips: Teaches fifth grade in Orange County, California; salary about $25,000; married, no children; sees herself as generally "moderate" on politics, voted for Carter in 1976 and Anderson in 1980.

Mark Reiss: Co-owner (with his father) of a carpeting business in Southern California; income averages over $110,000; married, three children; usually votes Democratic (including Carter and Mondale over Reagan), but feels he is becoming more conservative on some economic issues.

Carl Rohrback: Executive for large utility company in Northern California; income over $70,000; married, two children; conservative politics.

Harry Stevens: Retired in his early thirties, supports himself with what he terms a "comfortable income" from properties he built and now rents; also has invested in other housing and business development projects; lives in Reno, Nevada, area; recently married to a woman with a young son; very conservative political views.

2

At the Barricades

PUBLIC EVENTS

Isla Vista, California. February 25, 1970. A few minutes after 9 P.M. The line of sheriff's deputies filled the community's main street, the Embarcadero or "Loop," as the small business district was called. There were eighty-three of them, attired in full riot gear. They were confronted by a crowd of close to one thousand people that spilled out of the Loop and onto the side streets. It was a boisterous crowd, and some of its members were hostile to the police; insults and an occasional rock were hurled at the officers. Still, most hung back from the confrontation, curious but cautious, their sympathies perhaps divided.[1]

Virtually everyone in the crowd was young and white. The overwhelming majority were students at the adjoining Santa Barbara campus of the University of California (its nearest buildings were only a few hundred yards away). These were California's "golden youth," undeniably middle class, from predominantly conservative families. The remainder were non-student residents of Isla Vista, or "I.V.," as almost everyone called it. This latter group included a small number of "street people" —the local term for irregularly employed transients, or what the media called "hippies"—and other youths who were attracted to Isla Vista by the unique character of the community or who had stayed on after graduating from UCSB. Fronting on bluffs overlooking the Pacific and bounded on one side by the University campus and elsewhere by fields and marshes, with more than 13,000 residents (80 percent of them under twenty-five years of age) crammed into 340 acres, unincorporated Isla Vista was perhaps America's most clearly defined youth ghetto. Until now, UCSB had been known as the "play school" of the California university system, and Isla Vista was seen as its lively playground. The sun and surf were thought to more than compensate for the crowded, relatively expensive, and often rundown apartment buildings, the absence of a community government, and the paucity of basic public services. But the events of this Wednesday evening were to drastically alter that placid campus-by-the-sea image.

The confrontation that brought people into the streets of Isla Vista on this night had been building for over a month. There had been several police-student clashes on campus in late January and early February. The conflicts were kindled by mass rallies protesting against the denial of tenure to William Allen, a popular and decidedly unorthodox anthropology professor who had become something of a countercultural symbol. When protesters sat down in front of the administration building and blocked the doorways, the police were called in (Potter and Sullivan 1970: 69–70). Twelve students and three policemen were injured, a few windows broken, and several arrests made.

Most notable of these were the indictments of nineteen students as alleged ringleaders of the demonstrations. Suspended from school and banned from campus, most of the "Santa Barbara 19," as they called themselves, were members of the Radical Union (RU), a loose-knit organization of white activists that had come into prominence during the Allen controversy.[2] The allegedly political nature of these indictments and, especially, the calling of police onto campus now became major issues in the struggle.

In the final days of February, student unrest had spilled over into Isla Vista, and it had become clear that its roots went far deeper than the Allen case. Both the depth and scope of student grievances, particularly their feelings about the police, were dramatized by the events surrounding an especially acrimonious encounter between sheriff's deputies and I.V. residents on the afternoon of February 24. When patrolling officers tried to take a black student activist in for questioning about a recent burglary, a crowd gathered and scuffles broke out between the deputies and members of the crowd. The police took the activist away in handcuffs, but someone slashed a tire on one of the patrol cars and then doused the tire with gasoline and ignited it. A white student activist on the scene was arrested and beaten by the deputies as he struggled with them in full view of the crowd (Potter and Sullivan 1970: 73). On that evening, windows were broken in several realty offices and in the largest, most imposing structure in I.V., located in the heart of the Loop: the Bank of America building.

These attacks were not random. There had been periodic complaints from I.V. residents about police harassment over the past few years, and the recent campus strife served only to increase the antagonism. There were also complaints against the realtors. Real estate management companies were viewed by many Isla Vistans as unscrupulous agents of absentee owners who cared little for the community or its residents, being concerned only with making profits. As UCSB increased its enrollment ninefold from 1954 (the year it was established) to 1970, spawning an "instant town surrounding an instant university" (Stickney 1971: 16), zoning laws were changed and building codes revised to permit high-density construction. The lack of affordable and uncrowded housing was perceived as the number one problem in the community (see report of the Santa Barbara Citizens' Commission on Civil Disorder 1970). During the week of February 16, almost all the realty companies had declined to sign a standard rental contract drawn up by the Associated Students (UCSB's student government) in an effort to redress long-standing student grievances.

And the bank? It had been the focus of repeated student criticism for its alleged profit-making off the Vietnam War and its role in financing California's agricultural industry, an industry then engaged in a bitter labor struggle with Cesar Chavez's United Farmworkers. In response to these criticisms, the Associated Students voted in November of 1969 to withdraw their organizational funds from the bank. More salient than these specific charges, however, was the fact that the Bank of America was easily the most prominent "ideological landmark" in Isla Vista, a highly visible citadel of big business in a community that "featured nothing more imposing than small neighborhood stores" (Potter and Sullivan 1970: 47). As one student (quoted in Flacks and Mankoff 1970: 340) later explained: "It was the biggest capitalist thing around."

Finally, all of these local grievances were expressed in the context of a much wider movement in opposition to the draft and Vietnam War. "UCSB is no Berkeley," many were fond of saying, but despite Santa Barbara's reputation as an oasis of sunny tranquility, its students were becoming increasingly politicized by the intense national controversy over the conflict in Southeast Asia. Disaffection from the Vietnam War, more than anything else, constituted the substratum of dissent (see especially Smith 1971). Antiwar rallies and demonstrations on campus and in Santa Barbara in the fall of 1969 attracted thousands of people.

It seems clear, then, that the attacks on property Tuesday night—regardless of how much passionate rage or wanton frenzy they entailed—were selective and, for the most part, politically inspired. Yet, stormy as that evening's conflict was, it would soon pale in comparison to Wednesday's maelstrom.

Fire in the Streets

The hundreds of young people confronting the line of sheriff's deputies in the Loop on Wednesday night had been engaged for more than three hours in sporadic rock-throwing attacks on police and on real estate offices and businesses. Once again, the bank was a primary target. And, once again, the hostilities had been touched off by a street arrest. This time, however, there had been a large crowd already on hand.

Events unfolded this way. William Kunstler, the attorney for the Chicago 8, had given a scheduled speech that afternoon in the campus stadium. Seven thousand people attended. "It is better to conspire to create a world where black and white can live together," they heard Kunstler say, "where men and women are equal and poor people abolished, perhaps by the elimination of property as a private concept, than to destroy minds in the universities and beat heads with night sticks." And then he told them: "I have never thought that picayune violence is a good tactic —but on the other hand, I cannot bring myself to be bitter about it and condemn it. If resistance is not heeded, then it can lead to revolution. I hope the government is listening to what is being said. Fill the streets so they can see you."

As people made their way back into Isla Vista, some headed for a rally in Perfect Park, next to the bank, which had been called by the Radical Union. Numerous police cars cruised up and down the streets, elements of the heavy patrols that had been deployed in anticipation of possible trouble. Kunstler's appearance, on top of Tuesday's violence, had naturally created great concern among the police about further unrest. Further, there were many disturbing rumors circulating through the community, tales of Molotov cocktails and riot in the making. It was in the midst of this nervous activity and high-strung emotional climate that a patrol car stopped a former student, Richard Underwood, for carrying an alleged fire bomb (actually an almost-empty wine bottle). Four additional units quickly arrived. Underwood was arrested and, when he resisted, clubbed in full view of hundreds of spectators. An angry crowd marched down to the Loop. Stones and bottles were thrown at police. Similar attacks on realty offices and the bank followed. A patrol car was set afire, and the police on hand were driven off in a hail of rocks.

Now, at twelve minutes after nine o'clock, they had returned in force —at least with whatever force they were able to muster on such short notice. As they massed in formation on Embarcadero del Norte, the charred remains of the police car were smoldering a block away. Overhead, resting atop a fifty-foot pole, the Bank of America's familiar electric sign was dark, the glass shattered by dozens of rocks and bottles. The doors of the bank were broken open and most of the windows smashed (those that had not already been broken on the previous evening). A burning trash dumpster had been pushed into the lobby an hour earlier, but the flames had been quickly extinguished by students who were opposed to the violence. Hundreds of people had been parading through the bank—"like tourists," one observer said—with some of them sitting down to eat an ice cream cone or smoke a joint in the vault anteroom or in the board of directors' meeting room. The scene was a surreal melange of revelry and insurrection.

The police intended to sweep through the Loop and clear the area of rioters. They were, however, greatly outnumbered, and they lacked crowd-control equipment and training. This had never been a serious problem in the previous clashes on campus, though, when even larger crowds had assembled; whenever the police showed up, people backed off. And, true to form, as the police began to move forward on Embarcadero, some in the crowd began to fall back, joining others who had started retreating when the sheriff's deputies had first arrived. But then something very unusual happened. The remainder did not retreat. Instead, they charged. Heaving bottles and rocks, they stormed the advancing force. Overwhelmed, the police broke under the assault. They ran, and people ran after them. Small groups of policemen were isolated, surrounded, and nearly overpowered. Many were injured. An account published by the California Highway Patrol stated that it took almost half an hour for the police to "fight their way back to the bus that had brought them" (*California Highway Patrolman* 1970: 59).

Within minutes, the protesters had gained control of Isla Vista. Street barricades went up, including large dumpsters hauled into the middle of the roadways to block police movements. Police reinforcements arrived about an hour later but were unable to regain the upper hand. Held at bay by rock-throwing attacks, police remained on the outskirts, sealing the community off (Potter and Sullivan 1970: 74). While there were even more dramatic and startling actions to follow, actions that captured the attention of the nation and that came to stand as a symbol for the entire event, the unexpected charge at the police line was pivotal. Screaming and howling like banshees, several hundred sons and daughters of California's upper middle class had attacked armed riot police and forced them to flee in near panic. As one protester later put it: "That in essence broke the spell. They didn't have any power over us." Isla Vista, in the eyes of its most militant residents, had been "liberated."

Once the police left Isla Vista, the bank became the central focus of the protesters' actions. People were again roaming through the structure, some intent on wreaking havoc, most merely inquisitive. Many simply stood outside the doorway for a few minutes and peered in. "After a while," one protester who was at the scene remarked, "people simply got bored with it all. Even the 'Boy Scouts'—that's what we called people opposed to the violence—even the 'Boy Scouts' who were guarding the place got bored, and around midnight people left the scene."

But not everyone left. Upstairs, and in the board room, a small group of people made piles of furniture, loose paper, and material taken from emptied file drawers, doused the stuff with gasoline, and ignited it. Gradually, the fire spread. The mezzanine was soon ablaze, and in less than fifteen minutes the entire building was burning, the incandescent glow lighting up the night sky. "That's when the whole town came out again," a witness noted. "There was a constant two-way stream of students between the burning bank and the campus," another observer reported. It was estimated that as many as 5,000 individuals at one point during the night were on the scene (Potter and Sullivan 1970: 74).

The gathering multitude stood and watched the Bank of America burn to the ground. Some greeted it with cheers and threw things into the fire, symbolically participating in the arson. Dozens danced around it, singing and laughing in jubilation—"wild black figures capering about in silhouette against . . . the flames," as Edward Loomis' documentary novel of the event describes them (Loomis 1970: 8). "It was a collective kind of thing; it made it part of a group myth," a participant later recalled. "It was like this carnival . . . this blazing carnival," another stated (quoted in Stickney 1971: 19). Many others could only stare at the fiery tableau in disbelieving silence. Later, after the flames died down, a few even brought out hot dogs and marshmallows, roasting them over the coals.

It was three A.M. before local police, reinforced by units from neighboring communities and by the Highway Patrol, were able to move back into Isla Vista and regain control of the streets. Daylight found the bank reduced to a skeleton of blackened girders. A few wisps of smoke rose from the ruins as people started to gather around it once again. For those who had somehow missed Wednesday night's battle, it must have been a shocking sight; for those Isla Vistans who had watched the bank burn, it was a sobering reminder of just what had been done, with the surrealism of the night transformed into the cold reality of the day. In the final analysis, however, the bank burning probably contributed to a greater sense of empowerment in Isla Vista and a greater sense of daring. By Thursday evening, February 26, the conflict was raging once more, and at a more fevered pitch.

This time it began with a rally of some 200 persons "in which fears were expressed of a police 'vendetta' to retaliate for the last night's bank burning" (Potter and Sullivan 1970: 74–75). As the crowd grew, what can only be described as open street-warfare soon broke out. Police trying to occupy the area were assaulted with rocks and fire bombs. They began using tear gas, but the crowd kept throwing the hissing bombs back or covering them with trash can lids. Whenever police units moved to clear one street, the place they had just vacated was immediately reoccupied by the protesters. When word spread that a student had been run down by a police car, it seemed to heighten the level of violence. (This rumor later proved unfounded.) Molotov cocktails were used to "liberate" entire areas occupied by police. Later in the evening, a man was shot in the shoulder by sheriff's deputies when he tried to drive his car through a police barricade on campus. Police thought he was trying to bring supplies to the protesters. Even more ominously, the authorities reported sniper fire (these reports turned out to be inaccurate).

Shortly after 11:30, the sheriff's deputies withdrew from Isla Vista. It was only when National Guard troops—alerted earlier in the day by Governor Ronald Reagan—were sent into the community at half past two in the morning, accompanied by helicopters dropping tear gas canisters, that public order was restored. A dusk-to-dawn curfew was put into effect and ninety-seven arrests were made (compared with only thirty-six on Wednesday). By Friday night, February 27, with the Guard out in force and with torrential rains helping to squelch further outbreaks, an uneasy truce finally prevailed.

"If It's to Be a Blood-Bath . . ."

The burning of the Bank of America became, in journalist John Hurst's well-chosen words, "an instant symbol, a focal point used by all shades of the political spectrum, the flaming proof of everyone's political pudding" (Hurst 1980: 3). On the Left there were expressions of sympathy and support. *Ramparts* magazine, for example, in its special ecology issue, favorably contrasted the political consciousness of the Isla Vista protesters with what it saw as the often misdirected, fuzzy-minded politics of the budding ecology movement. "Burning a bank is not the same as putting banks and their system out of business," the editors stated, but they went on to speculate that what happened in Isla Vista might awaken people to the "real source of their misery." The statement concluded: "If it does, the students who burned the Bank of America in Santa Barbara will have done more to save the environment than all the Survival Faires and 'Earth Day Teach-Ins' put together" (*Ramparts* 1970: 4).

Within the student community at UCSB, there was considerable debate over whether the use of violence by the protesters had been justified. The student newspaper, *El Gaucho*, printed dozens of letters and commentaries on this issue, with the writers divided into three groups: those who were totally opposed to the use of violence by students and felt it was senseless or stupid; those who were critical of confrontation and violence as political tactics but were equally critical of the behavior of police, university authorities, and government officials; and those who argued that the rioting, whatever its moral status, had at least served to call attention to (and dramatize the gravity of) community grievances.

Some students took their response a step further, circulating an "anti-violence" petition that read: "We the undersigned, out of deep concern for our society and its problems, condemn the violence which occurred in Isla Vista as a self-defeating effort to correct society's problems." By March 4, over 6,000 signatures had been gathered.

El Gaucho editorials took yet another tack. "The burning of the bank may have been symbolic of revolution in America," the paper's leftist editors stated, "but it's doubtful that it was in itself a revolutionary act. For violence at this time means only suicide." A more promising strategy for turning Isla Vista into a "liberated territory," they wrote, was the building of community institutions:

> We must continue to fight those who oppress us, but we must at the same time create what we can for ourselves. In Isla Vista, this means that we must start to turn a depressing, dirty, fragmented and oppressive environment into a joyous, loving, communal place where we can try to build institutions of new humanistic culture. . . . We must live the revolution in our personal lives, in our community. Isla Vista is not yet ours, but we can make it ours if we pool our creativity and our energy and our commitment. . . . *Demandez L'Impossible! Pouvoir A L'Imagination!* (*El Gaucho*, 3 March 1970.)

Perhaps the most telling evidence of the effect of the bank burning on Santa Barbara's students, however, was a campus survey taken only two weeks after the event. "Forgetting about rational considerations for a moment," it asked, "was the burning of the bank emotionally satisfying to you?" Thirty percent replied in the affirmative (Smith 1980). Thus, when some enterprising graphic artists of the counterculture created posters of a huge facsimile of a Bank of America scenic check "illustrated with the burning bank in brilliant red and yellow tones" (Hurst 1980: 3)—the very same photograph that had graced the cover of *Ramparts*—hundreds of Isla Vistans hung them on their living room walls.[3]

Representatives of the business community and public officials were of quite a different mind. Understandably, their response to the rioting was one of astonishment and moral outrage. The Bank of America bought full-page newspaper ads throughout California and across the nation that vowed that they would "make their stand" in Isla Vista (described in some of the ads as a "normal American suburban community") and urged Governor Reagan to use "all the means at your disposal" to protect "citizens and their property." The ads went on to compare the rioters to Adolf Hitler's Brown Shirts and offer a $25,000 reward "for information leading to the arrest and conviction of the leaders of the mob violence in Santa Barbara."

Prominent politicians expressed similar characterizations of the protesters. Reagan flew to Santa Barbara the day after the bank burning and
called them "cowardly little bums," adding: "I wouldn't be surprised if
later reports showed outside agitators." The governor also noted that
he was "happy to hear that there were students on the other side who
tried to halt the burning of the bank—these appear to me to be far more
typical of the students." Vice President Spiro Agnew, in his address
to the National Governor's Conference the same day, stated: "Never in
our history have we paid so much attention to so many odd characters.
. . . Twenty-five years ago, the tragicomic action of such societal misfits
would have brought the establishments running after them with butter-
fly nets rather than television cameras." A week after Reagan's visit, Los
Angeles Mayor Sam Yorty spoke in Santa Barbara and claimed, almost
echoing the governor, that "outside agitators and Communist conspirators" were responsible for the Isla Vista disturbances. Reagan referred
to the bank burning again on April 8. Speaking to a meeting of the California Growers Convention in Yosemite National Park, he called for a
crackdown on campus dissent: "Appeasement is not the answer. . . . If
it's to be a blood-bath, let it be now" (Potter and Sullivan 1970: 53–55).

The already-infamous February uprising turned out to be only "Isla
Vista I." A second riot, "Isla Vista II," broke out on April 16, barely a
week after Governor Reagan's Yosemite speech. This new insurgency
began with a protest against the refusal of both the university's chan-
cellor, Vernon Cheadle, and Santa Barbara County officials to allow a
speech by Yippie leader (and Chicago 8 defendant) Jerry Rubin. Nancy
Rubin came to UCSB that afternoon in her husband's place. "All property is theft," she declared at a campus rally. "We've got to fight for
everything." Stu Albert, a Berkeley radical appearing with her, called for
the " 'rip-off' of pigs" (Potter and Sullivan 1970: 56).

Later that day, about 400 students gathered in front of the trailer in-
stalled by the Bank of America as a temporary office next to the ruins
of its predecessor. Like its predecessor, the temporary bank became a
target for rocks, as did realty offices. The protesters were initially confronted not by police, but by other students and residents who opposed
their violent tactics. Arguments ensued and taunts were exchanged. Observers later reported that while "there was some damage to property
from rocks and Molotov cocktails" during the evening, "the nonviolent
forces appeared to be succeeding" (Potter and Sullivan 1970: 76). Then,

apparently without warning, sheriff's officers arrived, riding in four dump trucks. The trucks had high metal beds and reinforced wooden panels. Four to six officers equipped with shotguns, antisniper rifles and tear gas deployment equipment, and outfitted in full combat gear—riot helmets, black jump suits, flak jackets, gas masks, portable radios, ammunition belts, and combat boots—were in each truck. They had dubbed their maneuver "Operation Wagon Train." Tear gas and birdshot were fired at the crowd, scattering militants and peace keepers alike (Potter and Sullivan 1970: 10). Six students were wounded.

This incident was followed by four days of street fighting, and by the most tragic event of that agonizing year in Isla Vista: Kevin Moran, one of a small group of students defending the bank against a rock and fire-bomb attack by 300 protesters on the night of April 17, was killed by a police bullet during another crowd-dispersal action. (An official investigation later ruled the killing accidental.) Isla Vista II ended with one dead, seven wounded by shotgun pellets, and ninety arrests.

There was even more violence that spring. In May, students at UCSB and across the nation responded to the U.S. invasion of Cambodia with marches, demonstrations, strikes, and moratoriums. In the city of Santa Barbara, 2,500 students rallied on May 5 and nearly one hundred draft cards were burned. The next day, radicals called a strike on campus and padlocked classroom buildings. That afternoon, close to 5,000 students blocked the freeway near campus. In response to these and other demonstrations, Reagan ordered the University of California system closed for four days. People were quick to defy the ban on campus protests, however; on May 7, some 3,000 UCSB students held an illegal rally and then marched to the freeway, which was blocked again. When the university reopened on May 11, it followed the lead of other campuses by attempting to channel the protest into more academic pursuits. Many classes met off-campus and official "National Crisis" courses were established, enrolling nearly 2,500 students.

The events of February still cast a giant shadow over the community, however. On June 3, news leaked out that seventeen people (including two "John Does") had been secretly indicted for burning the Bank of America. Police raided I.V. apartments looking for the alleged conspirators. The next day, a group of I.V. residents demonstrated in support of those indicted, and several hundred signed petitions accepting complicity in the bank burning. The fact that most of the seventeen were well-known political activists or public figures on campus, together with the revelation that two of them had been in jail at the time the bank burned, fueled suspicions that the indictments were politically motivated. During the support rally, the temporary bank and several realty offices were stoned yet another time. More confrontations took place between those advocating and those opposed to such attacks. The situation had a familiar look about it.

For three days, "the bank was the scene of intense but localized demonstrations and rock throwing" (Potter and Sullivan 1970: 98), but the "cool it" forces, aided by the county sheriffs, managed to prevail. Local officials were reportedly under increasing pressure from Sacramento to carry out a crackdown on student dissent, however. On June 7, the police broke up a community festival that had run several hours past the 7:30 P.M. curfew, announcing to the crowd that they had ten minutes to safely return home before arrests would begin. A large group— perhaps one thousand people—left the festival, marched to the bank, and attacked it in force, almost setting it afire. The police responded with sweeps through the residential areas of Isla Vista. Four days of renewed and heightened mass violence followed, and the Los Angeles County Special Enforcement Bureau was called in, along with the National Guard. Numerous instances of police misconduct—beatings, illegal apartment break-ins, indiscriminate use of tear gas, unlawful arrests, and verbal abuse—were reported (Santa Barbara Citizens' Commission on Civil Disorder 1970: 9–11; Potter and Sullivan 1970: 117–26).

"Isla Vista III" culminated on June 10 with a mass sit-in of students, faculty, and other adults at Perfect Park to protest police brutality. By 7 P.M. that evening, about 1,500 people had gathered in the park. Police helicopters and sound trucks warned the demonstrators to disperse or face arrest for unlawful assembly; the curfew deadline was approaching. About half obeyed, joining a crowd rimming the Loop. The scene resembled a battle zone, with officers in flak jackets and gas masks, and trucks and tear gas equipment ringing the field. Faculty members tried to negotiate a last-minute lifting of the curfew, but were unsuccessful. As the deadline arrived, a murmur of "sit down, sit down" ran through the crowd. The "Star Spangled Banner" and other patriotic songs were sung. At 7:45, the officers moved in and began making arrests. In the beginning, with some exceptions, the arrests were orderly. As the evening progressed, however, they became rougher. About 9:30, after some 300 had been arrested, deputies donned gas masks and warned that gas would be used if the order to disperse was not obeyed. An officer in a pickup truck then started a portable fog machine and aimed the nozzle over the crowd, who lay face down. Officers with night sticks then waded into the remaining protesters, dispersing them with force (Santa Barbara Citizens' Commission on Civil Disorder 1970: 11).

There was considerable public outcry against the behavior of the police, particularly the Los Angeles contingent. Twelve UCSB professors sent an urgent message to Jerris Leonard, chief of the civil rights division of the Department of Justice, asking for an investigation of civil rights violations in Isla Vista by law enforcement officers. "In this deteriorating situation," they warned, "there has been a serious and growing loss of confidence in the rule of law. A tragedy of unprecedented proportions may be in the making." A volunteer prosecuting attorney assisting the Santa Barbara courts resigned his position, stating: "The criminal conduct of a few young people is of lesser significance in comparison with official lawlessness conducted behind the badge of a police officer" (quoted in Potter and Sullivan 1970: 58). Even the *Santa Barbara News Press*, staunchly conservative and previously unrelenting in its criticism of student protesters, in an editorial of June 11 "urgently recommended" that "the sheriff take action to ensure that his men, or men under his control, do not illegally force their way into homes or apartments," that "all law enforcement personnel be warned to protect the safety and civil rights of all citizens," and that "acts of terrorism and intimidation by law officers as well as by demonstrators be vigorously prosecuted" (quoted in Potter and Sullivan 1970: 102). Few citizens were now willing to repeat Reagan's call for a "blood bath"; by this time hundreds of parents had come to Isla Vista to bail their children out of jail and suddenly realized whose blood would be spilled. (All told, there were 667 arrests during the eight days of Isla Vista III.)

Finally, County Sheriff James Webster met with several community leaders and announced a relaxation in the curfew and a sharp reduction in the number of police assigned to Isla Vista (Potter and Sullivan 1970: 13). "We felt [this] would be the best way to return things to normal and cool everyone off," Webster stated. With the reduced police presence, the number of confrontations did, in fact, drop significantly. On June 12, County Administrator Raymond D. Johnson conferred with Governor Reagan's office and then announced that the curfew had been lifted completely. After more than one hundred days of turmoil, a semblance of order had been restored.

The lives of several Isla Vistans were still very much embroiled in turmoil, however. Eleven people were scheduled to go on trial in August for burning the bank, each of them facing over twenty years in prison (indictments against six others had been dropped). The legal difficulties of others were not over, either. Those who had been arrested in connection with the campus demonstrations—the Santa Barbara 19—were still awaiting the resolution of their case. Additionally, there had been almost 1,000 arrests during the three riots themselves (although the charges against most of the Perfect Park sit-in arrestees had been dismissed). And even if they had avoided arrest, hundreds of young, white Californians had actively participated in something very like an insurrection. The bitterness lingered, as did anxiety over what might happen next.

It seems likely that the months of conflict had left a mark, in some way, on nearly everyone involved.[4] Many students had been "radicalized" by the actions of the police, especially during Isla Vista III. Others had been galvanized to oppose the violence actively, some going so far as to physically defend the bank when it came under assault. Even those students who had few, if any, political concerns and who had sought to avoid as much of the conflict as possible could not escape its ferocity. Tear gas seeped into almost every apartment, helicopters hovered over everyone's head, dusk-to-dawn curfews defined the parameters of every resident's life, and troops patrolled the streets that all had to travel. The war—at least for a while—had indeed come home.

PRIVATE IMAGINATIONS

In reporting on and accounting for the "Isla Vista rebellion," we have written of the political backdrop and the precipitating events, the surging crowds and the violent street battles. Portrayed in this fashion, the story assumes the form of a seething collective drama, a riotous performance with a cast of thousands. But what of the faces in the crowd? Our interest in this study is not so much in the historical drama itself as it is in the individual actors and their relationship to that event, in the interplay between history and personal experience. "History," William Irwin Thompson reminds us, "is in fact a process by which a private imagination becomes a public event, but any study that restricted itself

to public events would have to ignore the fact that history is also a process by which public events become private imaginations" (Thompson
1967: 235). We need to consider, therefore, the different ways in which
the events of 1970 in Isla Vista stirred the imaginations of individuals, to
see the events through their eyes, both as an initial step toward understanding this complex interplay and as a way of introducing some of the
men and women whose biographies we will be following in this study.

At the same time, it is through exploring the subjective side of the
Isla Vista rebellion, the intangible, emotional atmosphere in which it
occurred, that we can gain a greater understanding of its realities and
contradictions, and thus a greater appreciation of its legacy. In describing
the broad, collective contours of the struggle, we have tried to convey a
sense of what riot and rebellion looked like; now let us hear what it felt
like.

"I Ran Along with the Crowd, But I Couldn't Believe It"

Among the crowd confronting the sheriff's deputies in the Loop on
the night of February 25 was Roger Wade, then a twenty-year-old sociology major. Raised in an upper-middle-class San Diego suburb and in
a family that espoused liberal values, Wade was a recognized leader of
the Radical Union and one of its more articulate spokespersons. He was
also one of the Santa Barbara 19. That morning, Wade had helped distribute RU leaflets announcing the Perfect Park rally that was to follow
Kunstler's speech. "The idea in printing up these leaflets was clearly to
duplicate the previous nights actions," he recalls. "We wanted to get a
group together, a group that would be willing to get something going.
And that was all very open, although the leaflet didn't say 'come to
the park and riot.'" The question of whether the RU activists could be
successful in promoting such direct action soon became moot, however:
"The police managed to start it for us by beating up, in front of everyone, Rich Underwood. Completely unprovoked. So it didn't take much
instigation. We—this small group of people in the RU—we were continuously surprised in that first riot by the number of people who were
willing to take action, people who we had never seen before." But this
was the story throughout the uprising: the activists, who sought to lead
and guide a mass struggle (and the RU had clearly played a crucial role

in mobilizing support for William Allen), often found themselves almost on the sidelines as the students they had been trying to organize took matters into their own hands.

This new development was dramatized for Wade—as it was for other observers—by the crowd's response to the police sweep through the Loop on Wednesday night. "Lots and lots of people had gathered at the scene of that afternoon incident [Underwood's arrest], and the people in the Radical Union gathered there too. We stood around, and essentially helped inspire and participate in sort of . . . crowd anger-raising actions. Then the police appeared on the scene. I had participated in some street actions in Berkeley and had some familiarity with how crowds typically responded, and I knew that the pattern up there was that the police charged and everybody ran, so there really wasn't much aggressive behavior by the crowd in the face of a police line. And this was the attitude of most of us who were part of this 'hidden' leadership group—at least we thought we were leading. Then the police began sort of marching in a line toward the crowd and I started running back, assuming that we would throw some rocks and then everyone would run. And I was completely surprised when they started running forward, charging the police, and the police ran. And I ran along with the crowd, but I couldn't believe it!"

While Wade was unprepared for the militancy of the crowd, he did not hesitate to join it. "I participated in the riots extensively, and that involved street fighting. I thought the riots were the best thing that could happen to Isla Vista and did everything possible to encourage them. Most of my time I spent running around trying to organize little blockades, essentially. The police were, after that first riot, disorganized, and the only thing they could do was speed into town in unmarked cars and throw tear gas grenades, so whatever strategy evolved on the part of the rioters was simply an attempt to block these people as they sped around. We would push dumpsters out and other things to stop them. Unsuccessfully! So my efforts were essentially kind of loosely coordinative, without any particular effectiveness. That was my response to things." As for the bank burning, "that came as a complete shock. I wasn't involved, however, in burning the bank, and that has been a source of unending teasing [from friends]. I didn't even see it. But I would have been involved, had I been there."

"I Felt That I Wanted to Burn It Down"

Other Radical Union activists were equally surprised at the willingness of many students to engage in violence but had more ambivalent feelings about the raging street battle and, consequently, were uncertain about what actions to take. One of these RU members was Ed Pines, a twenty-seven-year-old recent graduate of UCSB whose involvement in the New Left began with the civil rights movement of the early sixties. A shy, soft-spoken, and often intensely self-absorbed man, he had spent most of his time during the three years prior to the 1970 events organizing against the draft, turning in his own draft card in 1967 and refusing induction a year later.

Pines acknowledges that he had strong feelings about nonviolent resistance, emphasizing what he terms "this Quaker side of me, these reservations about violence. The Quakers have this 'respect your enemy' ethic: Try to have a dialogue with them, try to respect them as people." At the time, however, Pines found himself wondering whether peaceful dissent was achieving anything. On February 25 in the campus stadium, he felt that William Kunstler was expressing many of these same concerns: "In his speech, Kunstler didn't come right out and urge violence, but he spoke of the massive injustice going on. We knew he understood the frustration we felt about the war, about what took place in Chicago, about the grievances here with the university, with the draft, the police, the realtors. He was sensitive to our frustration and powerlessness. He understood the need for people to take to the streets."

When Isla Vistans did indeed "take to the streets" only hours after the stadium rally, Pines was faced with some hard choices. "All through that afternoon and evening, there was this tension inside me: Should I get involved? Let myself go with the frenzy of the night, the spontaneity of the violence? Or should I hold myself back, maybe try to prevent violence, refuse to join in? My feelings kept shifting back and forth during the whole night." And this uncertainty was compounded by a certain amount of fear: "Some people were just into it—they loved throwing the rocks, but I was very cautious, because I didn't trust the police. I had been in Newark during the riots there, and I knew they could come out shooting; so I was very cautious and calculating throughout all of it." Thus, when the force of sheriff's deputies arrived at the Loop, Pines was one of those who immediately withdrew. "I went back to my apartment.

But the other people in the crowd were just 'freer.' Amazingly, they started attacking the police from the streets, from behind buildings." The police withdrew from the community, "and then it was just anarchy, in the sense that there was no authority around."

Despite his ambivalence and caution, Pines found himself becoming "wrapped up in the fever of it, the excitement of that moment, that whole period of time. I left my apartment, came onto the streets and appraised the situation. I was very frustrated the bank didn't take, didn't burn down when the dumpster was set on fire." Still, there were more questions, more political concerns: "I went to the bank, looked it over, and asked myself, 'Do I really want this bank to burn to the ground? Or is this just a symbolic sort of thing? Do we really want to make a statement? Do we want this bank up in flames?'"

Finally, he decided to act. "I felt that I wanted to burn it down. So, I went back to my apartment, where a friend of mine earlier in the day had left a fire extinguisher that was filled to the top with gasoline. To the amazement of my roommate, I took the extinguisher and left with the intention of soaking the bank down and lighting it up again. But by this time the bank was full of people. I couldn't do it. It was impossible for me to use the gasoline; it was just risky; it was dangerous. I was fearful that if the gas hit some smoldering debris, a flame might flash back to the extinguisher and explode. Ironically, I was also afraid of what my friends would think if they saw me walking about with a fire extinguisher. That could hurt my reputation as a radical. I'd lose my political credibility! They'd think I wanted the fire out. There was a good chance I'd get jumped by some of the rioters, or even worse, that one of the people who were actually trying to put out the fire [with genuine fire extinguishers] would get hold of mine and try to use it to douse the remains of the fire." Pines took his extinguisher and hid it in the park. "It wasn't needed. I wasn't needed. There were enough other people doing it. I didn't personally burn the bank, but I got tempted; I got worked up enough."

While other activists shared Pines's ambivalence, not all "got all worked up enough" to join the rioters. Fear and confusion exerted a considerable influence on some individuals, even as they were deeply moved by the drama unfolding before them. Sheila Barressi, a senior history major who had grown up in a radical, film industry family and who was one of several RU members in a leadership position on the student newspaper, experienced just this mixture of emotions. "I was walking around Isla Vista feeling really scared. And then I stood in front of the bank with Ed Pines, watching it burn and got . . . I felt very excited by it, exhilarated, but at the same time I was really scared, scared of the physical violence. I was afraid of getting hurt. I don't really think I felt as much of the anger that other people did. I didn't quite understand what was happening, emotionally. I remember walking around I.V. with a friend of mine, and I was saying, 'Why are people into throwing rocks? I don't really understand.' I was trying to get him to explain it to me. I felt outraged about what was going on politically too, but because I was timid, I didn't really translate that into physical violence."

"We Wanted Pig Blood"

While fear certainly took its toll, we have also seen how the hesitancy to engage in violence on the part of activists like Ed Pines was rooted in concern over the political "correctness" of the violence, over whether or not it would achieve the desired political ends. Thus, we have Pines asking himself, "Do we really want to make a statement? Do we want this bank up in flames?" Radical activists tend to have sophisticated notions of political theory, strategy, and tactics. Their outrage has been disciplined into organizational activity: they are typically too "rational" to become "adventurist." Roger Wade described the situation in much the same terms: "The political people tended to be very cautious about being in the spotlight, but there were all these craze-os who were completely into the whole thing and who were much more creative about their violence. They would go out and do very visible things."

This is not to say, of course, that the masses of young people on the streets during the riots felt no ambivalence whatsoever about violence. The reality was quite the opposite. As an active participant in the uprising told us: "There were street debates going on all the time about whether we should use violence. I can remember a huge marching rally through the Loop. People would throw rocks through real estate office windows and leave the Christian Science Reading Room windows perfectly intact, and every time that would happen there would be this big debate in this moving, marching mass of people and you would hear arguments going on everywhere: 'Yes, throw rocks, fuck them!' some people would say. 'No, don't throw rocks!' others would argue. 'But

they're ripping us off!' would be the reply. 'Mary Silvers [a widely dis-
liked realtor] should be in jail. In any other city she would be in jail, so
I'm gonna break her window!' "

The point, then, is not to make invidious comparisons between "politicos" and "craze-os," but rather to suggest that questions of political
strategy and organization were not only discussed and debated by New
Left activists during moments of confrontation, but were likely to be central to their day-to-day lives; in fact, such concerns were perhaps their
most distinguishing feature.

The Radical Union was an extraordinarily diverse organization, however. As in all other political groupings, its supporters displayed a wide
range of zeal, conviction, and assurance. Not all of its members were oriented to a programmatic style of politics; consequently, when the dam
broke and people spilled into the streets, not everyone in the RU was
held back by strategic considerations. There were some whose actions
were indeed very visible, whose thoughts were less tempered by questions of proper tactics, and who had little ambivalence about violence.
Barney Thompson, for instance, a twenty-two-year-old history student
from a conservative midwestern family, gave us this especially enthusiastic account of what he saw and felt and did on February 25: "I went
down to see Bill Kunstler speak at the stadium and came back with the
mob. I mean, we were ready for action. The verdicts, the outrageous
verdicts that came down in the Chicago trial . . . we were ready to give
our own verdict in the streets, and we did it. The pigs made it easy.
They were cruising around in their riot gear, bristling shotguns out the
windows, and people were stoning them.

"Finally, some guy was smashing the windows out in a cop car, just
being really bold. The pigs split; they immediately lost their aura of
invincibility and split. We hunted around Isla Vista for more pigs. We
wanted pig blood. I was part of this mob that came in front of this realty.
I actually broke the first realty window that night; it was a lot of fun. It
was a no-deposit Coke bottle I picked up in a vacant lot.

"You know, I was amazed at the fury that people showed that night.
Some tried to rip buildings apart with their hands, just tearing apart
realty offices; pigs fighting each other to get the fuck out of this community full of insane people that hated them; people charging like gladia-
tors, with trash-can lid shields, throwing rocks at the cops. I mean, the
whole night was just wonderful. It really illustrated what Marx said

about the Paris Commune: a festival of the oppressed. You saw people walking around with a light in their eyes and look on their face that you had just never experienced in everyday life. There were hours at a time when there was nothing to do but enjoy being in liberated territory. That's what people did most of the night, because there were no more cops. I mean, people occupied themselves with barricades and, you know, took care of business as best they could, but most of the time, all you had to do was experience the new feelings you were coming into."

Like Wade, Thompson missed the bank burning, an event which was almost anticlimactic for him after the high of having experienced "liberated territory." "I thought, 'Well, we beat the cops, we beat the enemy,' and that was it. I didn't really think beyond that. I didn't think about burning the bank. And as it got later and there were fewer and fewer people on the street, other people were drifting off, they were getting tired. I went home. But there were obviously people around who thought differently, who had a clear political vision and actually burned the thing to the ground, which gave the rebellion its worldwide impact. I heard about it on the radio and rushed back out. Saw the glow in the sky and was out there to enjoy the bonfire.

"One of my first thoughts as I watched it was, 'This puts Isla Vista on the map, and I'm from Isla Vista.' It's one thing to be a rebel and sort of groove on your 'fuck everything' attitude, but when you can actually fuck something really big, like the Bank of America—God, there's just nothing compared to it!"

"I Just Threw and I Ran!"

The street warfare captured the imagination of many other RU members, including Bill McNaughton, a twenty-six-year-old graduate student in chemistry. McNaughton was one of the few activists at Santa Barbara with a working-class background. Born in New England, the first member of his family to go to college, McNaughton had once planned on joining the Marine Corps and had taken ROTC training as an undergraduate. Unlike Barney Thompson, McNaughton did not take part in the battle of February 25. "I was over at the stadium, where Kunstler was speaking, and I walked over to the park afterwards, and then everything started," he remembers. "I stayed there until maybe 6:30 or so, and I was with some friends, and they suggested that I shouldn't be around then, because I was getting to be too well known [as a political person]. And so what I did was, I started walking over to the chemistry building, and I got over there, as I found later, just after they started pushing the dumpster into the bank the first time."

McNaughton spent most of the evening in his office and lab, working with several other graduate students and faculty members. "It wasn't until the next morning," McNaughton notes, "that I found out the bank had been burned. I walked past it that morning. There wasn't much there: ashes, some parts that were still standing and charred. The safe was still there, though. The safe hadn't melted. You could see the safe from all around the bank, the walls were all down and everything. It was a mess."

Later, McNaughton shed his caution and joined the others in the streets. The dump truck maneuver that precipitated Isla Vista II stands out in his memory: "I'll never forget the first night of the second riot. They had this temporary bank, and it was all fenced in except for the street. And I was standing there, just outside of the fence, and the trucks came. All of a sudden you hear this 'R-R-R-R!' and you look down the street and you see these lights that were just—you know, a car light is like, about two feet off the ground, and you just see these lights that were way up off the ground, and everyone's saying, 'What's that comin' up the street?' No one had ever thought about dump trucks. And now, all of a sudden you see these little 'Ch! Ch! Ch's!' going off, and I'm standing there watching it, and it was almost pretty, these lights that you couldn't make out. It was mysterious and spooky, all these things going up the street.

"Then you hear 'Bam! Bam!' and 'P-s-s-s-s, P-s-s-s-s.' All of a sudden someone says, 'Tear gas!' and then it clicked. I go, 'Oh, that's right, tear gas!' I turned and looked and I go, 'Oops! There's a fence.' I almost ran into the fenced area. I ran around the corner, but I remember all these people who were there trying to stop the riots were inside and they got caught in the fenced area, caught by the gas. But I'm runnin', and I'm runnin', and the first thing I was gonna do was go across the park, but the trucks pulled up, into the park, so I turned the other way. I got across the street and made it to a friend's apartment right ahead of the law, where I spent the night. Then I found out all the people in the park were getting shot with shotguns. God, all I had to do was turn that way and I would've gotten shot."

That realization did not stop McNaughton from going back out the next night and participating in hit-and-run attacks on the police. "I remember the cops coming down the street with their shields and everything, and just moving back and throwing rocks. And then they stopped and sent a bunch of reporters out to talk to us and tell us to go home and that we're going to get arrested. And I remember them watching the reporters walk back, and right after they walked back we just let loose with another avalanche of rocks. Then later on we went into the alleys." McNaughton pauses in his story, his voice now dropping almost to a whisper. "We were sneakin' down this alleyway to get really close to the Loop. There were cops standing all around the Loop, and we just crawled up these alleys. Everybody's got stones; there were about four or five of us, you know, just pockets full of stones. And you just let go, you don't even look at what you're throwing. You just got all these stones and your goal is to get down there and just unload every stone that you've got in your pockets and in your hands, as fast as you can, and then turn around and just run. I don't think I ever hit anything. I just threw and I ran!"

"It Was Sheer Terror"

While the activists knew that once the authorities were able to organize their forces, the police response to the rioting would be massive, few were prepared for the actual experience. As one put it: "I wasn't surprised that it happened, but when I saw it actually happening—it's like, 'I can't believe this is happening!' We were certainly aware that there was repression like this going on across the country, but when it happens to you, it's hard to imagine the reality. It's kind of a shock."

More than anything else, the official response demonstrated just how defenseless Isla Vista was against well-organized police power. Thus, for Kristen Van Duinen, an eighteen-year-old anthropology student (and Santa Barbara 19 defendant), one glimpse of "Operation Wagon Train" in action was more than enough proof of the protesters' vulnerability. "People built a barricade across this street because that would cut off the Loop, so dump trucks would come charging around the corner toward the Loop and we'd have this barricade there," she recalls. "And they came hauling ass, at like forty miles an hour, and they just went right through it. I mean, I don't know what was in that barricade, all kinds of mattresses and chairs and trash cans, and they just didn't even slow down, they just barreled right through it. I just went 'Whoaaa!' We were watching on the balcony of this apartment, and they're shootin' off their grenade launchers, and there's gas all over the place, and—Oh! It was a sense of . . . of their power, it was overwhelming, and they were there to put on this incredible show of force, and they did. God . . .

"I remember one night about fifteen of us [in the RU] got trapped in this apartment, and the pigs by then were doing their maneuvers on foot and skulking around apartments. And we were face down on the living room floor, with all the lights out, panic-stricken. And helicopters were circling overhead and tear gas launchers were going off. They were shooting tear gas from the Loop toward campus, and somehow it just went right through those windows, 'cause nothing was sealed and they just absolutely inundated that street. We were choking inside, and trying not to choke 'cause they're also walking around with their gas masks and their shields, and we're going, 'Oh God, if they ever walk in here.' We're just shaking on the floor, terrified. It was so unbelievable. It was sheer terror."

Other activists did experience police break-ins. Denise Saal, then an eighteen-year-old English literature student from the San Francisco area, had moved to Isla Vista six months before the riots. "A day or two after the bank was burned, I was at the house of a friend of mine [another RU activist] where I had sort of been staying. It was like two o'clock in the morning, and we were asleep in bed and the police came and kicked the door in, about twelve of them, with shotguns and stuff, and yanked us out of our bed. I think we heard them pounding on the front door and so we jumped up and sort of hurriedly threw on a pair of jeans and were rushing into the living room when the door came in. We were very, very frightened. We were very frightened for our lives. A few officers had been injured the night before, one of them had his eye put out or something, and we knew that the police were really out for blood."

The police pushed Saal and her friend against the wall, "threatening us a lot," she says. "It was very scary." A quantity of material from the apartment was confiscated by the police, who later charged Saal with having fire bombs in her possession and produced gasoline in gallon-size

wine jugs ("which we had never seen before," Saal insists) as confirma-
tory evidence. Both she and her friend were immediately arrested: "The
actual experience of being involved in a riot and an occupation was ever
so heavy. I mean, it taught me what it's like to live in a police state. It was
a real emotional, gut-level experience of repression which most people
don't have. Most radicals have never experienced it."

"We Were in the Sanctuary of Sanctuaries"

Disbelief, uncertainty, confusion, anger, joy, exhilaration, terror: the
emotional responses of these Radical Union members to the Isla Vista
rebellion were varied and often shifting, as were their forms of participation. At the same time, however, their feelings were linked by a shared
sense of political and cultural identity, by their sense of being part of
the movement (however vaguely this political community was defined),
which provided a common base for understanding. Their experiences,
then, taken as a whole, represent one distinct side to the Isla Vista rebellion, and their involvement was understandably intense. But there were
other, less politically involved students who were caught up in the rush
of events or who suddenly found themselves reluctant participants in
history. Consider, for example, the story of Warren Newhouser.

Newhouser, son of a conservative southern California business executive, was twenty-one years old in 1970 and one year out of the university.
He had stayed in Isla Vista after graduating, working as a part-time gardener. Newhouser was not a member of the Radical Union, although he
knew some of the activist students and had participated in a few of the
campus demonstrations against the firing of William Allen. "I was political—political in the sense of sharing a basic consciousness, a cultural
consciousness more than anything," he notes, "but I was not willing to
be involved in the grind of political activity. So I wasn't directly involved
in radical organizations; I didn't have the time or the interest."

In the early evening of February 24, Newhouser was driving back
into Isla Vista with his girlfriend after a day at the beach. "We saw this
mass of people in the street, out in front of the Bank of America. There
were people throwing rocks at the bank and stuff like that. My girlfriend
didn't want to have any part of it; she drove home in the car. But I got
out and walked around and hung out, and was sitting there smoking
joints with friends of mine out in the streets. And then I had to leave.

I was supposed to meet this other friend of mine. I walked away from the crowd, and that was my mistake, because the crowd was standing in front of the bank and as I was walking away, around the bank, I was arrested. The police were hiding in the bushes in the park, so when I walked around the bank they just grabbed me. I was just loaded and walking away from the crowd, basically. They claimed they saw me do this and that and this and blah, blah, blah. It was a pretty crummy experience."

Charged with malicious mischief—a misdemeanor—and taken to the county jail, Newhouser was released the next morning, February 25. (He was later convicted of this charge and served two weeks in jail.) That afternoon, he went to hear William Kunstler's speech in the campus stadium. "I knew something was happening and I expected something to happen that afternoon, because I knew the reality of the situation, because I knew there were a lot of people that were politicized and aware and angry throughout Isla Vista. I expected there would be an attack on the Bank of America that night. And I was out for a while in the streets that night, but mostly I spent a lot of time in an apartment that has a balcony that overlooked the area, and there was about twenty of us up there."

When he was "in the streets," Newhouser was drawn to the bank building, for it was clearly the conflict's centerpiece. By that time the bank was already broken into, its doors wide open. Without any hesitation, Newhouser entered the ransacked building. "I'd, you know, walk through the bank," he remembers. "It was great. It was a fantastic experience. We were in the sanctuary of sanctuaries. I mean, when you talk about corporate sanctuaries, what else can you talk about besides the Bank of America? It was such a great symbolic event. I enjoyed it immensely. It was fun—that's what I was thinking at the time it was happening. Not fun as a light kind of thing, because it was very meaningful. Fun can be a deep sense of taking control, handling your own destiny. It was fun in terms of being liberating and meaningful and enjoyable."

Newhouser did not simply "walk through" the bank, however; he introduced his own ritual into what felt like a countercultural celebration. "I spent a lot of time, when I was in the bank, with a wastebasket upside down in my hand, like a drum, walking around singing, chanting —you know, Indian chants or something—walking outside and inside and telling people to come in and look at it, that it was their big chance.

Demystifying the bank: that's exactly what I saw happening, bringing it down to a real human level. Like we were saying, 'Look, these are just fuckin' assholes here in the bank, right? I mean they just built this building and put up all these walls, and most of the walls are in your head.' So it was a cultural event. Isla Vista was a free zone that evening."

Later in the evening, as people began to drift away from the bank, Newhouser went over to his girlfriend's house and stayed there. He did not, he states, see the bank burn. "I was tired. I had been up all night the night before in jail, and went to the speech and everything. I think the bank burned at about 1 A.M. or something. I was in bed by midnight." Like many other Isla Vistans who slept through the fire, he was more than a little stunned the next morning when he discovered what had happened. "I remember getting up in the morning and going outside to look at the sun, and a friend of mine was walking down the street. I just started talking to him, and he told me that the bank burned. 'What the fuck? I missed it!' I said. I mean, I didn't expect it to happen, 'cause I saw people try and start it on fire earlier that evening and being unsuccessful just because it was such a goddamn concrete structure. So I was surprised that it had gotten burned. I would have stayed longer, probably, if I thought it was gonna get burned. But I was tired and I thought, 'Fuck, I'll just go to bed.' So I left."

But the police had a photograph of him inside the bank that afternoon. In their eyes, it was a damning piece of evidence. On June 17, he received a phone call informing him that he and sixteen others—including Bill McNaughton, Denise Saal, Barney Thompson, and Ed Pines—had been indicted for arson, rioting, and several other felony offenses.

"People Went Mad"

In 1970, Kenneth Essian was a nineteen-year-old Isla Vistan who had been a liberal arts student at UCSB during the previous year. He was sympathetic to the student movement but "not involved in the radical politics" of the Radical Union. For Essian, the bank burning and the I.V. riots represented the explosion of mass frustration, frustration that simply reached the flash point. "That winter seemed particularly gray. It seemed like everyone was shut in and there was a lot of pent-up frustration that got released during the riots. It was a monsoon; there was a lot of energy." And, he recalls, "There were reasons for it. Isla Vista was kind of a slum town. There were the conditions that prevailed there, and conditions surrounding Bill Allen."Still, he feels that the rioting itself could only be described as crazy. "There was a feeling of mob psychology and people went mad. There was no reason for what was going on [in the streets]. It seemed to me to be pent-up frustration and anger that was being released."

Essian found this energy "very easy to get caught up in; I remember having an intense curiosity as to what was going on." On the evening of February 25, he watched as the crowd threw rocks at the sheriff's deputies and burned the police car. "I remember being caught up in it, the feeling. I was out on the streets, partly out of curiosity, partly out of many other things. I participated in the riot that night a little bit, but not much. I wasn't there when the bank was set on fire, but I saw the bank burn after it was started and quite well along."

His feelings as he observed the fire were ambivalent. "It was a very heavy thing, not something that happens every day, and I was wondering what the implications of it would be. I wasn't thinking strongly that it was a bad thing or a good thing, but I had studied and read about Gandhi and nonviolence and it was a violent act. Perhaps I wasn't sure if that was the best way to accomplish certain goals."

There is no doubt that Essian's involvement in the February protests was peripheral. Unlike Newhouser, for example, he did not march about in the vacant bank, nor did he enthusiastically embrace the assault on the Bank of America building as a liberating act. But his story has another twist to it, a twist that brings it into convergence with Newhouser's. Three hours after the bank was set aflame, when police reinforcements and National Guard troops were in the process of "retaking" Isla Vista, Essian was one of several hundred residents on the streets. "I was standing in a yard. It was very late at night. Some policemen had come by with tear gas and had made a sweep down the street, and then they had left. Not all of the police had gone, though; some of them were waiting in the bushes. Clever guys! And so I heard this sound, and it was this policeman running to tackle me. And I didn't realize it was happening before it was too late, so when he went to tackle me, I kind of rolled with his tackle and then got up and ran. I ran to a neighboring house and the police came there also, and eventually arrested me—they came in there. We were taken to a place where they were holding people, and then eventually to the jail. I was charged with participating in a riot and failing to disperse, and released on bail a day or so later."

After pleading guilty to "failure to disperse," Essian was put on probation with a six-month suspended sentence. Although he did not take part in political activity during the remainder of the winter quarter or in the spring, and had no contact with the Radical Union, his arrest on the night of the bank burning had marked him, at least for the authorities, as a radical. And this made him an arson suspect. His picture was shown to those who claimed to have witnessed the attack on the bank, and on June 17, Kenneth Essian was charged with participating in its burning.

"I Remember Him Saying, 'My God, I Think I've Been Shot'"

To this point, we have considered the experiences of several Radical Union activists, as well as those of two students who were not particularly involved in political activity but who were nevertheless swept up by the sheer intensity of the riots and, in one case, inspired to join in. Now let us turn to the responses and impressions of individuals who, in sharp contrast to both the political activists of the RU and "cultural radicals" like Warren Newhouser, were part of decidedly more conventional student subcultures. These narratives will enable us to develop a more complete account of the event. Further, it is through such comparisons that the extraordinary influence of the 1970 Isla Vista riots on New Left activists and their sympathizers can be pointedly demonstrated, laying the groundwork for an understanding of the riots' long-range consequences.

We begin with Charles Johnson, an ex-Marine and Vietnam veteran. After being discharged from the military in 1967, Johnson enrolled in a Los Angeles–area community college. Two years later, at age twenty-three, he transferred to UCSB, where he majored in history. To help put himself through school, Johnson worked as a part-time manager at one of the small stores that dotted the Loop area in Isla Vista. Additionally, unlike most students at the university, he lived in Santa Barbara, his apartment a twenty-minute drive by freeway from campus. "I wasn't comfortable with the whole Isla Vista scene," he explains. "I thought that the apartment buildings were something of a rip-off, and there were over ten thousand people packed into a square mile."

Besides finding the physical setting unsatisfying, Johnson was also alienated from the cultural environment. "There were a lot of street people, just a lot of bizarre stuff that I was not really into. I was not heavily into the drug scene. I smoked a little dope—that was about it. And I didn't relate as well with people who lived there as I did with the guys who lived in my apartment complex in Santa Barbara, who were, by and large, working stiffs." In these ways, Johnson was very much a mirror-opposite of Warren Newhouser. Yet, like Newhouser, he would be drawn into the center of the storm.

Johnson witnessed the initial attempts to burn the bank during the afternoon and early evening of February 25. "From my perspective, it was just a bunch of kids who were bored, and had nothing better to do, and were just having fun and got carried away. And there was no more rationale to it than just doing something else to see what would happen next. There was nothing organized about it. It was a spontaneous combustion."

In the days that followed the bank burning, Johnson found himself totally at odds with those explanations of the incident that stressed its political meaning. "I was really disgusted and angry about what happened, and it made me even angrier when I saw the pseudo-explanations that came out. All of the arguments about the bank being a symbol of the military-industrial complex, that's just a rationalization, not a reason; that's a bunch of crap. I just didn't see it through the same eyes they did."

Johnson's anger simmered as the public debate and controversy over the February events continued. On the night of April 17 it boiled over as rioting broke out once again. "I came into I.V. again to see a girlfriend, who was not home. So I stopped at this little pizza joint, this little place on the corner across the street from the bank. They had cleared the rubble away by then from where the original Bank of America stood, and next to it, in a field, they had built a temporary bank." This makeshift structure was actually a trailer with a small porch fronting its single glass door. Several light poles were erected around the trailer, and at night it was bathed in brightness. As Johnson sat eating his pizza, he heard what sounded like breaking glass, and then he saw the lights around the bank go out. He walked outside.

"There was a crowd in front of the temporary bank building and I could see the same damn thing starting to happen again, which really disturbed me. They started throwing rocks, and they broke the windows out and the door out, and then somebody threw in a fire bomb, which consisted of something like a Gallo wine jug filled full of gasoline. And that triggered me. I didn't plan this, I didn't think about it or anything, it was just a gut reaction: I ran across the street and I had a motorcycle jacket on and I pulled that off, and I went through the door of the bank, being careful not to cut myself on the shards of glass. And I went inside and kicked the fire bomb away from where it was burning—it was by the drapes—into the center of the room. It was a dumb move. I just spilled gas all over the place, and I just started beating out the flames with my jacket. It took me three or four minutes, but I finally got them all out.

"I came back out and stood in front of the building. There was a little cement platform there, with a bannister. At that point I was joined by five other guys. So there were six of us there: myself, this guy Kevin Moran, Kevin's roommate, and three others. We all stood in line. I was near the end of the line and Kevin was standing next to me. And the crowd was still standing there. They weren't throwing rocks, but they were yelling obscenities and shouting at us to get out of the way. Everybody was screaming and shouting. I was really pissed. I was shouting, 'God damn it, you're not gonna burn this one down too!'

"Just at that time, big trucks of sheriff's deputies started screaming in from all different directions. I mean, those guys just came in like gangbusters from everywhere, and started piling off the trucks. And we just stood there, we didn't move, but the crowd scattered. They just started going in 180 different directions. And right at the height of all this—there was tear gas that was goin' off, and just a lot of noise and confusion—just at the climactic moment, in the midst of all this, Kevin sort of slumped against me, and I remember him saying, 'My God, I think I've been shot!'

"I grabbed him, and just kind of laid him out, and fumbled around, got his belt loose and got his shirt off. He had a wound in his abdomen. I thought it looked like a .22 slug. There wasn't much bleeding, just a little hole and a little bit of abdominal material that had kind of come through the hole and plugged it up. This sheriff's deputy came running up and I told him we needed a first aid unit, and he ran back to his truck and grabbed a kit and brought it back. I grabbed a compress out of that, and wrapped it around Kevin and tied it. I checked his pulse, but couldn't get a pulse. I remember saying to the deputy, 'My God, I think he's dead!' And I couldn't believe it, 'cause it was just like . . . two minutes. I guess he went right away. I don't remember him saying another word. I think he passed out after he hit the ground."

Kevin Moran had been shot by a high-powered rifle, not a .22. His pelvic bone was shattered, and bone fragments tore through his body; death was caused by massive internal bleeding. Although early reports labeled the shooting as the work of a sniper, this allegation proved false; the bullet that killed Moran came from the gun of an officer from the Santa Barbara Police Department, who later reported that his rifle went off accidentally as he jumped out of a dump truck. Johnson believes that the bullet could just as easily have killed him. "Kevin was standing right next to me, to my right, and the bullet came in from the right side, and if he hadn't been standing there, I would have gotten it. He was the only thing between me and that slug."

More jarring than that knowledge, however, was the shock of witnessing violent death in the streets of Isla Vista. "The thing that shook me up the most, more than anything else," Johnson emphasizes, "was just the whole unexpectedness of it. I had gotten inured to that stuff in Vietnam. Hell, when I stepped off the plane in Chu Lai, they rolled up with a truck full of dead marines, and I saw more than a few bodies after that in the six months I was there. But you know, that was a different world. A different set of ground rules applied there, and it was part of the job—you didn't think about it. I did not expect that to happen on a college campus in a civilian world. That really shook me up. It was so unexpected."

"One John Wayne Could Have Stopped the Whole Thing"

The Delta Omega fraternity house was located on a tree-lined street four blocks from the Loop. Delta Omega was one of the "straightest" frats on campus. Its members typically had good grades and were generally known as responsible young men who kept their alcohol consumption within reasonable limits. The use of other drugs—aside from an occasional sampling of marijuana—or any display of interest in I.V.'s "freak culture" was discouraged. As one former "Delt" told us: "Basically, for the most part, the fraternity stayed away from drugs. There were some guys that used them, but drinking was acceptable and drugs wasn't. You weren't supposed to do it. So if guys were doing drugs, they were doing it out of sight. If guys were drinking, that was completely open, 'cause we used to buy kegs for the house."

Since the Delts were geographically separated from the primary battle-ground of the Isla Vista riots, they were better able to keep their distance from the street fighting than were the members of other frats, whose houses were often surrounded by whooping, screaming rioters, rifle-wielding police, and billowing clouds of tear gas. This is not to say that the lives of the Delta Omega men were not affected by the conflict, or that their emotions were not inflamed by violent attacks on Establishment targets, the hit-and-run street battles, and the sometimes severe police response; the riots were too overwhelming in their scope to ignore. Nevertheless, the Delts whom we interviewed tended to take the role of the audience—disbelieving and sometimes contemptuous, oftentimes confused witnesses to what many of them felt to be meaningless anarchy. Thus, when George Dawes, a twenty-year-old economics major and ROTC cadet from Van Nuys, stood a few hundred yards from the Bank of America in the early morning hours of February 26 and watched the flames leap into the sky, his feelings were along these very lines. "It just didn't make any sense. I watched how that crowd psychology worked, and I just didn't understand it. It was amazing to watch."

Dawes's view of the Bank of America was very different from that of the students who were ransacking it. "The Bank of America, as far as I was concerned, just wasn't any more 'guilty' than the gas station or the university itself. The bank was making all the student loans for every-body to go there, at low percentage rates, lower than market, and they were the only bank that would open student checking accounts, when all the students were bouncing checks like crazy, and it was of course not profitable for them to open all these accounts with three hundred dollars in them. They also employed students. When you went in there, a lot of the girls working in there were either students' wives or students themselves. And they burned it down. Just didn't make any sense to me."

It was more than differences with the protesters over the contributions of the Bank of America that influenced George Dawes's reactions. His feeling that the bank burning "just didn't make any sense" was more fundamentally shaped by the conviction that the desired ends of the protesters were impossible to discern and that the means they were em-ploying were absurd. "The whole riots were a joke. I never could understand why they were burning things. We were burning the community we were living in, which didn't make sense. And it just wasn't exactly the French Revolution or the American Revolution, where you could understand that it had some positive goals to establish or something like that." Dawes's beliefs were shared by other Delta Omega members with whom we spoke. One recalled: "The burning of the bank—it galled me. Because to destroy someone else's property makes no sense to me. I mean, it does not solve anything. I can understand theft; I mean, theft, there's a reward for it. But rampant destruction makes no sense."

George Dawes also felt, as he watched the fire consume the bank, that "the authorities were foolish for not coming in and stopping it. The police and the fire department were all sitting back when I thought a little show of force at the right time would have just done it. I couldn't believe it when the cops didn't come. I was thinking that one John Wayne could have stopped the whole thing, 'cause it took them so long to burn it. I mean, it took hours and hours and hours of building up. It just seemed ridiculous, like a grandstand show. And it took no guts to burn it, 'cause there was nothing there to stop them from doing it. It showed no great courage, because there was nobody there to stop them. And it just seemed like, when the bank would burn, it would then become a great symbol of what they were doing. And there was no great symbol, there was no courage. It just kind of happened."

For Dawes, the activists in the Radical Union who supported the protests—people like Roger Wade, Sheila Barressi, Ed Pines—were worthy of little respect. "I never met one of the leaders that I thought I could get behind, and who I thought had a reason for what he was doing. I saw some guy make a speech one time on the [Nixon] administration's stance and on burning the American flag, and he absolutely made no sense to me. And I couldn't understand how he could get anybody to go along with him. The logic just wasn't there, his presentation wasn't any good, his facts were all jumbled, and what he wanted everybody to do seemed ridiculous." Similarly, the "lifestyle or the intelligence of the people involved in some of the stuff that was going on," to use Dawes's own words, was equally suspect. "They didn't know what they were doing, where they were going. It was kind of like the Vietnam War gave these guys something to do, rather than something they really believed in."

Ironically, Dawes himself was arrested during Isla Vista III, although it was simply a matter of being in the wrong place at the wrong time. "It was after the big demonstration in Perfect Park," he recalls. "A girl who was a friend got stuck in one of the fraternities after being at the thing and got gassed or something like that, and was all hysterical and everything. And she called and said she just didn't want to be there and was getting all messed up and was not too happy about where she was. And so a friend of mine and I got in our car to go down and pick her up and get her out of there, and we got stopped by a roadblock and picked up for not having passes—it was after curfew—and we were thrown in jail. We were charged with violating the curfew." The charges were dismissed two days later, and Dawes makes a point of reporting that when he was arrested "they were very nice to us, they gave us everything they were supposed to, they read us our rights, they did the whole bit. And nobody was hurt, nobody was abused."

As for the charges of police brutality, particularly during the third riot, Dawes thinks that "there was an overreaction, especially by the L.A. SWAT teams," but that "there were so many people that were just trying to cause problems that it was very difficult for the police to separate" the troublemakers from the innocent bystanders. If the police and National Guard made one serious mistake, he says, it was loading their rifles with live ammunition. "That was ridiculous," he feels. "A guy got killed."

"They Were Foreign People to Me"

Clark Jeffries, then a twenty-one-year-old economics major from San Francisco and a fraternity brother of George Dawes, was on his way home with a friend from his job at a Santa Barbara gas station late in the evening on February 25 when he discovered that they could not drive into the university or Isla Vista: all campus entrances and nearby streets were barricaded. It was Jeffries' first indication that something was seriously amiss: "We didn't know what the hell was going on. So we parked the car a mile away from school and walked in. As we started walking in, you could sense that there was a lot of commotion. You could see there was a lot going on in the center of town. So we walked on down to see, and we got there just about the time whoever it was decided to try and burn the bank set it on fire [by pushing the flaming trash dumpster into the bank]. I mean, there was just a big crowd of people milling around, and the next thing you realize, the place was on fire. And it was just kind of a madhouse."

In contrast to George Dawes, Jeffries was not especially upset about what he saw. "It didn't really make me angry that they burned it. I could see the protesters' point, that they had, you know, maybe a legitimate beef." At the same time, however, Jeffries thoroughly disagreed with the protesters' tactics and, like Dawes and others in Delta Omega, found the action severely lacking in rationality. "To me it seemed stupid, because I knew they'd come in and build another one. You're not gonna hurt the Bank of America. I would never do it. I guess I wasn't as angry as everybody else. I know that you're against the war and everything that's going on, but that just didn't, to me, seem to be the right thing to do."

In the days following the bank burning, Jeffries and his fraternity brothers were more intrigued than outraged by the turmoil: "During the next few weeks and months when everybody was being gassed and bombed and everything else like that, it was, I think, for the fraternity and the guys in it, more of a neat, of a different kind of an experience, than it was a protest or something. It was something so foreign to what we were used to that it was more or less kind of fun. It was more of a game to see how long you could stay out in the street before the tanks rolled down the street, and you know, every once in a while, one of the guys in the fraternity didn't make it in the window. Those guys [in the National Guard] would come and yank somebody out of the window. And then, you know, we'd have to go down the next day and get them out of jail and tell them the guy didn't do anything wrong, he just was out there running around. He was running around in his underwear seeing how long he could stay outside without getting caught." As Frank Morrow, another Delt, put it, "It was entertaining. How could it not be, watchin' all this go on?" And Mark Reiss, who agreed with Dawes that "burning the Bank of America was senseless," also felt that "there was an air of excitement" about it all: "This sleepy school, it had really turned into something!"

The police response, from Jeffries' perspective, was not excessive. "From what I saw, they were probably fairly fair. We had a few from our fraternity thrown in with everybody else. But they were either after the curfew or walking around the streets or doing like I was saying, seeing how long you could stay on the streets, seeing if you were the last one in the window and got caught. So you really didn't have much of an excuse as to why you got caught." This assessment is based on what Jeffries himself describes as limited experience of what was happening on the streets. "A lot of the areas where there was any brutality or whatever, I wasn't there. I was off in some other part of town doing something else. The Delta house was probably three or four blocks away, at least, from the bank area. We were a little bit far removed. I didn't really see what was going on."

The Delta Omegas at this point were a group of detached observers with little at stake personally in the struggle. Here the contrast between their feelings and reactions and those of most of the RU activists (and other individuals who, in various ways, became deeply involved in these events) is especially distinct. Clark Jeffries drew the boundaries between these two sides in this way: "I just never really got caught up in the protest or anything like that. And I think mainly it was because of my feelings for the fraternity, the group I was with. I don't think really any of them were that much into protesting. And it wasn't my thing, I guess. I thought the radicals were screwballs. I didn't know that many of them. I didn't really associate with them; I didn't party with them. And they were foreign people to me."

"It Was the Fall of Everything"

Once the steadily escalating conflict began to seriously affect the daily lives of even the most uninvolved students, once the police began to rely on force in their suppression of the protests, the character of the experience changed dramatically. Consider Clark Jeffries' account: "For a few days or weeks it was fun, you know, with tear gas thrown all over the place because it was such a different kind of experience and, you know, a chance to miss school and everything. But after a while, it got to be a little annoying. I was kind of fed up with it. I was there to go to school and have a good time, and it was getting in the way of doing that. I would just as soon had them get the school back to the way it was, get back to doing what we were supposed to be doing. I'm sitting here dodging bullets and dodging tear gas canisters trying to get from here to there and it just was, again, kind of an annoyance to me."

For others, like Larry Goodwin, a twenty-one-year-old history student and Bakersfield native who came to UCSB to play football, "it was the fall of everything. A little bit of utopia was all of a sudden marred in tear gas and plastic bullets. You say to yourself, 'Wait a minute, this isn't the world that I came to school at.' " Goodwin notes that he was "right there when the bank blew up." Speaking about the first attempt to burn it on February 25, he recalls: "I saw the flames. There were a lot of us there that were more interested bystanders than there were actual participants in the proceedings. A lot of people were intrigued or curious about what was going on. And I was, I mean, I was curious as to what these people were gonna do, and when all of a sudden a move was made to torch, you're saying to yourself, 'Whoa, now you got problems,' 'cause you knew the wrath that was gonna be incurred. And boy it came. It came just lickity-split."

Goodwin and two friends were caught out in the open during a series of tear gas barrages. "I remember the gas very vividly. All hell broke loose, and we got caught in it. We came back through campus, and down to the beach to get home, and that's when the cloud of pepper gas came down on the beach, and the helicopters were running up and down the beach with these big spotlights on 'em. Fuckin' ridiculous!" Later in the year, during Isla Vista III, he found even the most routine tasks of going to school continually disrupted by the raging battle that sometimes pushed itself right into his bedroom. "I was sitting there studying one night," he explains, "and all of a sudden the cops come blowin' in through a door 'cause they think they saw somebody run in. And this was at eight o'clock at night, but there was a curfew. It was like, you know, [they] grab you, throw you outside, 'Up against the wall!' " It was "police overreaction," Goodwin felt. "I suppose there's a degree of justification for it, but their handling of it was ridiculous—driving around in dump trucks, bringing in goon squads that rough people up and stuff like that. Come on! I mean, that was a little bit discouraging!"

Additionally, Goodwin had several run-ins with the authorities as he drove to and from work after the six o'clock curfew. "I used to get up at three and work from three-thirty until seven in the morning and load these bloody trucks. So I broke curfew every time; every day I'd get stopped by the same group of fuckin' people, same cops or National Guard. They'd search the car, make sure I wasn't carrying anything in or out, always a little melodramatic, you know, the jeeps with the red lights and all that, and I'd pass and I'd say, 'Look, you know I'm gonna be going down here every day, same time, same car. Why do we have to go through this?' And they say, 'Don't give me any shit. Get out of the car!'" And here Larry Goodwin laughs, struck by the craziness of it all: "Really bizarre."

In the end, though, he feels regret at the loss of that "little bit of utopia," that sunny, tranquil world that UCSB was supposed to be. "For something that had been so terrific all through three and a half years . . . the riots took away from all the enthusiasm that we'd had all through school."

"It Must Be a Bad Dream"

These feelings of regret and disappointment over what was lost because of the protests were shared by many of the nonactivists. Sometimes it led to bitterness, as the comments of Carl Rohrback, Delta Omega's president in 1970, reveal. "That year started out fine. We had a lot of good things going as a fraternity house and I was excited about the year ahead, and then we got into the second and third quarter and this whole situation started heating up. When the bank was burned, I was kinda shaking my head saying, 'I can't believe that!' I just couldn't believe that something like that was getting out of control. It got worse from then on out; that whole last quarter was ridiculous. I felt a little angry that my education was somewhat cheated. I felt like I was in a war zone."

While Rohrback "tried to stay away" from the rioting—"I don't have to chase fire trucks to go see things," he says—it soon reached the point where no place and no one was left untouched. "There's nothing like studying in my room and having helicopters overhead, tear gas in the street, mattresses burning, and loudspeakers blasting because the National Guard was driving through the streets telling us about a curfew! I just sat there and said, 'This is just ridiculous. I can't believe this, it must be a bad dream.' I was mad a little bit because the reputation of U.C. Santa Barbara was being damaged severely. I didn't enjoy going home and having everybody say 'Oh gee, you got a bunch of wild liberals down there.' A bad way to end a super college experience."

Rohrback's bitterness was generated less by the actions of protesting students than it was by the behavior of the university and county authorities and the police. "I was mad about the way the entire situation was handled, which was very poorly. The use of force just totally got out of hand. The students—even people like me—started to get a little hot about the approach that was taken. Here, under our own nose, in a very sedate, laid-back college community, we were just totally out of control." Mark Reiss concurs: "I was surprised by some of the police tactics; I got so frustrated [with the police behavior]. The guy who was killed, he was not a radical guy, he was a fraternity guy. And if we parted our curtains and looked out when the police drove by, they would gas us, just for parting our curtains! And I knew girls whose doors were kicked down, and then they were beaten up by the police. They weren't rebels. And when the police came into the 'House of Lords' [the residence complex in Isla Vista where most of the athletes lived] and beat up the football guys—God, if there were ever flag-waving guys, those guys were it!"

Other nonactivist students who witnessed or experienced the violence of the police and National Guard did not react as strongly as Rohrback or Reiss, although many of them also felt after Isla Vista III that the military-style response was unnecessary. A more typical reaction was to argue that the protesters were equally guilty, that insanity begat insanity and violence begat violence. Football team member Harry Stevens, for example, even found some amusement in it all. "I thought the police were way out of line, but my personal opinion was that both sides were at fault. You know, when I stood back and looked at the situation, in some ways it was kind of comical. Like when I was there in Perfect Park, for instance [the night of the June 10 sit-in]. I was just curious, I wasn't one who sat on the grass and refused to leave. A busload of cops came in there, and they sounded like a football team getting psyched up for the big game. You can hear them chanting and pounding on the floor and stuff with their feet, getting themselves all psyched up to go out after those hippies or whatever they thought they were. And then that would cause the students to do something just to aggravate them. And so it just kept going both ways. It was like two kids just aggravating each other to the point where there is a fight. And in a way it was kind of comical if you could sit back and see the humor in the thing, 'cause it looked like the war was right there in I.V., you know?"

Finally, some nonactivists tried to keep the two sides from going too far. Football team member Bill James, who worked as a resident advisor at a private dormitory in Isla Vista, remembers climbing onto the roof of his building to stop students from throwing rocks and bottles at the police and guardsmen below, while "helicopters were flyin' around with loudspeakers yelling 'Get off there' at me! And I was also trying to hold down the police brutality," he notes, "because that stuff was going on, you know; we had definite instances of that. The police would come in, break the door down, yank people out of the building. I had my hands full."

"It Seemed Like the Police Were Causing a Lot of the Violence"

On the night of February 25, Ginny Phillips and about a dozen other young women stood on the roof of Kappa Phi sorority house and strained to get a glimpse of the Bank of America building, almost four blocks away. They had heard on the radio that rioters had sacked the bank and that there were reports that it was on fire. "I remember being up there," Phillips states. "There was a bunch of us, trying to see as far as we could to the bank. All kinds of helicopters entered the air, and we couldn't see much happening at the bank. When it burned, we could see smoke and things, but we really couldn't see the activities, and the cops were telling us from the helicopters to get inside; they didn't want us on the roof!" Later, she and a few of the others "snuck on down to where the bank was, but stayed on the outskirts." There were people everywhere ("I remember not being able to see what was happening too much"), but Phillips was reluctant to try to get any closer.

Phillips' immediate reaction to the bank burning was that "it was kind of funny. I didn't really realize that it was quite as serious as . . ." And here she pauses, groping for a way to express adequately how she felt. "I was shocked but—I don't mean that it was funny, not like a joke, but the bank didn't belong in Isla Vista. And it was a symbol for big business. I was just as happy that it wasn't there." It would be a mistake, however, to attribute her reactions to strongly felt political concerns or to involvement in the student movement. Few Kappa Phi's were politically active (in fact, more than one Kappa told us that they were best known on campus for being "blonde, beautiful, and rich"), and Phillips was no exception. "I never even thought about demonstrating. I went to a couple of rallies on campus and signed petitions, but I don't remember getting honestly involved with anything." Nor was she politically aware. "I never read the paper in college. I didn't watch much TV, so I wasn't watching the news. I didn't really know a whole lot about what was happening." Finally, she was not especially sympathetic to the more radical perspective on events of which she had some direct knowledge.

William Allen's case for example: "I was in favor of his being fired. I resented the fact that so many kids took that class and would get an *A* for doing nothing. His class was one of these free-thinking classes. I guess I'm not a free-thinker. I just thought it was kind of bullshit." Her anti-big business feelings, like the feelings of other nonactive students on other major issues of the day, were more a product of the general political and cultural atmosphere in Isla Vista at that time than the result of any political analysis or ideology. "Isla Vista was like heaven to us," Phillips says. "It was where we lived and played, and we didn't want to see it change," to see "big business" encroaching on "our territory."

Three blocks to the east of Kappa Phi's sorority house, Mary Casey, then a twenty-one-year-old Kappa who had her own apartment, was also watching the flames shoot up from the bank. "I remember going out on my balcony and seeing the bank burning down and thinking, 'I've got to get out of this place!' " Casey was frightened. "I lived there with three other girls, and we listened to the radio. Everyone was being told to stay in their apartments, and I pretty much stayed where I was supposed to stay. We saw the police with the tear gas canisters, and just a lot of people running around the streets, a lot of hysteria, and seeing the flames and just feeling pretty scared." Still, she also notes that "you sort of got caught up in what [the people in the streets] were doing." Casey was not active in politics in any way, and despite its "scary" aspects, the riotous conflict—at least at first—was somewhat captivating.

It was not long before fear took over, and for Casey and Phillips and so many other Isla Vistans of all political persuasions, the police behavior was by far the most frightening aspect of the whole experience. Whereas several of the Delta Omega men reacted angrily to the bank burning and blamed the protesters for most of the turmoil, most Kappa Phi's reacted much more sharply to the police violence (almost certainly a "gendered" response). Casey is typical: "I didn't think it was great that the bank burned down, but I was more concerned about the police being around. I remember walking down Trigo Road to this drug store one night after the bank burned. It was past seven o'clock, and we were all supposed to be in, and I was standing next to some guy, and the police started hassling the guy and they just grabbed him and took him away. I thought, 'God, that could have happened to me,' and I just slowly walked back to my apartment. And that shook me up a lot. I think that affected me more than even the bank burning down. I thought it was a pretty sorry thing that the bank burned down. I thought that things were being carried away a little bit, but the thing that affected me the most was the violence of the police: seeing people getting grabbed and roughed up by the police, the tear gas. I definitely was more upset by the violence of the police than by the violence of the protesters. You feel, when you grow up, that the police are supposed to be the upholders of the law and supposed to help people, and it just didn't seem like they were helping people. It seemed like they were causing a lot of the violence that happened. I didn't think that they were helping the situation at all."

Phillips had similar reactions in the weeks following the bank burning. "It was actually like a siege. There were just police all over. I can remember [during the third riot] driving down the street that the Kappa house is on and having a policeman come right up to the car with a rifle and point it right at us. You hear about riots where people are hurt. We heard about Kent State where the four kids were killed, and it seemed to us that they hadn't done anything wrong. It scared us. We thought maybe it could happen to us. We hadn't done anything wrong either, but we were on the streets. I guess it was after curfew. I was actually scared of being shot, being mistaken, being in the wrong place at the wrong time, like Kevin [Moran] was, and being killed for absolutely no reason."

Rhonda Miller's account parallels Casey's and Phillips' in several respects. In 1970 Miller, also a Kappa Phi, was a twenty-year-old junior majoring in English. "I didn't care about the bank burning. It didn't make any difference to me. I thought it was a crime that kid got killed. So what if a bank burns, nobody has to be killed because a bank burns down. Everything that happened afterward was just too much for what, to me, wasn't that big a deal. I remember when we would be in the house, and seeing those dump trucks driving around with the guys with the guns; it just used to infuriate me. You get those clowns out there with guns and someone is gonna get killed."

Once again, it was the direct experience of living in a community under siege, rather than any specific political position or even general political awareness, that determined Miller's response. Miller says she never read the newspaper, watched television, or listened to the radio. "So I was just totally out of it in terms of what was going on in the world," she recalls, and as was true of the other women of Kappa Phi, it was when something touched her personally that she was moved to react.

"It Was a Full-On War"

Lucy Lizotte was also a Kappa Phi. But unlike many of her sorority sisters or the men of Delta Omega, this twenty-one-year-old sociology major was not mystified by the bank burning and rioting. "I was aware before the riots came that there was a segment of the school population that were becoming very angry over the war. I saw it mostly with my sociology classes. I saw it with my professors. I saw them becoming very concerned, encouraging people to go to different political functions. I went to a few of them out of curiosity." While Lizotte's curiosity was not translated into sustained political involvement, she was sympathetic to the antiwar movement and sometimes, "just for the fun of it," she had joined the noon-hour "peace vigil" in front of the library. "I kind of watched what was happening on campus," Lizotte explains, "and took it all in." Two weeks before the February 25 explosion, she had participated in her first political rally, a demonstration in support of William Allen, who was also one of her teachers. "I was kind of for him not to be fired. I thought he had a statement to make, and I found it kind of interesting."

In all these ways, Lizotte's thinking was more to the left than that of the other members of her sorority. Still, her reluctance to leap from vague sympathy to active participation kept her from venturing into the streets during the rioting. "I spent most of my time watching television, because we weren't able to go outside. I wasn't going to risk getting arrested. I was still very much into staying at UCSB, I was too close to graduating to flick it all in! Basically, I heard what my parents or anyone else heard on television. I was almost that far removed."

Almost—but not quite, as this story makes clear: "I was having an exam, right after the bank was burned, and they had a curfew, yet some of us had tests to take. The curfew started at seven but our test wasn't over until nine, so we had permission to go to our final and take a bus back home. The Kappa Phi house was right on Embarcadero, so I figured I'd be the first one dropped off. It was kind of sad, because I figured it would be kind of neat to get a bus tour right now with the riots going on to see what was going on. I was the *last* one dropped off. They turned and they zig-zagged all the way through I.V. for like an hour. There were trash cans burning, a car or two on fire, police chasing after people in the streets. It was a full-on war. It was what Vietnam must have been like. It totally freaked me out. It really made an impression. I'll never forget it."

Later expriences convinced her that the police were the ones most responsible for waging this "war." An incident during Isla Vista III drove this point home. "I was sitting inside the sorority house. The curfew was on, and they started indiscriminately putting tear gas all over I.V." Clouds of gas began seeping through the closed doors and windows. "Our little 'house mother,' who was like eighty years old, was coughing, and I was really afraid for her life. I just thought all that was just bizarre. That really did it. And the stories that I heard afterward from the people who got arrested, who weren't doing anything wrong, pulled and yanked out of bed, girls in their nightgowns being pranced down the street—bizarre happenings. That's when I started getting behind the riots."

Other members of the sorority expressed their sympathies even more directly, as Melissa Meyers, another Kappa Phi, recalls. "Ten or eleven girls got involved in the [June] protests. That was kept very quiet, though, and it was done very individually. I don't know if the alumni chapter would have appreciated their girls going out and yelling obscenities at the police or really having their lives endangered!"

It is evident, then, that by the spring of 1970 even some of the members of UCSB's largely apolitical fraternities and sororities had been politicized by the Isla Vista rioting. Yet there were distinct differences between the experiences and emotional responses of nonactivists (the men and women of Delta Omega and Kappa Phi, the football team members, and conservative students like Charles Johnson) and those of the Radical Union activists or movement sympathizers. These responses to the protests of that year were closely bound up with the sharp difference in the cultural worlds these two groups of people inhabited at that time. Further, the stories of the nonactivists are most often those of observers; they typically watched the battle in the streets from rooftops, from bus windows, and from doorways or sidewalks. To be sure, they also choked on the tear gas, dodged the probing search lights, and, occasionally, were nabbed by the police patrols, but their involvement was characteristically unwilling. In contrast, the stories of the radicals display a dramatically different kind of participation and a willful political commitment. Even where their accounts display few signs of active involvement in the rioting, the 1970 events were nevertheless experienced by these more radical youths as having profound political meaning. Disparities such as these practically leap out from the stories, and are the pivot on which our analysis will turn.

Still, the rioting had a tremendous emotional impact on all of these men and women, activist and nonactivist alike. For close to four months, their university and their community had been in a state close to civil war, a struggle that had ended with little sense of what it all meant or, perhaps more disturbingly, what might follow. What did in fact follow is the subject of the remaining chapters of this book. Having set the stage by recounting the Isla Vista riots through the narratives of its participants and observers, we can now begin to explore the personal legacy of that extraordinary experience, the lasting imprint of those events on the lives of people who lived through them.

3

Visions of the Apocalypse

In this chapter, we turn our attention to the immediate aftermath of the Isla Vista rebellion. Our focus here is on how people sought to make sense of what had happened during those four and a half months of turmoil, and the changes in belief and identity provoked by that extraordinary experience. These changes, we will find, had a profound influence on the direction their lives took.

REVOLUTIONARY CONSCIOUSNESS

If there is one theme that stands out above all others in terms of the changes in identity and consciousness that took place during the riots, it is "revolution." To be sure, even before the Bank of America was set ablaze and hundreds of rioters filled the streets, the few dozen activists who then made up the inner core of the New Left at UCSB had begun to think and talk of militant confrontation and overthrowing "the system"; they even began, as several told us, "to recognize ourselves as revolutionaries."

The expression of "revolutionary consciousness" was shaped, however, by the conditions that existed at UCSB and in Isla Vista at that particular time. While impulses to revolution had been promoted and encouraged by frequent protest actions in places like Berkeley, Cambridge, and Madison, the movement in Isla Vista had not yet grown beyond the limited circles of a few radicals who were still searching for ways to build and inspire mass action. There were periodic flashes of mobilization, but no sustained challenge could be mounted. For the most part, alienation and disaffection among the wider student population assumed cultural rather than political forms.

Then came the William Allen controversy. And then came February 25. The gap between militant consciousness and militant action abruptly and explosively vanished. Imagination was now overwhelmed by events, and "revolution" suddenly became something very tangible and real, not only for the inner core of experienced activists but for recent recruits to the movement as well. In the midst of this compacted civil war, Isla Vista radicals became convinced that their community was a microcosm of America, that the nation was on the verge of a cataclysmic upheaval. A collective vision of the coming apocalypse was brought into being, a vision that gripped people's imaginations and penetrated deep into the fabric of their daily lives.

What people meant by *revolution* was, of course, as varied as the people themselves. Moreover, they had no precise plans or models for what might happen. Still, the Isla Vista activists universally recall sharing a conviction that "there was a shit storm a-comin'," that something had to give. For one activist: "In this whole time period leading up to the bank burning and the riots, there was a sense that we were all embarking on some path that was ultimately leading toward revolution, of whatever nature—and it was very undefined. During all those demonstrations and riots there was a sense that revolution was imminent; it was just around the corner. The downfall of the State was coming." "It just got crazier and crazier," another activist emphasized. "Things began to take on an apocalyptic tone, and everybody did actually believe that the revolution was at hand."

Even for those who did not see revolution as "just around the corner," there was still an expectation of increasing civil strife, a sense that a new stage of struggle had been reached. Now, anything was possible. "I certainly had a sense that things were building inexorably toward a climax," Roger Wade recalls. "I didn't really believe the movement could be defused. I assumed things were going to get hotter and hotter and that's what was certainly governing most of my actions. I certainly wasn't thinking we were going to win in five or ten years—I know I was thinking protracted struggle—but I just had a sense of ever-increasing conflict." Others echoed Wade's remarks: "I thought revolution could happen. I didn't think it was imminent, but I thought if we worked on it, that it probably could happen. I was gung ho, ready to do it." While many concurred with this anticipation of cataclysmic change, some saw, instead of an expanding Left, the possibility of a takeover by the Right, perhaps even the establishment of a military dictatorship.

These images of total social breakdown, of violent civil strife and chaos recalled by our respondents were common to young people all across the country and were to some degree a reflection of public events during the late sixties. The year 1968 alone conjures up a seemingly continuous stream of violent and traumatic experiences: the leading advocates of peaceful change, Martin Luther King and Robert Kennedy, are assassinated; protests at the Democratic national convention in Chicago are answered by police violence; Columbia University students seize five buildings in a dramatic display of "direct-action politics"; ghetto uprisings occur in Washington and other cities; the black power movement gains increasing support and public attention; the Tet offensive deals a devastating blow to the U.S. war effort; Russian tanks crush the Czechoslovak uprising; the French student and worker strike nearly topples the DeGaulle regime. Globally spotlighted, these moments embodied images of order and authority crumbling in the face of spontaneous mass action or shocking acts of violence. Dramatic representations on the nightly television news as well as in popular culture—films like *Easy Rider*, *Z*, *Medium Cool*, and *The Battle of Algiers*, and rock songs like the Rolling Stones' "Street Fighting Man," or the Beatles' "Revolution"—reflected these events and created even more heightened visual and aural images of apocalypse.

The collective action that exploded out of American campuses in the 1969–70 school year reinforced and deepened these sentiments. As Sale has noted:

> The scope of this violence was quite extraordinary. It took place on a larger scale—in terms of the number of incidents, their geographical spread, and the damage caused—than anything seen before in this century. It was initiated by a sizeable segment of the population— perhaps numbering close to a million, judging by those who counted themselves revolutionaries and those known to be involved in such acts of public violence such as rioting, trashing, assaults upon buildings and confrontations with the police—and it was supported by maybe as much as a fifth of the population, or an additional 40 million people—judging by surveys of those who approve of violent

means or justify it in certain circumstances. And, above all, the violence was directed, in a consciously revolutionary process, against the state itself. . . . for the first time since the Civil War, and over far more of the country, violence struck against the institutions of American government and those corporations and universities seen as complicit with those institutions, with an explicit aim of destroying or at least shaking that system. (Sale 1974: 634–35.)

This is the cultural and political context in which UCSB activists came to believe that the Isla Vista bank burning and subsequent rioting—with dusk-to-dawn curfews, martial law, the violent death of Kevin Moran, hundreds of arrests and injuries—were "the crest of a great wave," as Sheila Barressi put it, a wave that "was going to start coming down with greater and greater force every day." The massive protests against the invasion of Cambodia, which occurred in May of 1970, only a few weeks before Isla Vista III—protests that were marked by the deaths of four students and the wounding of nine others at Kent State and the deaths of two students at Jackson State—served as a final confirmation of this apocalyptic vision: what was happening in Isla Vista now seemed to be happening everywhere.[1]

Nor were students alone in such imaginings: one has only to recall Reagan's "blood bath" speech, the sometimes inflammatory proclamations of President Richard Nixon and Vice President Spiro Agnew, the flood of vitriolic newspaper editorials, and the public sense of fear and alarm that was, in part, generated by these pronouncements. Like the New Left radicals, many public officials and commentators believed that the crisis was deepening. The President's Commission on Campus Unrest (1970: 5), for instance, when reporting in the early fall of 1970 on the violence of the previous winter and spring, warned: "If this trend continues . . . the very foundation of the nation will be threatened. A nation driven to use the weapons of war upon its youth is a nation on the edge of chaos."

REFUSING THE FUTURE

To New Leftists at UCSB and elsewhere, the signals were clear: people everywhere were on the move, revolutionary change was not only urgently necessary, but possible. This image of revolution had a deep emotional appeal not simply because it seemed to explain what was actually happening in the world, nor because it seemed to flow logically from the ideological commitments of the activists. For insofar as revolution necessitated the abandonment of personal interests and private goals, it offered the prospect of continuously living in history rather than having to face the expected limitations and boredoms of ordinary adult life. As Roger Wade describes it: "It was a tremendous sense of purpose gener-ated—we were making a new society—but I think it was more just the pure energy that was being generated by being involved in this massive movement. It was captivating and contributed to our ability to not be so very concerned with what happened to [us] as individuals."

Another RU member adds to Wade's account: "There was so much going on in the world and all around us—there was just one thing after another and each advance seemed very significant and very earth-shattering—that there was a sense that you couldn't afford to pay atten-tion to details of a personal life. The feeling was that you should devote all your time to politics." "It was sort of like becoming a nun," Denise Saal says. "You dedicate your life to something and renounce everything else because that seemed to be what the choice was at the time. Be-cause here we were, working around the clock—just an incredible level of energy and time commitment was necessary—and that's what we were living and that's what we knew as political life." And the percep-tion of politics had itself been drastically altered. While proving oneself through taking personal risks had, by 1968, become a central element in these New Leftists' ethical commitment to embody the struggle within their own lives, political activity and risk-taking were now frequently defined in terms of willingness to support and, if need be, engage in military combat. Where "putting your body on the line" once meant, in its most extreme form, a willingness to go to jail, a readiness to "make real sacrifices to stop this horrible machine," as one man recalled, many RU activists were now talking about "how prepared you have to be to lay down your life," to follow the "heroic example" of the Cuban and Vietnamese revolutionaries.

The prevailing mood of campus radicals as the school year ended in 1970 was, therefore, intensely focused on the prospect of revolution and their responsibility to fulfill themselves as revolutionaries. At that mo-ment, many of them believed that they had solved the question of how their individual lives could be made congruent with their principles: the answer lay in merging their fate as fully as possible with the imperatives of revolution. As one woman expressed it: "For us there was no future. Revolution was the future." By 1970, alienation from adulthood was propelled by events as much as it was animated by countercultural values. "We were caught up in this intoxicating feeling that came from believing that we were part of this nationwide movement that was really shaking up the whole society," Sheila Barressi remembers. "I really did think a revolution was coming, and I really didn't think about what concretely my life was going to be like. I really didn't have any sense of it at all. All I saw in my future was being part of a revolutionary movement." "I thought my future was in the hands of history," another RU member states. "I didn't think about my own future. I really didn't think about it. The present seemed overwhelmingly important. It seemed like every day the world was in a crisis. Since everything in the world was gonna change so much, the future seemed academic, at that point, to think about."

If people did think about the future, they typically concluded that they would ultimately have to go underground or go to prison. Or die in the streets. Roger Wade, for example, recalls: "At that time, I thought a lot about prison, and about going underground. I assumed that at some point going underground would be very likely, that either repression would become stiff enough that they were rounding up people or that I would be involved in something so that I would have to make such a move. I remember thinking about it, wondering how it would be."

Those were not the only disturbing thoughts. Wade also remembers having "mental images of gun battles with the police as they were rounding people up, as the street fighting escalated." David Carroll made similar preparations for the inevitable showdown. A sophomore from Acadia who had been committed to the Kennedy style of liberal politics and active in the ecology movement before getting involved with the RU, Carroll went out and bought an M-1 rifle and hid it in his closet. "I was committed to the fact that it was just going to come to a big shoot-out. A lot of my fantasies at that time were suicidal—trying to shoot a few politicians and take out as many as you could on the way out yourself. You know, when you're really afraid and your mind starts working, daydreaming—those are the kinds of daydreams that would come up in my mind. Subconsciously, emotionally, that's where my fears were at. That's where I thought things were headed. And whether I liked it or not, I thought I was being swept up with it and that I had very little choice in the matter of what was going to happen." Bill McNaughton at the time "didn't give a damn about being thirty years old. I just decided like I might be dead in the streets—'The Last Hurrah,' 'Charge of the Light Brigade,' or something."

In sum, convinced that the apocalypse was imminent, many activists regarded the question of their personal future—of how to live in terms of commitment to social responsibility and personal liberation—as resolved. History would determine one's fate; the individual would be liberated through selfless immersion in revolution.

"TIME TO GET ON WITH LIFE"

For some UCSB students, of course, these beliefs made little sense. The political community and cultural world they inhabited bore little resemblance to either the revolutionary epicenter of the radicals or the unstable powder keg of fearful residents and outside observers who anticipated the worst. The atmosphere they breathed was not laden with apocalyptic fantasies or nightmares. Such was the case with the nonactivists we interviewed: their impressions of the political meaning of the Isla Vista riots—what these events presaged for the society and for their own lives —were quite different from those presented in the preceding pages. The significance of the apocalyptic vision can thus be further underscored by considering the perceptions of those students who did not share the political perspective of the New Left.

The nonactivist students did not see the attack on the bank as part of a nationwide insurrectionary upsurge; they typically thought of it as a confusing, localized outburst of insanity. Tending to be thoroughly apolitical, often insisting that they had little knowledge of political events, several of these individuals initially reacted to the rioting as—recalling Clark Jeffries' words—"more of neat, a different kind of experience than as a protest or something." Once the conflict began to affect more seriously the lives of even the most nonpolitical students, once the police began to rely on force in the suppression of the protests, the novelty of it all and the sense of being part of a "neat experience" quickly wore off. "It was exciting a couple of times, at first, then it got scary . . . extremely frightening . . . like a siege," Jeffries says. "A bad dream," Carl Rohrback calls it. Even at this point, however, even as the helicopters and tear gas and troops turned Isla Vista into a war zone, even as many fraternity and sorority members became outraged at the behavior of police, not one nonactivist in our sample felt that Armageddon was at hand.

Jeffries, for example, puts it this way: "I thought [the radicals] were sure as hell making their voice known, but I didn't think we were on the verge of revolution. All I really had to do was drive a mile away from I.V. and there was no National Guard. The city of Goleta wasn't rioting, Santa Barbara wasn't rioting—it was just all happening in Isla Vista. People just got carried away a little bit. So I didn't think the world was coming to an end at that time." And George Dawes tells us: "I thought the riots and the reports that things were falling apart [in the country] were being exaggerated by the news media. I mean, they made Santa Barbara sound like everybody was crazy, and everybody in Santa Barbara was not crazy. And everybody was not that liberal, and they weren't gonna burn everything down." As for the spread of protest on a national scale, Dawes "just didn't see it as that big of an internal strife, didn't see the pressures as that great."

While the riots had created a situation whereby almost every I.V. resident had to face the same circumstances, these circumstances were interpreted in distinctly different ways. Within the world of the movement, Isla Vista appeared to be the harbinger of revolution. And Isla Vista, together with other revolutionary battlefields like Berkeley and Madison and Ann Arbor, was the only "real" reality. When I.V. activists cast their gaze over the nearby suburban neighborhoods of Goleta, they believed that they were looking at the last outposts of a dying culture, a decadent way of life that would soon be replaced by the new revolutionary vision. For the nonactivist members of our sample, however, the more conservative adult world outside Isla Vista was the real one.

Moreover, because the nonactivists did not feel especially alienated from that world, they did not think of their days in the university as a time for working toward fundamental cultural and political change. Rather, they saw it as a time for experimenting with culturally acceptable forms of youthful exuberance, as a time for "fun" before they had to get on with the serious business of living like an adult. In this sense, they did not view youth as real either; it was but a steppingstone to the more significant world of adulthood. As one Delta Omega told us: "You gotta live within the system in some way. And for me, I just wasn't the person like that, the person to fight it. You know, you can do a lot of things when you're young, but you couldn't exist on something like that."

Predictably, when these men and women left the riot-torn streets of Isla Vista behind, they embarked on conventional post-student careers. As Clark Jeffries puts it, "It was time to go on and get a job and get married and get on with life." After school ended in June of 1970, Jeffries did just that, taking one week off before getting married and starting work as a computer programmer—at the Bank of America. Other Delta Omega's also followed well-worn paths toward adult responsibilities in the years immediately following the riots. Carl Rohrback, who also graduated in June of 1970, moved to San Francisco and was hired by a large utility company as a "first-level" manager. That same summer, he went to the army's summer camp at Fort Lewis, Washington, to complete his officer training. Because of a football injury, however, he was declared medically unfit for military service. Within two years, Rohrback married and was promoted. Larry Goodwin decided that he wanted to go into international management and work overseas when he graduated, so after traveling around the country on a motorcycle for four months—his last fling at the carefree life, he says—Goodwin started graduate school in business. At school he became interested in advertising, however, and when he received his master's degree he went to work for a major advertising agency in New York City as a marketing executive. George Dawes received his B.A. from UCSB in the winter of 1972, twenty-two months after the bank burning. His first obligation after graduation was the army, but as the Vietnam War was winding down, he served only three months. Immediately upon his discharge, Dawes started graduate school at the same institution that Larry Goodwin attended. He stayed in international management, however, and after getting his master's, went to work for a large American bank as an auditor for their South American division.

The story is much the same for the other nonactivists. Harry Stevens graduated in 1971 and immediately went to work for a modular housing firm in Southern California (his father was on the company's board). Later, Stevens decided to go into the housing business for himself. He and his brother moved to Nevada and, with help from their father, bought two lots and took out a construction loan. They began building a duplex on each lot, doing nearly all the work themselves. To support himself until the houses could be finished and sold, Stevens worked the night shift as a dealer at a nearby casino. Charles Johnson also graduated from Santa Barbara in 1971. From there he went on to graduate school in history at another California university, hoping to go into college teaching and research. After two years, however, he dropped out of graduate school and began teaching high school and junior college courses at a state correctional facility. Bill James married immediately after graduation and took a job as football coach at a small southern university. Frank Morrow went to work as a manager for a large steel company. Mark Reiss enrolled at UCLA's business school. After receiving his master's in business administration, Reiss went into business with his father, managing a large catalog store in Orange County. Others took jobs as sales representatives and executives in private industry.

Among the Kappa Phi's, Ginny Phillips traveled to Europe after graduation and then moved in with her parents and began her "fifth-year" studies to earn teaching credentials. After receiving them, Phillips began working as a junior high school teacher in Southern California. Rhonda Miller stayed in Santa Barbara for two years after her graduation, working as a secretary in the biology department at the university. In 1972 she moved to the Los Angeles area, married her boyfriend, a horse trainer at a local race track, and got a secretarial job at the track. Mary Casey married her college sweetheart immediately after graduation and went to work at a large Southern California department store as a management trainee, helping to put her husband through law school. Lucy Lizotte began studying for her teaching credentials at UCSB in the fall of 1970 and lived in Isla Vista during that year. After teaching for one year in a coastal community south of Santa Barbara, Lizotte moved to Los Angeles in 1972 and taught elementary school in the San Fernando Valley suburbs. She was married that same year. Melissa Meyers also married soon after graduation and became a housewife.

None of this is to imply, however, that the burning of the bank and the four months of turmoil had left no imprint on the lives of nonactivists or their political attitudes. The "police overreaction," as several of them termed it, and the response by the authorities to the protests, had a marked effect on their thinking. Lucy Lizotte comments in this regard: "When I saw what the police did, and the way the university handled it, then I kind of got into it . . . I became more sympathetic." Additionally, their attitudes toward the war changed over the years they attended

UCSB. In some cases, it was attitudes toward racism and the position of blacks and other minorities that changed. "Where I grew up in Texas, blacks were always referred to as 'niggers,'" Bill James tells us. "But at UCSB, I took a course in [contemporary] black literature, and we read Eldridge Cleaver, Malcolm X—I just wanted to know what was goin' on." He was one of two white students in the class. Remembering the black students' hostility and his own angry reactions, James also feels that he learned a lot from the experience. "I grew," he says simply. "To me, that was the value of the education I had at the university." Moreover, while many of them had entered the university as strong supporters of America's Vietnam policy, by the time the bank burned nearly all had become opponents of that policy. In short, their experiences at college had, to varying degrees, "liberalized" these fifteen men and women.

One indicator of this liberalizing process is their voting record in the 1972 election. That contest offered a fairly clear-cut political choice: George McGovern versus Richard Nixon. Because McGovern lost in a landslide defeat, a vote for him was a distinctly minority position. Seven of the fifteen nonactivists voted for McGovern, six voted for Nixon, and two did not vote. (The women from Kappa Phi, who tended to be more upset than were the Delta Omega men about the police violence during the riots, provided five of the McGovern votes.) Thus, the majority of these nonparticipants in movement and counterculture shared, at least peripherally, their generation's distinctive political outlook: in that 1972 contest, eighteen- to twenty-four-year-olds were the only age group that supported McGovern.

Although we will want to consider how the political views of the non-activist cohort changed as time passed and the events of 1970 receded in memory, our focus for the remainder of this chapter and the next now shifts to the activists. The Delta Omega's and Kappa Phi's had embarked on conventional careers, and the pattern of their lives over the next several years generally followed the normal sequence of school, marriage, and career. It is the story of those whose lives and thoughts were caught up in the apocalyptic vision that calls for a detailed telling.

RESPONDING TO APOCALYPSE

The belief that insurrection was imminent persisted among campus and Isla Vista radicals through 1970 and 1971. It is important to note that many others in Isla Vista, in the wake of the riots, were also caught up in the apocalyptic vision, and persisted in drawing political inspiration from the memory of the bank burning. A survey of UCSB students taken one year after that event found that, when asked how change would occur in the U.S. over the next twenty-five years, 25 percent answered "revolution."

Moreover, significant numbers of students were willing to endorse—or at least seriously consider—the use of violent tactics in protest. For example, in that same survey, 12.5 percent approved of "bombing as long as it is confined to property destruction," and another 28 percent said they might approve of property bombing "under some circumstances." About 9 percent approved the kidnapping of government officials, with another 18 percent answering that they did not categorically reject such actions depending on the circumstances. One in four thought that violence against property was a "good tactic."

With respect to the Isla Vista riots, only 6 percent felt that the violent acts committed by protesters were "more objectionable than police violence," while 43.5 percent felt that police violence was the most objectionable; the remaining 45 percent answered that the use of violence by both sides was equally objectionable. Finally, 21 percent agreed that "peaceful protest no longer works," and 42 percent were unwilling to reject violence as a political strategy.[2] If these responses are projected onto the total student population of fifteen thousand, it is clear that both the revolutionary expectations of the activists and their espousal of militant tactics were shared by hundreds of other students who were not committed members of activist circles.

If, in those months, one had been listening to the rhetoric and observing the scene in Isla Vista, the revolutionary mood would have seemed all-encompassing. Huge murals, whose iconography celebrated guerrilla fighters and ethereal "heads," decorated every bare wall. Each weekend large crowds of young people would gather for free music, dance, and camaraderie. The place was a kaleidoscope of countercultural and political energy, with an air of exuberant abandon, but shot through with occasional cold blasts of paranoia. It was a time when anything seemed possible, from a new age of human understanding to the end of everything human.

We have already seen that this mood was not shared by our nonactivist respondents, who, at least in retrospect, seem not to have even been aware of it, and who took up the very round of career, marriage, and family that was being questioned by so many of their peers, acting as if they had never even heard the questions, let alone considered them. But as we pieced together the recollections of our activist respondents, we found that several of them did not fully share the revolutionary mood of the bank burning's aftermath. Indeed, beneath the apocalyptic sensibility, some activists were pulling away from the community. Not all were able or willing to give their lives over to history or to put aside all concern for a personal future.

This was especially true of students who had begun training for professional careers, who had not completely rejected the possibility of combining vocational commitment and authentic political commitment. The small number of activists who were so oriented found it increasingly difficult to reconcile a commitment to life as a revolutionary with their interest in a profession or discipline, especially one that required training, institutional involvement, and certification that the movement itself could not provide. Such tensions only worsened as apocalyptic perceptions came to the fore and an atmosphere began to grow in which vocational interest was likely to be regarded within the movement as "bourgeois."

"I Was Having Increased Doubts About What I Saw Going on Around Me"

This was just the sort of inner conflict that troubled Martha Koch, a Radical Union activist and Santa Barbara 19 defendant from Northern California who had been active in the New Left since her high school years. Koch, whose parents were both physicians, had wanted to be a doctor for as long as she could remember. In the apocalyptic climate of the late sixties, however, she found that her status as a pre-med student routinely provoked criticism among her friends in the movement, even though her goals were decidedly humanitarian. "We would have lots of talks about what's the best thing for us to be doing, as groups and as individuals, but a lot of it focused on individuals," she recalls. "I was always the butt of a lot of criticism because I wanted to go to medical school. I got tremendous amounts of flak from people who I was doing politics with, because going to medical school was the wrong path for a revolutionary to take. At that time, there was a general sense that doctors were pigs, as kind of the outstanding representatives of the upper echelon of the bourgeoisie."

As the political climate heated up in the 1969–1970 school year, the pressure of politics intensified, and personal futures were increasingly seen in revolutionary terms, the level of criticism also escalated. "We went at a tremendous pace during that time. We were constantly just writing this leaflet, writing that analysis, organizing this demonstration, going to that demonstration, organizing these classes, building toward the next thing. There was always something to react to. So I think on the whole, it was hard for people to focus on 'Where am I going to be next year?' because things were changing fast, and there was so much happening. I don't think at that time most of the people involved had thought through what they wanted to do when they were adults. There wasn't a lot of real goal orientation among most of the people who were involved in politics. So at that point people were very critical of my wanting to go to medical school. I was very much on the defensive."

Koch was not immune to these criticisms. "I had a lot of questions in my own mind as to whether or not it was the right thing to do," she states. "I sort of felt more than anything else that I didn't want to close off my options." Collective pressures from others within the movement, made even worse by the press of events, prohibited any open discussion of these feelings. When Koch did voice her concerns, it was usually in self-defense when others criticized her lack of dedication. More important, she defended her commitment to medicine in terms of the cataclysm to come. "My response to people was, basically, 'What's going to happen if you have your revolution and then you don't have any doctors to take care of all the people that have been injured or, you know, to take care of people that are in the underground, or to take care of people who can't go to regular doctors because they don't have enough money or whatever?' Which was an adequate defense to all the criticism at the time, because revolution was imminent, and clearly we would need doctors in the revolution. I really believed that," she insists. "I felt that you had to have doctors on both sides, 'cause then it was very clear: our side, their side—this was deeply felt. I think I emphasized this more than I otherwise might have, for the purpose of defending myself, but I really believed it."

The morality of having career ambitions was not the only thing troubling Martha Koch. "I was having increasing doubts about what I saw going on around me during the rioting," she reports, "in terms of my feeling like some people who were supposedly on my side were acting irrationally—attacking policemen, getting carried away on the destructive side of things." While Koch had earnestly participated in the rock-throwing during the February conflict, and remembers the "pure fun" (her words) of venting her hostility toward the system as well as "the tremendous high in confrontation," she also felt that the rioting lacked strategic direction. "I wondered to myself what we were achieving, if anything. I am relatively resigned to the fact that violence is necessary at certain points in history—you need to go through violence to achieve revolution—but, personally, I thought those should happen only when they really need to. And should happen in a way that's organized strategically so that you can do the least amount of violence to achieve what you're trying to achieve, and that certainly wasn't true of anything we were doing in Isla Vista. It made me feel uneasy." Here issues of personal importance are interwoven with tensions within the movement, and caught up in turn with the political turmoil of that period.

The fact that Koch had been arrested as a result of the William Allen demonstrations further complicated the situation. "I started spending an inordinate amount of time dealing with the legal system and going down to the lawyer's office and raising money for our defense, and so on. It was increasingly at odds with what I was trying to do in terms of going to school. And as important as the firing of Bill Allen and the Santa Barbara 19 case was to us at the time, I know that it was not a crucial issue in the world. I mean, it was important on a symbolic level —what kind of educational system we have, what education is and who should teach—and I thoroughly believed in the importance of that, but I also knew that it was not a crucial world issue. Yet at that time I knew that it might seriously interfere with what I wanted to do with the rest of my life. The only way I did get through that winter quarter academically was that I had a friend help me out, in terms of just spending a lot of time with me going over the stuff I missed in lectures, doing organic chemistry and biology and stuff like that."

Koch did not discuss her misgivings about the violence or the effect the upheaval was having on her personal life with other people in the Radical Union. "I never criticized those things openly then, at that point, to anybody. I guess, on some level, it was out of fear that people were going to accuse me of not being politically correct."

So Koch chose "to just move out of town," to put some distance between herself and the fire storm of emotion in that community. "I decided, 'It's getting too crazy here, I can't focus on other things that I need
to do.' So I said, 'Enough is enough, I'm leaving,' and I made a decision
to transfer to Berkeley, and I moved two weeks later, just before spring
quarter started. I left very precipitously, and I didn't really talk to many
people about it. I told people I was leaving because I was ready for a
change."

Although she now lived in Berkeley, Koch did not break all her ties to
Isla Vista. "Spring quarter was a very schizophrenic time for me, because
I spent a lot of time in Santa Barbara even though I was officially going
to school in Berkeley. I had legal things to do with the '19' case, and I
wanted to see my friends." More important, leaving Isla Vista in the middle of the riots did not end her involvement in politics. "I couldn't stay
out of it. It was like there was too much going on. And then Cambodia
happened [in May], which had to be responded to. You couldn't not respond. I went to demonstrations, worked with some groups doing stuff
around Cambodia and doing leaflets, things like that. All that year, my
political feelings never changed, the motivating forces behind my being
involved in politics never changed. I didn't really want to get out of politics when I left I.V. so much as gain a little bit of a better perspective on
what I was doing."

This "better perspective" was achieved, Koch feels, largely through
contact with other left-leaning people in Berkeley who were interested
in health-related political issues and who did not view work in medicine
as hopelessly bourgeois. "For the first time I met people who linked
health to some kind of political movement. We read stuff that was put
out by MCHR [Medical Committee for Human Rights, a group of radical
health-care professionals], and I started getting some awareness of how
the health care system fit into everything else. That was very valuable.
And I also met other people that wanted to go to medical school who
were political, which was a tremendously supportive occurrence."

Martha Koch spent the remainder of her junior year and all of her
senior year in Berkeley, completing her pre-med studies, "probably putting a lot more time into doing politics than into studying," as the
political situation in Berkeley was at times as volatile as it had been in
Isla Vista. The revolutionary vision had not yet dissipated. "I remember many nights when we would go outside our house and be greeted

with a National Guard rifle or something to that effect. I tried to go to classes (I couldn't miss my labs and stuff), and so I'd go to labs and get tear-gassed on the way! There was still a sensation of revolution around town at that point; it was hard not to believe in it there." Now, however, revolutionary politics was not something her friends perceived as incompatible with vocational goals. "Now I had found other people like myself, people I could talk to."

"After I Got Arrested I Got Very Scared and Intimidated"

The concerns of a few Radical Union members went even deeper than misgivings about becoming totally committed historical combatants; some were frightened by the apocalyptic vision and withdrew from political activity altogether. The violence, the arrests, and the police occupation of Isla Vista gave rise to fears for their own safety. Political paralysis set in, and often personal paralysis as well, with the constant threat of jail (or worse) turning them into prisoners of their own fears. Students who had been arrested during the disturbances and who were relatively new recruits to the movement were especially vulnerable to these paralyzing fears. These men and women had been swept up by the rush of events before they had a chance to get their political bearings, to develop a sense of how they fitted in the movement. Their life was suddenly turned upside down. Additionally, in the apocalyptic atmosphere of Isla Vista in 1970, there was little opportunity for open discussion of fears or doubts about what was happening. As a result, some people were emotionally overwhelmed. In the midst of one of the most intense mass insurrections in recent American history, they felt quite alone.

Terry Lennox experienced these feelings. Prior to 1969, he had very little contact or involvement with radical activists at UCSB. "I certainly didn't consider myself a political person," he recalls. Moreover, while he had grown up in what he describes as a "progressive" family environment—his parents were both professionals, Jewish, very liberal politically, and intellectually inclined—he had no previous interest or involvement in either politics or cultural rebellion. For example, Lennox notes that "in high school there was this group of outcasts whom we called 'the folk singers,' and they were the only 'conscious' group of people in the whole school, but to me they seemed like weirdos. I just wanted to run track and play poker. I really had no political thoughts of any sort."

As for national political events such as the civil rights protests of the early sixties, Lennox "remembers them being on television, and being moved by them, [but] they didn't have any real effect on my daily life. My parents considered them important, and it was just sort of accepted [in our home] that liberal and nondiscriminatory ways of living were correct, so the protests did seep in, but it was more of an emotional thing than it was political."

Arriving in Santa Barbara in September 1966, Lennox had little sense of direction, "no specific ideas of what I wanted to do, no particular goals." Yet there was one thing that he knew he did not want: "I didn't want to become a professional like my father." His vague desire for a different life led him to gravitate almost immediately to the Isla Vista youth culture. By his sophomore year, he had formed a rock band, and playing music—especially the "new music" of the period, music that he often wrote himself—became his primary focus over the next two years, his primary vehicle for expressing both his alienation from the conventional middle-class lifestyle and his identification with the counterculture. It was through the band that Lennox became involved, in a limited way, in the political scene. When the "New Free University" (an "alternative" educational project run by radical students and professors) was established in the student union building in the winter quarter of 1969, his band often played there. "That seemed to be a role I could play in the thing," he recalls, a way to contribute to a movement with which he identified but which he knew little about. "I don't think I had much perception of any movement at large. I was very much against the war, but I didn't really think in political terms. I really did not have much knowledge. I pretty much only knew what was going on in Isla Vista, and that's pretty much what I considered 'The Movement.' "

It was also through the rock band that Lennox met Sarah Glenn, a twenty-one-year-old philosophy student from Sacramento. They quickly became very close. In the fall of 1969, he started working for the campus newspaper as a reporter. (Glenn had been writing for the paper since 1968.) "I needed a job, and *El Gaucho* was hiring," Lennox notes. While the fact that Glenn was on the paper was clearly a factor as well, that was as far as it went: "There was no political motivation in me to join the paper." Nevertheless, there were definite political consequences. While working on *El Gaucho*, both he and Glenn came into contact with people in the Radical Union, some of whom, like Sheila Barressi, also wrote

for the newspaper. Barressi invited the two of them to an RU meeting
—the radicals were always looking to recruit more *El Gaucho* people—
and they eagerly accepted. Their motivations, though, were again more
personal than political at that point. "Sarah and I wanted to make some
friends, and we felt just sort of really neat that we had been involved,
included, in this group. It seemed that the people in the Radical Union
were thoughtful, intelligent, nice people, and Sarah and I were in sort of
a plastic bubble and needed to get out of it."

The focus of that meeting was William Allen's firing and how the RU
could rally student support behind him. "I had a very listening role. I
felt like I was an observer more than anything else," Lennox reports. As
he began attending Radical Union meetings, however, he became very
excited about the RU's style of, in his words, "combining the personal
and the political." The theme of women's liberation had a particularly
strong influence on him in this regard. "I remember this meeting when
a couple of women got up and said to these guys, people who did most
of the speaking and who were the leaders, they said, 'You know, we're
tired of listening to you guys talk. We're going to start being a part of
it now.' When that happened, it hit me in my heart. I felt very much in
agreement with what they were saying. And people tried to incorporate
women's liberation into how they structured their politics, which meant
to include women and give everyone a voice, to respect people. So my
feeling about politics was that these two things, the personal and the
political, could be welded, and it had some meaning."

As Lennox's identification with radical politics grew, campus events
reinforced his commitment. Within a few months after his first RU meeting, the Allen case was generating a great deal of controversy, and
Lennox was quickly thrust into the middle of things. Both he and Glenn
were assigned to cover the escalating conflict for *El Gaucho*, and their
frequently coauthored articles attracted considerable attention. Here the
"ego boost of seeing your name in print and having a voice that people
listen to" played a large part in reinforcing political involvement. And
personal needs and political commitment, movement ethos and historical events blended together, "I began to get caught up in that whole
feeling, [that] heady atmosphere, the whole youth culture approach to
life. We felt we were the first group to have so much strength between
us." His political concerns now extended beyond Isla Vista, and he be-

came aware of "a general slow movement of changing consciousness which was beginning to happen throughout the country, something that was erratically progressive. Revolution seemed inevitable. I didn't have any overall perspective on how to wage the revolution. I really did not have any scenario. I wasn't one of the thinkers, but I was moving very quickly and doing what I thought I should do."

Lennox covered the large rallies in support of William Allen in late January for the student paper, rallies that ended with the deployment of three hundred police on campus to remove demonstrators from around the administration building. Three days later, the Santa Barbara 19 were arrested, and Lennox discovered that he had been charged as a 'co-conspirator.' Enthusiasm and excitement now dissipated into fear. "After I got arrested I got very scared and intimidated. I realized I was getting into something that was too . . . more than I wanted. I was just too scared." Yet Lennox was not ready to give up on politics completely. He continued writing for the paper ("reporter-in-exile," he was called, due to the suspension and banning of the arrestees by the university administration) and continued to associate with the politically active students.

The bank burning came three weeks later. Lennox had covered the Kunstler speech for *El Gaucho* and was with Sarah Glenn in the Goleta office of the paper's printer on the night of February 25, writing up his story. "I heard on the radio that the bank was being burned," he remembers, "and we tried to come and get on campus but you couldn't. You had to go all the way around because the roads were blocked off. We came and stayed in the *El Gaucho* office until early that morning, when we walked home past this charred bank where people were roasting hot dogs on it." Lennox had no urge to get involved, however, for fear now turned into paranoia. "During the riots in the ensuing days, I would stay in the newspaper office or in some apartment. I didn't participate in any of the rock-throwing or the riots that went on after that. I just stayed completely away from it. I was even afraid to walk by the bank because I had this great paranoia that I would be picked out, just like with the Bill Allen arrests. I hadn't done anything in that demonstration. I was there as a reporter, I had a pen in my hand, standing close to the podium, and I felt I was innocent, but I was arrested. So I had my paranoia. I had it very strongly!"

Lennox's withdrawal from organized political activity was noticed by others in the RU, but no one called particular attention to it, and he did not bring up the subject: "I felt that I was doing about what I could, and I think people understood that I wanted to lay a little low." As the political tension—and thus the personal strain as well—increased through the spring of 1970, Lennox turned increasingly to Sarah Glenn for support. "Sarah meant more than anything else to me then. It seemed everything else was secondary. When we started to get more deeply involved in politics, I would try to affirm with her that no matter what happened we still had each other. That seemed to be far and away what was important."

He and Glenn were married in April, their wedding staged as a movement celebration. "You are my revolution," he wrote in a poem to Sarah, and it was in their personal life that he now sought to practice the political values that he was afraid of acting on in concert with others. "After we got married, I had a vasectomy because Sarah said the pill was really doing her a lot of damage, and it seemed like it would make sense for the man to take responsibility on himself for birth control. And [there also] was the fact that over-population seemed to be important—it would be a good, ecological thing to do—so I felt that it was the correct thing to do."

Despite his desire to avoid the public arena, Lennox was to be pushed once more by events onto the center stage. On June 3 he and Glenn were eating dinner in their apartment when he received a telephone call from a friend telling him that there was a warrant out for his arrest for burning the bank. His worst fears were realized, and all the anxiety and paranoia came surging to the surface once again. "I was flabbergasted. I was scared. I knew I was in over my head, getting indicted for the bank. I knew I just wasn't a 'political being' in the way the government had seemed to lump me in. I hadn't been involved in these things for months, in any political activities. It was an incredible shock."

Starting in August and lasting over three months, the trial of the Isla Vista "bank burners" tied up the energies, skills, and financial resources of the radical community. For Terry Lennox, its psychological impact was even more pronounced. "Most every day was spent at the trial, and when I would come home I didn't really desire to see anybody. People would come over once in a while and try to be supportive, and I would try to smoke dope with them, but I was just going through the motions of living. I wanted the trial to be over. That was really all I could think. I wasn't in any place to begin to reach out and make friends. I was just too frightened. Even though there was a great deal of sympathy for us, it was still myself who faced all this time in a state prison, and I was very frightened."

Lennox was sure that agents of the Federal Bureau of Investigation were watching his house and that his phone was tapped. His relationship with Sarah disintegrated under the pressure. "I was just wanting to shut myself in and not think about anything except getting free, and she was very involved, maybe because or in spite of what was happening, with women's liberation. She had a real need to bust out and meet other people, and I was just a very confining influence. So there we were: I was not wanting to be involved in politics because I was very intimidated, and she was wanting to get more involved in politics because she felt she had to make herself, her voice heard. We were going in very opposite directions at that time."

The trial ended on November 7 with the acquittal of all defendants on all the felony counts. (Several individuals were convicted of misdemeanors.) Lennox was free at last of the terror he felt about going to prison. Yet the conclusion of the trial did not bring complete peace to his personal life. "I felt Sarah and I should be together, but she felt that I should go. She felt she needed some space. If she had wanted me to stay I would have stayed, but she felt I should leave." Their marriage, born in the spirit of hope and revolution, had lasted less than one year. "I took off for northern California. I had no idea what I wanted to do, I just was getting the hell out of Isla Vista." While the break-up of his marriage was pivotal, there were additional motivations for leaving. Most important was the nagging fear that it could all happen again. "I felt very uncomfortable in I.V. I just felt like a little anonymity. There were reports that police had the pictures of radicals on their dashboards, and I felt I was too well known. I felt as if this [one particular] cop had his eye on me, so I guessed it was time to go."

Politics had shown itself, at least in Terry Lennox's eyes, to be more of a threat to personal life than a unifying, self-enhancing force. It was time, in his words, "to regroup and look inside," to rebuild his life. He got a job as a dishwasher in the Bay area and took up writing on a regular basis, even trying his hand at a novel based on his Isla Vista experiences.

No longer were Sarah and the "whole feeling" of Isla Vista at the center of his life. As he put it, "learning and growing, these just seemed to be the most important things."

"What Needed to Change Was Within Me"

Another respondent who was put on trial for burning the bank and ended up fleeing Isla Vista as a result was Kenneth Essian. As Essian emphasized in his account of the Isla Vista riots, he was not active in the Radical Union, nor did he participate in any student demonstrations before the riots; he did not even know the RU activists. Essian's arrest during one of the police sweeps through Isla Vista apparently marked him as a suspect, however, and when a person who claimed to have witnessed the bank burning identified him as a participant, he was arrested. To make matters worse, he was also charged with violating probation from an earlier sentencing for possession of marijuana. Consequently, he was held in the county jail without bail during the entire bank-burning trial.

Essian's sudden notoriety led to an almost complete break with his parents. Essian's father, an air force officer, had already expressed his displeasure with what he viewed as his son's "weird ideas"—his pacifist leanings, his distinct lack of interest in athletics, his involvement in "freak" culture—and his father ran out of patience altogether after the "participating in a riot" arrest was followed four months later by the bank-burning charges. Neither his mother nor his father came to visit him while he was in jail. "It was too hard for them to face—that their son was locked up," he says.

He did "a lot of thinking" during his time in jail. Confined there day after day, with hardly any visitors, his only break from the isolation being the hours in the courtroom, afraid of what would happen if he was convicted, Essian concluded that he and only he was to blame for his trouble. He feels that the experience, because it was so traumatic, served as a catalyst for changing his life. "I was in jail and didn't like being there. I realized that I did not want to be in jail for the rest of my life. I was tried for a crime I didn't commit, and I didn't like that. I didn't like the whole scene. And I realized that at some level the way I had been living my life up to that point had brought it all about. I realized that something had to change, and what needed to change was within me."

Additionally, Essian decided while in jail that the heated emotions and sharp divisions in the broader Santa Barbara community over the riots had been the result of "arrogance on both sides." "People didn't listen to each other's side of the story enough," he says, and so he began talking to some of the activists on trial and other friends about the need for reconciliation and dialogue, for more communication, more effort at "understanding people in different positions." The political climate both inside and outside Isla Vista was far from being conducive to reconciliation, however. Given the bitter divisions between students and police, between revolutionary activists and vindictive authorities, Essian's advocacy of dialogue met with little positive response, further distancing him from the Isla Vista scene.

One personal change that followed the jail experience involved religion. If peace within the community was not possible, he felt, perhaps he could at least achieve peace within himself. Through his brother, Essian was introduced to the teachings of Kirpal Singh, an Indian master of Sant Mat—literally, "path of the masters." The "Path" had great appeal for Essian, not only because its emphasis on meditation and the focusing of one's energies on self-transformation seemed to offer a way out of his troubled situation, but because it was based on the values and concerns that were already important to him. He had read Gandhi's autobiography and some of his other writings while still in high school. "Something struck me very deeply when I read his teachings. There was some . . . some echo of truth about it to me, about what he said. And the whole way he lived his life, his commitment to truth, was not at all superficial, was very, very deep. And it made sense to me, and it seemed like a very high thing." Sant Mat was devoted to this same search for truth, Essian felt, to the quest for "higher things."

When he was released from the county jail, Essian stayed with friends for a few weeks and then left Isla Vista, moving back home to live with his parents. If dialogue between students and authorities was not possible, perhaps he could still achieve a reconciliation with his family. "I wanted to mend the pain I had caused them by winding up in jail," he explains. Next came a trip to Europe with a girlfriend (they spent nine months there) and then a decision to go back to school, but this time at a different campus and with an entirely new intellectual direction: he would study entomology and horticulture. "I got a job with a beekeeper, and it appealed to me. I enjoyed working outdoors part of the time. At Santa Barbara I studied liberal arts, but I didn't see myself doing anything with that. I decided to choose something a little more practical that I could make a living at, that I enjoyed doing." And when the education he received was not as practical as he had hoped, he dropped out and set off for the Pacific Northwest and a job as a farm machinery mechanic. Finally, however, he was able to return to California and a job as groundskeeper and gardener for a large housing development that had its own orchards. It was during this period that he was formally initiated into Sant Mat. Spending his days working in the orchard, tending to his garden, and devoting time to his meditations, Essian believed he had found the inner peace he needed.

"I Didn't Have a Fear of It the Way Some of the Others Had"

Although Terry Lennox and Kenneth Essian were acquitted on all charges, four of the people we interviewed were convicted of riot-related offenses. Ed Pines and Warren Newhouser were found guilty of rioting and malicious mischief (both misdemeanors) in the bank-burning trial. Barney Thompson was convicted of participating in a riot (a misdemeanor) after he was arrested in the spring of 1970 in a demonstration called to protest against Governor Reagan's visit to Santa Barbara, and another RU member, Steve Rubin, was convicted of battery on a police officer (a felony) in a separate trial. Responses to these experiences varied enormously.

Ed Pines remembers finding out about his indictment from a friend who heard it announced over the radio. "Some clerk who was sympathetic got the list of people indicted and leaked it to KCSB [the campus radio station], and they were reading it on the air. I was charged with seven or eight counts: arson, attempted arson, burglary, malicious mischief, rioting, battery on an *L.A. Times* photographer. Somebody with me broke the photographer's camera. I didn't do it. When I found out [about all this], I left my apartment and hid out for a few days, up in a friend's house in the hills. We all hid out, all of the people indicted, until we got lawyers and got organized. Then we turned ourselves in and spent a few hours in jail 'til we got bail."

Like Terry Lennox—and, for that matter, all of the other accused "bank burners"—Pines was stunned by the news of his indictment. But the possibility of going to prison was something Pines had faced when he refused induction in 1967, and that, he feels, enabled him to avoid the emotional breakdown that Lennox experienced. "I had been through the whole prison thing. I wasn't welcoming it, but from the moment I turned my draft card in, I was expecting to go to prison. I waited twenty-two months for it, until I was declared 1-Y. So I had spent time investigating the whole prison stuff. We, the Resistance, even put out literature explaining what prison would be like, and we wrote an essay on fear of prison, so I was very familiar with prison and I didn't have a fear of it the way some of the others had, facing those sentences."

This stance carried over into the trial itself. "There were differences in the degree to which people wanted to take the thing on, face the fear of going to prison and all that. [Some] just escaped from it, went into drugs, came doped to trial, spent no time working on the thing, just succumbed and passed it over to the lawyers, gave themselves over to professional hands. I was just totally immersed. I saved people's cases by my investigations." One dispute involved the timing of the first attempt to burn the bank, by pushing the burning dumpster through the doorway. Several defendants had based their defense on testimony that they were elsewhere at the time the arson attempt was made. Pines was able to dig up a photograph that showed the bank clock singed by the flames from the dumpster, settling the time question in favor of the defendants. "As it turned out it was a great experience, facing the system right up front. The ones who escaped it, rather than get involved, had more trouble coping with it."

His involvement in the trial provides an interesting contrast with his feelings at that time concerning the call to total revolutionary commitment. Several years older than most of the RU activists and, more important, a veteran of seven years of political activism, Pines was not nearly as caught up in the fervor of 1970 as were the other members of the RU. "That time wasn't a peak for myself, not a peak of expectations. I had more hopes in '68; I thought my actions back then could make more of a difference. By [the time of the riots] I had gone through quite a few experiences and got my hopes dashed. Like, by 1970, I had faint hopes about the Vietnam War ever ending. It was just going on and on. I was at that time even becoming suspect about the impact of collective political action on a goal like that—to end the war—and was realizing it takes so much effort to get so little effects, results."

It was not only his age and political experience that kept Pines from embracing the apocalyptic vision, however. Equally influential was what he describes as "this humanistic-psychology side of me": "I guess I evolved out of the SDS thing. I went from this SDS phase into this more humanistic-psychology phase and wasn't as active in the organizing in 1970. So I wasn't a straight politico. I was as much into the human potential movement as I was into radical politics." While most activists felt that the choice facing the New Left at that time was between sacrificing themselves to history and total withdrawal from political activity, Pines felt uncertain about what he describes as "single-minded, sustained total commitment." Although respecting people who could "give themselves" totally to the struggle, and feeling "some guilt compared to [those] people who worked with no private life as such," he acknowledges: "I didn't do that. I had moments of personal retreat, disengagement, periods of reflection."

For Ed Pines, then, the key problem was blending political commitment and personal life, collective needs and personal development. Somewhat like Martha Koch, he sought to develop an approach to politics that did not result in being consumed by the movement but resisted the temptation (and security) of withdrawal. Thus, while Pines states that he "wasn't one of the active organizers [in the riots]," he also emphasizes: "I still had a subculture. All my friends were political, so I was out there in the bank thing. And I never lost my political identity, the [feeling that the] way to change things is through political work. Encounter groups or humanistic psychology are a means to change your personal life, but you still have to have political struggles against the system."

Despite Pines's effort to keep some distance between his own thoughts and actions and the totalistic demands of the movement, he remained strongly committed to activist involvement. Sentenced to one year in the county jail, he continued to organize against the war while awaiting the resolution of his appeal.

Barney Thompson, in contrast, made no effort whatsoever to distance himself from Isla Vista's revolutionary vision. If anything, he was caught up more than ever in the apocalyptic tenor of that moment. One day after completing his ninety days in the county jail, Thompson went on trial for burning the bank. The experience, in his case, did not lead to reassessment; instead, his militant convictions hardened. "I realized that what I liked most in my entire life was what I was doing right then: being a rebel." When the bank trial concluded, Thompson began working with a group of lawyers and I.V. activists who were setting up a community law office in the area.

"I'm Never Going to Turn Myself In"

Warren Newhouser's actions represent yet another response to the threat and experience of prison. The three months of trial were difficult. "Let me assure you, the trial was a bitch. It was heavy. It was extremely heavy to be the one accused of these huge crimes, to actually suffer through these lackeys pointing at me saying I did something which I positively did not do. And which I had eight or nine witnesses testifying that I was with them in this apartment [when the bank was burned]. Which was in fact the truth. It was a bummer." Unlike Pines, Newhouser did not become deeply involved in preparing the defense's case. Instead, he relied on a little black humor to cope with the pressure. "The only thing I decided to do during the trial was to read Kafka, *The Trial*. I think it made [the prosecutors] upset. It was perfect, absolutely perfect. That's what I did during the trial, was sit there and read this book during most of the stuff."

After the trial concluded with only misdemeanor convictions, however, the prosecution was faced with the decision of whether to ask for a retrial on the felony charges. Several months went by before they announced their decision not to prosecute. Additionally, the defendants appealed their misdemeanor convictions. All this left Newhouser with a lot of time to think about his future: "It went on, and fuckin' on, and fuckin' on forever, and during this whole time I was trying to figure out, trying to get a handle on, what I was gonna do. And I had this girlfriend, [and we were] talking about if we were gonna stay together at all . . . and, you know, it was all a confused mess in my mind."

There were few people Newhouser could turn to for assistance or advice. Most of the other activists we interviewed received support from their parents, but this was not an option in his case. He and his father, Newhouser notes, had "incredible fights," with his father telling him, "You can't come to this house, I'm not gonna have a dirty mess like you there!" He felt cutoff from his family. "My father was worried, I think, about soiling his good name. My mother was concerned, but they never came to see me during the trial. They didn't help. They didn't know what to do, and I didn't ask them for anything."

Moreover, Newhouser formed few close bonds with his codefendants. Thus, when his appeal was turned down, Newhouser had to choose a path almost completely on his own: "I remember just thinking one day, 'These fuckers are serious about this! I mean, they're gonna put me in jail for this. This is not a joke, this is really true, this appeal is just bullshit.' I had done two weeks of county jail already, and it sucked. I didn't want to do any more time. I just made one of those basic watershed kind of decisions where I said, 'I'm never going to turn myself in. If they catch me, they catch me, and they take me kicking and screaming. Fuck them. I am not turning myself in. Period. That's just the way it has to be.'"

But going underground was not something to which Newhouser had given careful thought. It was circumstances, more than political commitment, that put him into this dilemma to begin with. While this decision to flee seemed to resolve one set of problems, it also presented a whole array of new and equally perplexing ones. "From that point, I just tried to get a handle on what I could do, where I could go, how I could live. I didn't know anybody who was living underground at the time. I didn't have a feel for what it meant. And there was no way to really know how vindictive the forces of law and order were going to be."

It soon became clear, though, that he could get help from the underground network that developed in the United States in the late sixties. While Newhouser never considered joining a radical underground group —"I wasn't committed to revolution in the way you'd have to be for that," he notes—he nevertheless found that politically based "support systems" were readily available for people in his situation. "It turned out to be a lot easier than I expected. It wasn't as traumatic as I feared. I was offered identities before I left. I could get new identity papers and use them, and I could just be a new man. I drove away with a friend of mine, a long way away, just to live out in Nowhereville for a while, to have no connection with what's going on and no way to trace me."

Eventually, Newhouser made his way to the mountains of New England. He was hoping to build a new life, but was still unsure about what that life should be: "I didn't have a plan when I left, all I was hoping to do was survive!" And there was still the fear that his past would catch up with him. Life underground was unstable, and political involvement seemed, at least at that point, extremely risky. Although Warren New-houser felt that he had achieved some measure of "victory" against the system—he was "free"—he was the one who was in hiding, who had to give up all that he had known for a life of uncertainty and paranoia. It was, to say the least, an ambiguous victory.[3]

"I Started to Turn to the Ocean"

Steve Rubin was the only RU activist to do "hard time." Rubin was the youngest son of an upper-middle-class Los Angeles family whose politi-cal values were left-liberal. His older brother had been active in the early days of SDS. Soon after arriving at UCSB in 1968, Rubin began work-ing with Roger Wade, Ed Pines, and other activist students on draft resistance issues. A self-described "real roustabout" and "flamboyant young radical," Rubin's emotional involvement in politics was especially intense. During the William Allen protests, and particularly during the riots, he was a leading participant in the street action. Convicted in the spring of 1970 for assaulting a police officer, he was sent to the state peni-tentiary for ninety days' "observation." (This came on top of a month in the county jail earlier that year for another riot-related offense.) The observation would determine whether he would serve more time in jail or be released on probation.

"The ninety-day thing was especially psychologically excruciating," Rubin recalls. "My lawyer told me when I went down there, 'Don't worry, I'm sure you'll get probation,' and I figured, you know, they sepa-rated you from the community, you were in trouble and in for ninety days, and then they'd let you out. But I found out when I got down there, and started reading the commitment notices, that 75 percent of the guys committed on a ninety-day program are sent back to the joint. And that got me worrying pretty heavily! It means that when you're up for observation you can't hit anybody that hits you, 'cause you can't afford the chance of somebody saying, 'Well, I saw Rubin swing the first blow, actually. It's part of his violent character, and we ought to give him a negative recommendation.'" Once "written up," Rubin could be denied probation and would have to serve at least a year in prison, perhaps even three or four.

Moreover, being incarcerated in the state penitentiary for any length of time—observation or no observation—was tremendously demoralizing. It was a real shock for someone who had grown up in a well-to-do family and was attending the University of California. "When they slam the door you go, 'Fuck, what am I doing here?' You're not bred to believe that you'll end up in a place like that. You go, 'Oh my God, this is for real; they mean business.'" The atmosphere was tense, often violent. "It keeps you looking over your shoulder. I mean, like I got upset when they'd shut down the whole prison for a missing spoon, and I was walkin' down the halls, always looking over my shoulder, 'cause I didn't know who the fuck had the spoon and who they were gonna use it on, and whether for a neurotic reason they would want to come after you. You know, I kept thinking maybe guys were jealous that I was a white middle-class college student, and would want to take a whole life of oppression with a swing of the knife. There is no way to describe what the experience of prison was like. I mean, that is an experience beyond . . . just scary, just frightening as shit."

Being raped in the shower two weeks after his arrival did not help matters. In addition, Rubin was marked as a "political" prisoner by the prison administration from the beginning, subjected to petty harassment by the guards, and watched carefully. More disturbing than this, however, was the "complete feeling of helplessness that [the people who run the prison] can do what they want with you. And that's a special shock for a student, for someone who's always had bourgeois times, always had a soft kind of, you know, backing to fall back on if you ever got into trouble, financially or otherwise. In the joint, it's dog-eat-dog; you're just one number. Conditions are just overwhelmingly inhumane. I saw a lot of destroyed people there."

Much to his relief, Rubin was given probation at the conclusion of his observation period and was released from jail in late August. Prison had a marked effect on his thinking, both about politics and about himself. For one thing, some of his ideas about the politics of imprisonment—ideas that many in the New Left were espousing—were modified. "Some of the guys I met there, it really made me deal with the question about what a criminal orientation is," he told a fellow RU member (who was recording the conversation) one year after his release. "And it made me deal with how you selectively do two things: go about building a genuine system of rehabilitation, and go about ordering an efficient means of isolation, keeping people who are real human criminals, who are a threat to the population at large, keeping them in isolation. You know, when I went in there I had all sorts of utopian ideas about freeing all prisoners, that all prisoners were political prisoners because of their crime against the state or their crime against capitalism. I came out of there thinking that was absolutely bullshit. You can't let some guys run loose. They're psycho-sexual murderers; there's nothing political about it. Their origins may be political insofar as they're the products of the socially degenerate, wasting society, but you can't unleash them on society."

Rubin still felt some commitment to restructuring that "degenerate society" and its institutions, however, and that included the prisons. After enrolling at UCSB for the fall term, he became involved in the "prison movement" for a few months (this was a time when radicals were being strongly influenced by George Jackson's writings and books like Eldridge Cleaver's *Soul On Ice*), working on various prison reform projects. The fact that he had done time in jail made him a natural participant—people expected him to be involved in such issues—yet the lingering effects of his experiences were taking a toll on his political commitment. "I wanted to run away to the mountains and live in a little cave for a year. I was really freaked out a little bit, and I felt myself changing to a nonrevolutionary stance. I wasn't interested; I was repressed. I was frightened of going back, and I didn't want to take part in any of the real revolutionary things. There were things to do, but I was staying strictly away from it, because I wanted to get my degree and get off probation and all that shit. So I stayed pretty much away from it and did little things on the sidelines—you know, wrote a leaflet to sneak into the county jail to strike and shit. But I started to slowly evolve out of the political thing."

What Steve Rubin "evolved" toward was far removed from New Left activism, but not far away from the countercultural quest for authentic personal freedom: "I started to turn to the ocean. The year after prison, I rented a Boston whaler for the summer, and I buzzed in that fucker every day. I got bronzed and tan and grew my hair out about eighteen foot long. I decided maybe I'd be a fisherman or something. I succumbed to this addiction to the ocean." Although Rubin talks of how his father took him fishing as a child and he dreamed of being a deckhand on a sports fishing boat, it was the nightmare of the penitentiary that moved him to try to make that dream a reality. As it had been for Terry Lennox, political activism for Steve Rubin was no longer a means of personal salvation; it was now something from which to flee.

THE FATE OF SIXTIES COMMITMENT: TAKE ONE

Martha Koch, Terry Lennox, Steve Rubin, and Warren Newhouser were among those who felt estranged from the revolutionary totalism that their friends and fellow indictees were espousing. Such estrangement, at the time, seemed idiosyncratic in the face of what appeared as an overwhelming consensus about impending apocalypse. Moreover, no one who knew any of these people at the time would have been likely to see them as falling away. Indeed, as they tell it, their estrangement was not rooted in disillusionment with the beliefs of the movement, with which, for the most part, they still identified.

In retrospect, these stories of early departure and distancing seem best interpreted in light of the eventual dissolution of the student movement as a whole. Perhaps these seemingly idiosyncratic experiences offer clues about why the movement eventually fragmented; perhaps they reveal some of the ways in which the movement contained the seeds of its own disintegration. Rather than reading these as stories about the failure of revolutionary commitment, they might better be read as revelations about the inability of the movement's modes of organization and operation to sustain commitment beyond the moment of intense upheaval.

A key to understanding the movement and the counterculture as frameworks of commitment is to see them not primarily as systems of beliefs, codes of conduct, or waves of mass action. The concrete experience of movement participation in the sixties had mostly to do with face-to-face relationships in small groups. The beliefs and codes of movement and counterculture were brought home to individual young people, not simply or mainly through images on television or magazines or pamphlets, but in close circles of friendship. When young people gathered, they came not one by one but together with their friends. Indeed, the sociology of institutions—of education, of popular culture, of mass media, of bureaucracy—tells us that beneath all visible structures of influence and control is a proliferation of informal primary groupings, which mediate and channel formal messages and measures aimed at mobilizing and directing individual energy. To a great extent, in any institutional setting, members neither obey nor protest as individuals but do so in reference to the primary groups with which they are involved.

Student life is particularly replete with such primary group formations, as several generations of social researchers have found.[4] Students, like inmates in other institutional settings, band together in order to cope with authorities, rules, and demands that infringe on their interests and limit their freedom. In addition, adolescent and youth friendship groups have often been interpreted as sources of emotional support as members try to manage the sharp break with the nurturing environment of the family. Adolescent peer culture, from this perspective, is "functional" in that it enables the transition to adult independence. Perhaps most important is the way in which friendship groups and intimate interaction provide opportunities for identity testing and validating, for learning who one is, for deepening capacities for "role-taking," empathy, self-expression, for finding others for mutual caring and love. If youth is the moment in the life-cycle when identity is the primary issue, then the intense intimate associations that seem to characterize youth are understandable as crucibles for identity (Eisenstadt 1956; Erikson 1968; Flacks 1971).

Student and youth friendship circles, though formed spontaneously, do not exist in isolation, but are likely to be oriented to broader "youth cultures" and "subterranean traditions" of value, style, and taste (Matza 1961). Today's "preppies" and "punks" represent the latest variants of earlier youth subcultures, such as the "collegiates" and "beatniks" of the fifties.

The movement and the counterculture in the sixties were, like other youth subcultures, the expression of a myriad of friendship circles formed locally in campuses and communities across the country. The formation of national movement organizations, and the publicity the sixties revolt received in national media, attracted and focused the consciousness and activity of a rapidly growing number of others not in the originating circles. However, the friendship groups of the sixties youth revolt were more intensely involving than those characteristic of conventional youth subcultures. By the late sixties, in places like Isla Vista, student activists were involved with each other in an all-encompassing regime, highly consuming of time and energy. Moreover, participation in their circles implied shared involvement with fundamental issues of value, purpose, and ideology. The activist groups did not just share tastes and symbolic affinities, they became arenas for working through basic beliefs at a deep level. More than most youth groups, those embedded in the movement became consciously concerned with mutual resocialization—the elimination of bourgeois values, racism, materialism, authoritarianism, and sexual repression, and the fostering of self-sacrifice, revolutionary dedication, collectivist responsibility, and antiauthoritarian assertiveness. Each member was likely to think of himself or herself as becoming "new," actively breaking with values and traits one had been raised to have, abandoning personal hang-ups that limited one's capacity to share, give, express, and risk.

In Isla Vista, and in many other student communities, this work at personal change began unsystematically, but gradually many friendship groups self-consciously declared themselves to be collectives. "Collective" usually implied sharing household arrangements and always entailed the creation of explicit rules about mutual commitment. Such commitments were deeper than the ties of formal organizational membership and more definite than those associated with conventional friendship. All the RU people we interviewed were deeply involved in such collectives. The emotional atmosphere of movement collectives was heightened by the sense of shared threat arising from involvement in civil disobedience and disruptive protest. As the movement activists increasingly defined their aims as "revolutionary," they increasingly felt bonded by the sort of spirit associated with combat.

The experience of belonging to movement collectives, then, was crucial in establishing and maintaining activist identity and commitment during the sixties. The small circle of friends was the seedbed for the collective action and for the ethical code that defined the student movement. The fraternity of these collectives enabled members to take the risks and make the sacrifices required by militant action. The validation, warmth and, often, love experienced in these groups was a major reward for taking such risks. The friendship groups and collectives were, therefore, functional for the movement as well as for the individual members. But the stories we have just recounted suggest that cohesion and moral pressure exerted by these groups resulted in serious and often hidden costs as well as benefits for both the movement and its members.

These stories can be read as having a single theme with many variations. The theme is that, beneath the exhilarating experience of mutuality, sharing, and oneness, there was a growing, nagging discomfort and apartness. The discomfort began with a private awareness of needs, feelings, interests, and aspirations that were at odds with the expressed norms and ideals shared by the group. It led to a desire for distance and exit when one discovered that it was not possible to express these private feelings openly within the collective without risking shame and disapproval.

Obviously, all group situations create dilemmas of this sort for individual members. Tension between collective identification and individuality is pervasive in all social interaction. In ordinary daily life, such tension is eased when individuals have multiple ties to groups that do not demand the total commitment or prescribe the total identity of the member. But because movement collectives came to demand total commitment, tensions between collectivity and individuality could not be managed by maintaining a larger network of interests and loyalties. Any effort to do this would, in itself, be a violation of the emphasis the movement placed on integrity and commitment. Because members shared an expectation that each participant was striving to fulfill the group's defined ideal, efforts to express interests or feelings that ran counter to that ideal were incompatible with membership.

The point is not that movement collectives imposed alien standards or ideologies on participants. These were not sects, demanding conformity to a highly elaborated belief system. The problem experienced by Koch, Lennox, Rubin, Newhouser, and Pines was not a crisis of belief. They do not describe disillusionments like those frequent in the communist movement of the 1930s, disillusionment rooted in sharp conflicts between members' experience of external reality and movement claims about it. Instead, what each experienced was a crisis of personal development. In retrospect, it is obvious that, however much individual members believed that they should transform themselves, the personal changes fostered within the collectives inescapably conflicted with fundamental aspects of members' individuality. Resistance to change was inevitable, yet the collectives lacked effective means to overcome such resistance—not least because most members presented themselves as enthusiastically committed, publicly affirming the "newness" of their being. But the ideals and norms expressed in these groups were often both too narrow and too far-reaching to mesh with members' developmental needs and interests, and the atmosphere of these groups did not at all encourage the free expression of these dilemmas.

Martha Koch's desire to pursue a medical career put her at odds with her closest political friends in Isla Vista. Hers was not an isolated experience. In the climate of the late sixties, any career interest was viewed with suspicion, since it implied a willingness to join the "system," to put private interests ahead of political priorities. Most activists harbored the hope that their own futures could be decided within the framework of the movement rather than the established occupational structure. But there were some, like Koch, who could not reconcile such sentiments —which they shared—with intense personal interests, especially those that required training and certification that the movement itself could not provide. Koch found that she could not expose her perplexity to other group members, since the cohesion of the collective rested on the assumption that all members were committed to the same ideals and had abandoned their pre-movement, individualistic selves. To question this assumption was to endanger the group's solidarity and one's acceptance within it. Instead, Koch left Isla Vista and found a political home in a social circle made up of left-oriented medical students. But the collective, as such, never seriously confronted personal issues of vocation and career, never tried to determine how these could be integrated with political engagement. The failure of Koch's Isla Vista collective to be a resource for her development mirrors the failure of the student movement as a whole to deal with the social and political relevance of members' skills, interests, and training. Instead, at its revolutionary peak, the movement turned these into matters for scorn and shame.

Vocational issues were not the only source of conflict between personal need and collective ethos in the movement, as our members' stories suggest. Terry Lennox and Steve Rubin experienced fear in the face of prison, while Warren Newhouser was nagged by fundamental questions about the strategic directions and tactics prevailing in the movement at the time. Their problem was, of course, that fear and doubt were not supposed to be admitted and voiced within the collective. Instead, members were expected to present themselves as eagerly, toughly ready for combat, confrontation, and the threat of repression. Members often strove to outdo each other in displays of revolutionary manhood and conviction. Terry Lennox could not admit to paralyzing fear in such a climate. Steve Rubin was unable to confess his doubt that all prison inmates were persecuted political prisoners or his reservations about pursuing actions that could return him to a prison experience that he had found horrifying. Warren Newhouser's doubt that revolution was really impending was not heard within arenas of political discussion in which he participated, for such doubt would have undermined his credibility if voiced. Lennox and Rubin drifted out of organized politics because of their private fears and doubts. Newhouser remained committed, but the groups he participated in, obsessed with apocalypse, did not draw upon his insights and wisdom. And for someone like Kenneth Essian, whose involvement in movement activities was minimal, there was even less chance that his need for reconciliation, for pulling back from the brink, would be heard.

Such suppression of private fear, doubt, and inadequacy was extremely common in the experience of movement activists in the late sixties and early seventies. If one's collective embarked on an organizing project, members expected each other to become instant organizers, free of anxiety about talking to strangers, confidently able to argue a position publicly, perfectly at ease in roles that most people would find intimidating. In some cases, members were challenged to abandon sexual hang-ups about monogamy and promiscuity. Collectives were frequently arenas for competitive display of macho toughness and disdain for bourgeois creature comforts, soliciting vows of poverty and promoting communal use of personal property. Activists who had belonged to such collectives are likely to recall the experience as painful because of the unacknowledged gap between public profession and private feeling— and the shame and guilt that resulted.

The repressive atmosphere of these collectives was not imposed from above by central committees or charismatic gurus. Instead, it arose spontaneously out of the group's shared effort to interpret the cultural and ideological climate in which it was embedded and the political situation it confronted. Yet the expectations members held of each other were accepted with enormous collective naiveté, for they were rooted in the assumption that instant and total change was possible. The movement collectives made no provision for the great burdens of anxiety, guilt, and pain produced by demands for personal change. By blocking open expression of that pain, by demanding that it be denied, the movement collectives were sowing the seeds of their dissolution.

"WE ARE ALL OUTLAWS IN THE EYES OF AMERICA"

If some activists were distancing themselves from Isla Vista in the year or so following the bank-burning, unable or unwilling to continue riding the wave of "revolution," most of our activist respondents continued to embrace the vision of impending revolutionary transformation. In that period, most devoted themselves to a strategic vision grounded in the idea that youth ghettos could serve as "liberated territories" within which revolutionary values could be institutionalized and from which social transformation could be launched.

The RU activists were not alone in adopting such a community-focused strategy, of course. For some other I.V. residents, as well as progressive students and faculty, it was the only alternative to continued violence and suffering. As one person wrote in a letter to *El Gaucho*, just weeks after the February riot:

> Isla Vista can either continue in its cultural conflicts—riots and street fighting—or it can become the first of the New American communities—an autonomous life space where rules facilitate and sanction youth culture. Police can be a service agency respecting youth culture, landlordism can give way to communes and co-ops, with credit unions supporting change and banks not supporting the status quo. The University will have to come to see itself as a builder of this, and not a servant of business interests in the surrounding community. (12 March 1970.)

Even *El Gaucho*, whose editorials had been a major voice of the New Left at UCSB, cautioned (on March 3) that "violence at this time means only suicide." Nevertheless, whatever one's political perspective, institution-building was difficult even to consider when the community was the scene of pitched battles between police and students. With the restoration of some semblance of public order after Isla Vista III, however, the organizing began in earnest.

There were more complications. The University of California presented itself as another advocate for Isla Vista. The Trow Commission, appointed by the regents to investigate both the riots and the university response, recommended that UC recognize its responsibility toward that community, fund a variety of community programs, participate in forming a police foot patrol (to bring the sheriff's deputies in close contact with the people), and work toward improving local housing. The regents approved the recommendations and voted to allocate $600,000 for Isla Vista aid, almost a third of which was to go to the foot patrol. Then, on top of UC's decision, the Bank of America announced its plans to fund community programs in Isla Vista. "We have recognized," the bank said, "our social responsibility."

These plans for using university or Bank of America funds in Isla Vista generated a great deal of debate among radical activists and in the wider community. Both the propriety of accepting the money and the intentions of these established authorities in allocating it were questioned. Many perceived it as an effort to undermine militancy and weaken the movement. Superficial "pacification" programs in the guise of "community assistance" had been instituted after the urban black rebellions of the 1960s, these skeptics argued, and now "they" were trying to pacify Isla Vista. "I thought it was really kind of a cop-out—the institution building," one woman told us. "I thought that the Bank of America was trying to buy the radicals off, and I wouldn't involve myself with that. I didn't like it." Denise Saal held similar beliefs: "We saw it as a buy-out, a sell-out, a group of liberals coming in to set up a sort of 'reform government' in I.V. to quiet down the natives." However, others argued that the community desperately needed public services and that by emphasizing community or collective control, revolutionary and anticapitalist institutions could be created, regardless of the university's wishes.

While the debate continued, the "institutionalization of humanistic culture" activities also went on. There was simply too much romantic enthusiasm and utopian fervor in Isla Vista, and too much real need, for things to get bogged down in ideological quarrels. The university's money facilitated the development of a variety of organizations and institutions: the Isla Vista Community Council (an elected body that had only advisory powers in county government but was nonetheless perceived as a first step toward political representation), human relations center, Open Door Medical Clinic, Isla Vista Planning Commission, credit union, food co-op, tenants' union, Isla Vista Department of Justice (a community legal clinic with a radical perspective), Isla Vista Parks and Recreation District, and a variety of others. Some, like the tenants' union and food co-op, had a somewhat radical and explicitly collective character. Others, like the planning commission and the community council, became political arenas where progressive concerns could at least be discussed.

The radical collectives and their members sought to maintain a "revolutionary perspective" in whatever community activities they became involved in. Bill McNaughton and Paul Little, another RU member and accused "bank burner" who had been a student government officer during the prior school year, ran for community council positions and were elected. Other activists became involved in the tenants' union. The collective project that received the most attention, however, was an alternative, "underground" newspaper. Called the *Strategic Hamlet* in order to draw parallels between Isla Vista and the barbed-wire-enclosed camps into which Vietnamese peasants were moved to "protect" them from communist guerrillas, the paper published its first issue in the early fall of 1970, soon after students began returning to Isla Vista after the summer break. Roger Wade, Sheila Barressi, and Sarah Glenn were among the former RU members who worked on the *Hamlet* at different times.

At the same time that these community projects were being organized, the collective members began to prepare themselves for "armed struggle," spending hours in the isolated foothills behind Santa Barbara learning how to shoot guns and developing other military and survival skills that would be necessary in the approaching cataclysm. As one person states, "We felt that violence was becoming more and more necessary. There was a lot of debate over essentially Weatherman-type strategy—this idea of going underground and committing violent acts of sabotage." Plans were sometimes discussed for such actions, as well as for self-defense against the expected fascist onslaught. Moreover, as they steeled their bodies for revolution, they readied their minds. Discussions of revolutionary theory and strategy became much more intense in the wake of the riots, and ideological lines began to harden (although the doctrinaire sectarianism that had consumed SDS a year earlier and continued to plague most movement groups throughout the country never won out). In many instances, debates over revolutionary tactics were quite consciously carried on in public, with the *Strategic Hamlet* serving as the forum. One exchange was headlined, "To Bomb or Not to Bomb." There was also a series of articles on armed self-defense. The introductory essay (entitled "In Defense of Self-Defense") stated: "As the system becomes more repressive, the pigs begin to go beyond this normal role of arresting people who are then dealt with through the courts, and instead begin to function as armed executioners in the streets. This attack is direct and physical, and their goal in many cases is to kill. Under these conditions, armed self-defense is necessary" (14–28 October 1970). Later articles discussed shotguns and handguns. Additionally, the paper published articles on revolutionary struggles in the Third World and repression against radicals in the United States, as well as communiqués from the Weather Underground. "That was the kind of stuff we did," one of the paper's former staff members says. "We saw the *Strategic Hamlet* as preparing people for armed revolution."

This revolutionary asceticism was combined, in characteristic Isla Vista fashion, with continuing attachment to cultural romanticism. Because of the strong coalescence of "freaks" and "politicos" in I.V., the political effort to turn the community into a liberated zone was equally an attempt to territorialize this cultural revolt. The political significance of "mind-expanding," "consciousness-raising" hallucinogenic drugs was a major topic of discussion among activists, and many were enthusiastically committed to the use of such drugs.

Thus, the *Strategic Hamlet* did not restrict itself to articles on armed struggle. It became equally absorbed with cultural matters: essays on "people's art" (tie-dying, macrame, batiking, candle-making), on community self-sufficiency (the creation of community gardens on "liberated land," starting a compost heap, the formation of a whole-wheat co-op, how to make homemade beer), and on such intriguing topics as "edible plants of the southwest," "getting naked," and "how to make your own moccasins," were printed side-by-side with accounts of shoot-outs between Black Panthers and police, the latest action by the Tupameros, reports on Vietnam, and poems commemorating the death of Weather Underground members Diana Oughton, Terry Robbins, and Ted Gold. Indeed, while others had proposed community building as a substitute for militancy and violence, the *Hamlet* collective argued that "community consciousness" had been forged in the flames of the burning bank, that revolutionary militancy and community were inseparable. An essay entitled "Isla Vista: Toward a New Culture" in the second issue of the *Hamlet* began:

> Up until late February, 1970, Isla Vista was little more than a geo-graphical entity containing something under 15,000 residents, 85% of them students. The first riot changed all that: it signaled the violent emergence of a new Isla Vista, a mythical and visionary Isla Vista. It heralded the creation and enactment of a dream for an alternative culture/society . . . not simply a counter-culture, but one positively working for practical solutions/alternatives to society's problems. After the bank-burning, Isla Vista broke out of its womb of com-

munity non-responsibility. People began to realize that although they lived in I.V., the community would never be theirs until they seized control of the social/political and economic framework. (14–28 October 1970.)

Community organizations that attempted "to meet the daily life needs of the populace" and that were cooperatively run so as to "translate the democratic will of the populace into effective power" over their daily lives—such as the food co-op, credit union, community gardens, and tenants' union—were singled out for special attention in this regard.

The quest for a fusion between political and cultural transformation and for an opportunity to experience this liberation led several activists to undertake what can perhaps best be described as cultural odysseys during the months following the riots. Sheila Barressi and Kristen Van Duinen, for example, went on a month-long cross-country trip in the early summer of 1970, intending to join a group of yippies who were planning a visit to Cuba. Although the Cuban trip fell through, Van Duinen remained on the East Coast for several months, fascinated by Jerry Rubin and the yippie style of "revolutionary youth-culture" politics. Cynthia Spivak, another RU activist who participated in community-building efforts before deciding that she needed to experience other, non-Western cultures, moved to Singapore for a year and traveled to India and the Soviet Union before returning to California.

A six-month trip to India by *Hamlet* staffer Ellen Hemmings was yet another odyssey. Hemmings, then a twenty-year-old history student from the Los Angeles area, was one of the Santa Barbara 19 defendants. Raised in a conservative family, with a brother serving in Vietnam, Hemmings came to UCSB in 1969 uncertain of the wisdom of the war and thus deeply affected by the antiwar and draft resistance efforts on campus. The countercultural life of Isla Vista had an equally profound influence on her thinking, however. By the time of the community-building period, she recalls, "I was fed up, really, with Western culture, and I wanted to see alternative ways of living and thinking. I had seen so much that I didn't like in the West. I felt I had experienced the West to the ultimate, and I wanted to see the opposite way of thinking, because the East is so much more collective in their thinking and lifestyle."

Hemmings' search for alternatives did not end there, however. After returning from India she traveled to Cuba on one of the first Venceremos Brigades. "I believed in communism, and I wanted to see how it functioned. And it was a very beautiful country. Everybody was so optimistic there. The majority of the people worked hard and got results. The Cubans I talked to felt very involved in their country's government, and the kids were extremely enthusiastic too. I was impressed with their schools and health-care facilities. I remember when I came back, I thought it could be really great here, in the U.S., to have communism because we could be free from that struggle for economic survival [that Third World nations face]. There's so many other things we could do with our minds."

Throughout this period of heightened revolutionary commitment, these men and women did indeed try to live free from such economic pressures, did try to live as "liberated youth." Thus, even as they called for institutions that would meet the community's daily needs, they gave little serious attention to the mundane problems, such as economic survival, that movement activists faced. Because vocational careers were seen at that time as, in one person's words, "corrupted by the structure and morality of somebody else's society," people sought to get by on part-time, low-wage jobs and, on some occasions, "ripping off the system." "We did a little shoplifting," one person recalls, "and we used to make [illegal] long-distance credit card calls, and we did a 'lost' traveler's checks type thing, and supported ourselves for a few months on that. I would waitress for a few days, but I was dropping acid every night and I didn't manage to keep that job." In keeping with this line of action, the *Strategic Hamlet* published "Living Off the Fat of the Bacon," a series that included pieces on "Ripping Off Sears" and "How to Fly the Friendly Skies for Free." While there was more than a touch of yippie-style humor in all this, there was an equal amount of serious attention to the revolutionary politics of such practices. The article discussing shoplifting, for example, was followed by this editor's note: "Hopefully this scheme will not be used to fulfill the materialistic fantasies of the participants. While we can indeed see the constructive aspects of an act of theft against a large corporation, it would be erased if that theft is motivated by something other than need. Selfish or accumulative motives are not deserving of any praise in our movement and, hopefully, will one day disappear along with Sears Roebuck." (*Strategic Hamlet*, 14–28 October 1970.)

The most telling statement regarding these cultural impulses, how-ever—and perhaps this entire revolutionary period as well—is provided by a woman activist: "I remember my favorite song that summer was [Jefferson Airplane's] 'We are all outlaws in the eyes of America.' I really totally identified with that. I and my closest friends really saw ourselves that way. We really saw ourselves as outlaws."

4

Confronting Reality

THE FATE OF SIXTIES COMMITMENT: TAKE TWO

The belief that revolution was imminent was rooted in the expectation that the Vietnam War would continue to escalate—that the Cambodian invasion of 1970 portended further expansion of the ground war, that further intensification of the bombing of Vietnam would lead to massive civilian casualties—and that, therefore, only further effort to "bring the war home" through massively disruptive direct action had a chance of affecting the policy. This would be followed, activists reasoned, by more concerted government repression of the movement—rounding up of activists, aggressive suppression of protest, deepening and more violent polarization. Surely, in this climate, the ghetto revolt would become increasingly politicized and systematic, and the white response to such a development would accelerate the drift toward a fascist-like atmosphere. Given such anticipations, and fueled by the rhetoric of national politicians and of some black and white revolutionary leaders, images of "armed struggle," of "outlaw armies of youth," of "liberated zones" and "urban guerilla warfare," seemed like plausible pieces of an impending scenario.

As the school year of 1970–71 wore on, it became evident that further escalation of civil strife was unlikely. The campuses—including UCSB—were, in fact, relatively calm in comparison with the fury of the previous year, and no mass confrontations equaled the unprecedented national upheaval of May 1970. Thus, despite the persistence of youthful discontent and the flourishing of insurrectionary faith among some sectors of the student population, there was considerably less collective action.

A primary reason for this relative demobilization was that the most dire expectations of the activists were not being confirmed by events. Instead of further escalating the war, the Nixon administration embarked on a complicated policy that combined negotiations, withdrawal of U.S. troops, and intensified bombing. Furthermore, a movement in Congress to cut off appropriations for the war was building, and there was hope that the Democratic nominee for president in 1972 would be a strong advocate of U.S. withdrawal. These developments provided, for the first time in years, a rationale for conventional political strategies rather than confrontation as a framework for the Vietnam opposition.

Meanwhile, the draft lottery had served to reduce the threat of the draft for many young men, and conscription itself was soon halted. An amendment lowering the voting age to eighteen was quickly adopted after the Kent State protests. Enforcement of laws dealing with marijuana possession was relaxed in many college communities. In short, instead of a relentless iron heel of repression after 1970, there were increased opportunities for political expression and a relaxation of the threats to personal liberty that youth had been experiencing during much of the sixties.

The polarization of the society seemed also to be reversing. A flood of popular writing, epitomized by Charles Reich's *The Greening of America*, attempted to explain the youth revolt to Middle America in terms quite different from the epithets previously hurled by some leading politicians. The burden of the literature was that the youth movement, despite its excesses, was a harbinger of a more open and liberated society. Even the president of the Bank of America, Louis Lundborg, contributed to this discourse; his book, *Future Without Shock*, based on meetings and discussions that he initiated with students in Isla Vista, advocated opposition to the Vietnam war and understanding of the legitimate grievances of the young. Such public pronouncements undoubtedly resonated with the personal experiences of the thousands of families in which parents were compelled to deal with their protesting offspring. As parents put up bail money, struggled to make sense of the new language, and coped with the pain of dealing with defiant children, they were more and more receptive to the idea of a dialogue, rather than a war, between the generations.

Indeed, in the aftermath of the 1970 events, such dialogue was increasingly prevalent in Santa Barbara. A blue-ribbon citizens' commission strongly criticized police conduct during the riots. A candidate for sheriff was endorsed by Isla Vistans (and elected on the strength of the I.V. vote) after he promised to punish police officials responsible for excessive force. The regents provided funds for community services after receiving the results of a study that laid much of the blame for riot-inducing conditions to university neglect of the community and a lack of student voice in community affairs.

In Isla Vista, New Left activists defined their participation in community development as a start at creating a revolutionary liberated territory. In college towns and youth ghettos all across the country, many participated in such efforts as an alternative to direct action, confrontation, and riot. Institution-building, the development of self-government, the creation of ongoing grass-roots leadership and organization, were seen as ways to provide voice and power to the constituencies of the movement and the counterculture that could be achieved before, or instead of, "the revolution." These were, moreover, ways by which the movement could overcome its narrow social base and reach out to the nonyoung, nonstudent, nonprotesting Americans without whose consent little significant change could be possible. And, it was argued, such local efforts could promote reform of police practices, housing conditions, land use policies, and other local conditions, while providing resources for the development of alternative institutions and countercultural enterprises. Some successes were persuasive, inspiring some activists to redirect their energy from scenarios of revolution to strategies of community organization and institution-building.

At the same time, national and local authorities increased the costs of "revolutionary" activism. The existence of a movement underground (consisting of Weatherman and other revolutionary collectives) and the rhetoric of movement leaders provided grounds for launching extensive grand jury investigations in which scores of activists were called to testify, under pain of imprisonment for refusal to answer questions. FBI and other intelligence agencies carried out programs of harassment and surveillance of questionable legality. Such activities were widely publicized, and ultimately a paralyzing paranoia spread throughout the youth and student communities. Youths questioned whether the risk of extreme physical danger was a reasonable price for confrontation with authority.

As applied to revolutionary-style activism, such questioning is bound to have a dampening effect, especially when coupled with disillusioning experiences. By late 1970, as described in the previous chapter, the movement scene was increasingly repressive, rancorous, and torn by factionalism. The movement's failure to live by its own principles of comradeship and love, combined with the risks of continued participation provided many adherents with grounds to withdraw. Indeed, despite the evidence that the protest and ferment of the young were affecting many levels of policy and social life, there was a pervasive feeling that militant direct action was no more effective than moderate tactics. The war was still being carried on, and despite the removal of American troops, the air war was intensifying. For some, the seeming immovability of government and society provided additional reason for disaffiliating from movement commitments.

THE PERSONAL VERSUS THE POLITICAL

In an essay written in the summer of 1971, an Isla Vista activist reflected on the movement's demobilization and dissolution:

> It's the end of another year, and the war is still going on. It's the end of another year, and the revolution hasn't come. Our frustration has set in—it's been institutionalized. Alienation, confusion, cynicism, fear: cliches of our collective psyche. War, racism, sexism, repression, poverty, pollution: so all-pervasive in our daily lives that they, too, have become cliches. Everyone, even President Nixon, knows that basic conditions haven't changed. . . . In every aspect of the Movement, people come up against the ubiquitous dilemma: how can we show our militancy without being ripped off? How can we be militant and not isolate ourselves from the masses of people in this country who want the war ended, who want clean air, good jobs, and the pursuit of happiness? Can the war and racism be ended without a revolution? How do we make a revolution? What is revolution?

The individuals in our sample who remained in Isla Vista were affected by these aspects of the "ubiquitous dilemma" in a number of ways. Representing those who concluded that "making revolution" was a pipe dream, Bill McNaughton says, "I finally realized there wasn't a social revolution going on, and that there wasn't going to be one, when I looked at a Gallup Poll in the newspaper and realized that I was part of what was only a 10 percent that could easily be ignored or eliminated. And what were they doing to that 10 percent? They were killing them in Chicago; you know, just busting in in the middle of the night and murdering them. They had this big witch hunt—the grand jury, conspiracy charges. I decided there was no possibility at all of revolution."

Roger Wade also felt that "the repression had become quite real" and had led to a dampening of militancy. "It wasn't that you could see the effects of repression as a precise point, but gradually the death toll mounted up, and people slowly became more and more aware of that." Although Wade did not share McNaughton's belief that repression could wipe out the New Left or his utter despair about the possibility of radically transforming American society, he too was shaken by the realization that the movement had a dangerously narrow base of support. More than anything else, the recognition that Isla Vista was hardly a microcosm of America and that radicalized youth and black revolutionaries were not going to make the revolution on their own caused him to reconsider his political stance. "Gradually, as the tear gas dissipated, I became more aware of my surroundings. I started to recognize that it wasn't good to just write off the rest of the population—it was suicide. That there really were two hundred million [Americans], it now meant something more than just an abstract number. I mean, it meant a whole lot of faces, a whole lot of hands. I mean, we were completely impotent."

Some shared Wade's sense of the movement's predicament but attributed it to an excess of self-righteousness that came, as one person stated, from "the feeling that you're doing moral battle" and was fueled by "the rush of confrontation." "There was so much evidence that right was on our side, as the movement grew in intensity. That easily spilled over into feelings that right was on our side in every other respect. I think we all suffered from the feeling that what was obvious to us was something that should be clearly obvious to other people, that there was no problem, that other people would see the right and everything would just be beautiful. It was so easy to get isolated from the rest of the world, being surrounded by people who basically felt the same way that you did about things."

Questions about the "military preparation" focus, more often than not, came from female activists. All the talk about guns and violence, they argued, encouraged people to be macho and tough, to substitute revolutionary style for political substance. This division between men and women in the RU was, of course, not new: during some of the most turbulent weeks of the previous spring, women resisted the call by the largely male leadership for a strike that would include padlocking classroom buildings and harassing strike-breaking students and faculty. The women suggested a less militant strategy, but the hard line prevailed as men argued that conditions required toughness. One year later, the environment had changed, and such criticisms were more openly and confidently expressed. Increasingly, activists felt that if revolution was still possible, it had to be conceived of as a long-term (perhaps life-long) process of mundane and patient political work, work that would require bridging the vast gulf of mistrust and misunderstanding that had opened up between the movement and the "straight," nonyouth majority.

This long-range perspective on revolution is dramatically illustrated by Sheila Barressi's experiences. In 1971, Barressi was chosen to travel to North Vietnam as part of a "People's Peace Treaty" student delegation. "Going to Vietnam made me see how much incredible patience it takes to make a revolution—how much patience, how much tolerance, how much understanding," she recalls. "I really wanted to emulate their courage, I wanted to emulate their patience. And also the way they related to one another, the incredible loving attitude people had toward one another and toward us—it was just mind-boggling. I really saw them as being quite saintly." These feelings led to some soul-searching on her part. "I remember thinking that we really weren't serious. If we really saw ourselves as revolutionaries, we'd have to develop some of the qualities which I'd seen in people in Vietnam. One of the main things was not just talking to ourselves, stop acting like fools and hating people [because they were] in favor of the war or because they weren't speaking out against the war—having a more compassionate attitude, having more patience."

Similar sentiments were expressed by another activist in an "Open Letter to the Movement." One of the New Left's principal failures, this person wrote, was "an orientation almost exclusively around crises and events," an orientation that reflected their "immaturity and impatience":

> This mistake, which is still being repeated, is based on an incorrect political analysis. . . . The revolution won't start one day and end on another, as T.V. and history books would have us believe. . . . The often used analogy between riots and orgasms isn't far-fetched. Our

emotions build up inside us; then something happens, a climactic event which sparks off the release of all our emotions; it happens. Bill Allen is fired, thousands demonstrate in front of the Administration building; it feels good to scream out together. The police arrive; we scatter. And it's all over. We go back to our daily routine, letting it build up again until the next climactic catalyst. We put so much energy into these events (thinking that if we do the revolution will begin) that sometimes we lose the ability to react at all when we need to.

The image I have in mind of those events is a long-haired male college student, fist uplifted, running through the streets, pissed off and screaming. The emotions are real, the need to react is real. But that's not the point. The point is, we need more than to just react. We need to see events and crises as part of a process, a long-term protracted, multilevel process of social change.

In sum, many activists were coming to feel that the movement's own actions and rhetoric, particularly its totalistic revolutionary posture, were self-destructive and served to heighten the already isolated position of the protesters. This isolation, which was endemic to youth and student movements to begin with and exacerbated in the late sixties not only by the New Left's apocalyptic vision and governmental repression but by hostile media coverage as well (see Gitlin 1980 for a discussion of this issue), meant that the movement had to go beyond the campus and expand its limited base if the goals and values it embodied were to survive and have a chance of realization.

These reassessments produced a personal as well as a political crisis for many movement activists. Their totalistic commitment to revolution, and the resulting estrangement from everyday life, had not only heightened the barriers between themselves and the nonyouth, nonmovement American majority, but had also created a barrier between themselves and their own futures as adults. Apocalyptic predictions had provided strong moral and practical grounds for avoiding serious efforts to make personal choices about identity and vocation. Belief in the imminence of revolution resolved the tension between individual need and movement demands by short-circuiting it.

But it was now obvious that the future had to be lived after all, that questions of long-term vocation could no longer be avoided. As Sheila

Barressi says, "After I went to Vietnam, I really felt that being dedicated to revolution wasn't something . . . I didn't want it to be a frivolous phase of my youth, I wanted it to be a life-long endeavor, tied in with what the reality of our lives was. I mean, we weren't gonna be students anymore, so what were we gonna do with this political consciousness that we had?" Moreover, the fading of apocalyptic expectations made it much more difficult for the movement collectives that formed in the immediate aftermath of the riots to serve as all-encompassing frameworks for sustaining identities. By the early seventies, then, all of our respondents had to come to grips with the issues of direction and commitment that only a few had been concerned with when Isla Vista was in the grip of revolution. Their political crisis was intertwined with a crisis in personal development—a "life-construction crisis," Foss and Larkin (1979) have aptly termed it.

"Could I Be Completely Political? I Decided I Couldn't"

The Isla Vista radicals responded to these interrelated political and personal crises in several ways. One response was to withdraw from politics and the seemingly insurmountable dilemmas created by political engagement. For some, politics and political organization became increasingly alienating, filled with risks and tensions that seemed unnecessary in light of a growing sense that little was being accomplished anyway (see Jacobs 1978: 486).

Ellen Hemmings' experiences are representative in this regard. After returning from Cuba, Hemmings continued to work with the Venceremos Brigade on information and public education projects. She soon became discouraged with this work, however, feeling that people in the brigade "were trying to manipulate me." "They were really into political coercion," she recalls, "trying to convince you to do things, whether you wanted to or not." One of the things about which Hemmings had misgivings was the increasing emphasis on waging armed struggle: "They were using a lot of guns, and I didn't want to get involved in that, I'd already decided against that."

Significantly, Hemmings was not objecting to these tactics on moral grounds—she had been fully committed to them at one time and, like other activists, had prepared herself for "revolutionary violence"—but rather because she sensed that at this point, many months after the riots, "it was just futile": "We used to have these grandiose ideas, we used to plan the revolution. I began to really question that. And then I came to realize that it was really stupid. I just didn't see that blowing up buildings was going to change anything." In fact, Hemmings' feelings of futility now extended to all forms of political activity. "I felt tremendously burned out, tired of the whole thing. It's like, there's no way you could do anymore. I guess 'cause we had done so much. We didn't really have anything that we could put our finger on and say, 'Okay, this is what we've accomplished.' It was like we'd run a race, it was finished, and that was it."

But it was more than just anxiety over the New Left's effectiveness and burn out that undermined commitment to the activist stance—it was also the erosion of the "intoxicating feeling," the "sense of selflessness" that people had experienced at the peak of mass protest. When the streets of Isla Vista were no longer filled with hundreds of defiant youths, the movement's ability to compel people to put collective ahead of personal interest was seriously weakened; consequently, the movement's demands for self-sacrifice were now felt to be blocking aspirations for self-expression and growth. Here is how Bill McNaughton describes these feelings: "During the time of the riots, you yourself was the very last thing you should be concerned about. In the movement it was the world of social justice. There was an initial attitude to forget about yourself and take care of the extremely important things that were happening in this society and commit yourself to a better society, without taking care of yourself. There was this attitude to make you feel guilty if you weren't devoting twenty-four hours of every day to the movement. I voiced that too, but that can only go on for a certain amount of time. It was very easy to do for a while because there was a very close bond. All of a sudden you wake up one day and you realize that you are just standing on really thin ice. Ultimately, I started realizing that you have to be concerned with yourself, because if you don't take care of yourself, you're not going to be much help to any cause. I was feeling trapped. I just lost a lot of my own identity to more of a group identity. I felt like I was suffocating."

For others, alienation from political involvement was marked by a personal effort to rediscover what was felt to be the lost spiritual or communal promise of the movement, a promise broken during the violent street battles of 1970 and the "preparing for revolution" period that followed.

The case of David Carroll illustrates this response quite clearly. At first Carroll was caught up in the apocalyptic vision, but the nightmarish fantasies of dying in a blazing shoot-out with the police that he experienced during the 1970 events led to what he terms a "profound spiritual crisis" in the aftermath. "My personal life was shattered, my idealism destroyed" by the months of turmoil and violence, he states; political involvement had become "too painful," the movement was "drifting away from reality." He began to "become more and more alienated from people in the movement at that time." With their "unrealistic" hard-line militancy, they were operating at "just the surface level of politics," while for him, politics "always had a kind of religious dimension, kind of a 'depth' dimension—personal identity, social justice, truth with a capital T—all those things, all those kinds of values that had been traditionally associated with religion, in a sense." These were the values that first attracted him to the New Left, he said, but they had been lost in the chaos and fury of the Isla Vista rebellion.

"I was just so blown away by the whole thing and in such a state of shock, and people in the movement began to be crazier and crazier," Carroll emphasizes. "Things didn't have a ground, and everything was just kind of floating around, and no one knew what was going to happen next. It was like suspended animation. I had no answers at that point; all I knew was that the old answers didn't apply anymore. There were still very real things that needed to be done, but I didn't know what. The whole political thing needed to be rethought at that time, and maybe people were trying to struggle with that, but in their conscious lives they were still spewing forth the same old platitudes, and they were still operating on the same level that they were the previous year. And the incredible things that had happened in Isla Vista . . . I just didn't see how they could still be in the same head-space. That's when I started drifting into Yoga and Eastern thought, and trying to put things together into a different kind of framework."

His turning to the East—initiated by taking up the study of Hinduism and Buddhism at the university and continued later by learning (and later teaching) Yoga and meditation—was motivated in part by what he describes as his "alienation from Christianity." Brought up in the Baptist Church and "terrified weekly by hellfire and brimstone," Carroll "left the church in disgust" at age seventeen "because of the cold treatment my mother was getting as a divorcee." The religious feelings—"the strong feelings about the world and the future and about suffering,"—never left him, however. A religious studies professor who was a native of India was also an important influence. "He started me on the path to reclaim my spiritual tradition. It's like I discovered a whole other world then that did not negate anything that I had experienced but sort of included it. It was sort of a wider spectrum, like here's a political view of things and then there's kind of an expanding horizon . . . putting it in a larger context. And Eastern thought, especially, sort of did that."

It was also at this time, Carroll reports, that he met Julia, the woman he married in 1973, only a few months after his graduation from UCSB. He was finally starting to put the pieces of his life back together. "Slowly," he states, "I began to have some peace of mind." In the fall of 1973, he and Julia left for a round-the-world trip, planning to make their way (by hitch-hiking and other equally adventurous methods of travel) across Australia, Asia, and Europe. Carroll had no specific job plans or prospects, no well-thought-out ideas about what he wanted to do when he returned. (As it turned out, he ended up taking a job in northern California as an unemployment claims clerk for the state, chiefly because "it was the first thing that came along, and less alienating" than working in the business world. "I couldn't become a management trainee for anyone!" he says.)

David Carroll's withdrawal from the New Left, then, did not represent a return to a conventional career or lifestyle. "I didn't go out and try to get a job in a big corporation and repent of my past ways or anything like that. I felt everything we did then was true and valid and right, but just the constant frustration and futility of the enterprise really took its toll. My life just really was at a low at that point. It was really a kind of a sterile, hopeless environment. The main thing with me was to be healed inside. Things were just too painful."

Further insights into this type of withdrawal from activism can be gleaned from the story of Joyce Weston, another Santa Barbara 19 defendant and RU member. Weston grew up in the sprawling suburbs of Los Angeles, the oldest of three sisters in what she describes as "a very conservative, middle-class family." Her introduction to the sensibilities of the sixties and the counterculture came through books she started reading in high school, such as Abbie Hoffman's *Revolution for the Hell of It* and Tom Wolfe's *Electric Kool-Aid Acid Test*, as part of, as she puts it, "a very conscious rebellion." When she arrived at UCSB in the fall of 1969, Weston started attending RU meetings, in large part, she says, because the activists provided "a real community" of people with whom she could identify.

While Weston was hesitant to participate in the street actions during the riots, she continued in her political involvement in the months of "community building" that followed, working on both the *Strategic Hamlet* and *Wildflowers*, a local feminist publication. But the rioting and the apocalyptic visions it spawned had changed the nature of interpersonal relations in the activist circle. Weston became increasingly concerned over what she felt was a disregard in the Isla Vista movement for people's emotional needs. In the face of the dilemmas and strains that activism inevitably produced, the movement was failing as a community of support. "I really felt that while we were all supposedly brothers and sisters in the revolution, there was very little sensitivity among the people. I felt there wasn't much emotional support from the other people involved. I was really unhappy with the kind of support I was getting, or not getting, from other people."

In response to these problems, Weston grew more and more despondent and finally decided to leave Isla Vista and transfer to a college in northern California. "My last three or four months in Santa Barbara," she remembers, "I went through a really severe depression. I didn't go to classes. I just sat around in my apartment, and I was sort of taking a lot of psychedelic drugs and kind of staring at the wall—just reading a lot of Camus and Kafka, and writing in my journal. I would spend days sitting and writing. I moved out into the country and had nothing to do with political commitment." In this new environment, she hoped, that elusive "community" could perhaps be found. And she was not disappointed: "Up in Mendocino, I lived on ten acres with ten other people. We had like three small houses that were divided between us, and there wasn't any kind of political connection. We just all lived in the same place. But we became a really pretty tight community, just simply because there are ten people you see all the time. Financially, we were all pretty separate, but we were very communal in spirit."

Weston also became closer friends with Terry Lennox and David Carroll after moving to the northern part of the state. The three of them were kindred souls, hurting inside, seeking refuge from what had happened and was still happening in Isla Vista without knowing where a safe harbor might be found, looking for the right synthesis, experimenting with possibilities, postponing the question of whether and how to "settle down."

Some of those who withdrew from activism did find their interests meshing with established institutional frameworks, however. Ellen Hemmings and Bill McNaughton, in response to their feelings of futility and "suffocation," began postgraduate training in the fall of 1972—Hemmings in nursing, McNaughton in chemistry. For both, this decision represented a return to career paths that they had left after becoming involved in the student movement. Moreover, the decision to undertake career training was defined at first as an expression, rather than an abandonment, of activist commitment. Hemmings, for instance, started nursing school in Santa Barbara when she was still involved in political activities, working at a free clinic in the city and living collectively with other radicals.

In both cases the withdrawal from activism was gradual. Hemmings explained her interest in nursing, at least at first, as both a political response to the movement's failings and a personal response to the problem of vocation. "Initially, I saw it as kind of a political action. I was getting involved in something that I thought was useful, that I could use, because we were all really effete; we just talked a lot and didn't do much. After having gone to Cuba, I realized that it was important for me to have some sort of job that I felt was important, because the Cubans were very dedicated to what they were doing and they all had certain roles that they played, whereas I didn't really feel that I had a useful role. If there was revolution in this country, what could I actually contribute to it? I didn't have anything I could really contribute at that time, and I felt like I should do something with my life which was worthwhile."

At the same time, when the level of protest declined, Hemmings' use of psychedelic drugs increased considerably, leading to less concern with political responsibilities, and her relationship with her boyfriend (another member of her living collective) slowly began to assume more and more importance. Dropping out of nursing school for a year and working as a tutor in English and history with a group of radicals who were attached to the Learning Center at City College did not reverse this shift away from politics, however; it only prolonged the withdrawal. "I was sort of a part-time political person and part-time drug user, part-time hippie. Didn't really do very much. Just kind of dropped out." Eventually, Hemmings decided to move to San Diego and resume nursing at a junior college there, withdrawing from politics completely, her desire to do something worthwhile no longer tied to commitment to the movement. "Meaningful work" was something the now-fragmented New Left could not provide.

Like Ellen Hemmings, Bill McNaughton was not so much fleeing from painful memories or crushing anxieties as he was looking to expand personal horizons, hoping to fulfill personal needs that could not find expression within the confines of the movement. "Could I be completely political? I decided I couldn't," McNaughton says. "Politics had become too much of my life; it just became too much. I just finally started going through a personal withdrawal. It cost me too much of myself. I really got disoriented after awhile. It's just not me. I had to find my own identity. There was a lot about me that I had to discover." In response to these feelings, McNaughton "really quit politics, really put it away. I mean, when I finally broke away, when I finally broke away from all that, I just didn't want to have anything to do with politics at all, just because it held me so hard."

"Breaking away" was followed by "exploring other things, just personal things," as McNaughton puts it. "Without any desire, just so I could get money," he enrolled in graduate school again, "and just really, really started wandering for a while." He reports that he "explored a lot of outdoors," thought of quitting school and "getting involved in farming," took up guitar playing and "explored music for a long time," and then finally came back to where he had left off two years before: science. "I finally decided that, you know, I guess I'm what everyone was telling me I should have been since I was that high—a scientist, a chemist. The problem is that people shouldn't have told me. I had to find out for myself."

It would be a mistake to interpret such withdrawal as an abandonment of the moral framework that the movement had provided for these young people. Hemmings and McNaughton were leaving the movement as it was then constituted, but even as they began their professional careers, there was a reluctance to settle for conventional identities, a concern about becoming ensnared in mainstream institutions. McNaughton vowed never to work for private industry, never to use his scientific skills for capitalistic purposes; Hemmings, after completing nursing school, went to work at a Veterans Administration hospital. Veterans "got a bad deal," she thought, and she wanted to help people who really needed it, who were being ignored by the socially irresponsible health-care system. She spurned supervisory roles, preferring to work directly with patients, and was outspoken in her criticism of elitism and racism, particularly among the doctors. Both Hemmings and McNaughton were still convinced that radical social change was necessary. Unable to reconcile themselves to the established order, they felt a certain amount of guilt about their inability to continue in activist opposition to it.

COLLECTIVE EXPERIMENTS IN EVERYDAY LIVING: ACTIVISM WHEN THE APOCALYPSE DOESN'T COME

These stories illustrate the continuing dissolution of the collective identity around which the movement had crystallized. Ironically, the call to transform one's life, which had been central to the moral legacy of the New Left and the counterculture, by the early seventies seemed to some participants to be better fulfilled in some nonpolitical, nonorganizational arena.

But such individual pathways were still the exception. Despite the warning signs of the splintering and dissolution of their movement, most of the Isla Vista activists sought collective, politicized solutions to the intertwined personal and political crises they had come to recognize. As visions of apocalypse faded, these men and women sought to create durable frameworks that would integrate personal life and social change over the long haul. For each, the key question was: "How do I find a vocation (or at least a subsistence livelihood) that will allow me to sustain myself and be a serious activist at the same time?" For this, they had few models or institutional structures to rely on. What seemed obvious, however, was the need to remain in a politically minded social circle. As one activist stated in an interview conducted at that time: "Collectives are really important and possibly the only way to maintain your sanity in [this] kind of situation. Isolation is the best way to kill someone's political and moral commitment in this country, and that's what this country is based on—individualism and isolation—and it's a real effective way to destroy peoples' commitment."

Discussion in activist groups in the early seventies revolved not only around individuals' needs to make a living in a political context, but also around the equally compelling need to reconstitute the movement as revolutionary visions and models faded. By this time, the organizational structure of the New Left had collapsed; no national framework rooted in the sixties' mass movements existed to provide strategic direction. Despite this apparent vacuum, activists across the country remained committed to the movement's values and vision (not to mention its concrete goals, such as continued opposition to the Vietnam War). Within this loose, and frayed, network there was a consensus that the movement needed to be reconstituted in such a way that its isolation from the American majority could be overcome. Activists began self-consciously to strip away the generational and student character of the movement, to question their language, styles of operation, demeanor; to search for long-term ways to connect with the everyday concerns of mainstream America. For thousands of New Left veterans, the burning question was how to find a vocational and political direction that would be both personally sustaining and politically meaningful.

It is crucial to recognize that these directions had to be developed virtually from scratch. For, unlike their counterparts in the industrialized nations of Western Europe, the American New Leftists had no institutionalized political party or other existing framework that could allow post-student activists to merge leftist political practice with long-term vocational commitments, nor permit left-oriented intellectuals and professionals to connect readily with party structures and cultural institutions. Compared with graduates of student movements in other countries, Americans were likely to find that sustaining radical identity beyond the youth stage was much more difficult (Laufer 1976). By the early seventies, student movement veterans were seeing that institutional alternatives that could nurture radicalism, that could provide supportive environments even in the absence of mass action, had to be invented. Yet, despite the difficulty, there was a pervasive feeling that the effort to be social inventors provided considerable personal, and political, promise.

"It Was Necessary to Build a Base Beyond the Student Community"

Early seventies' efforts in this direction took several forms. One especially visible collective experiment that proliferated in that period was the creation of "alternative institutions." They represented the clearest collective effort by New Left graduates to continue the political and cultural logic of the sixties in ways that would mesh with the personal needs of members for livelihood, and the political need of the movement to connect with the everyday concerns of the larger society. Alternative institutions were "capitalized" by the professional skills of recent college graduates who were motivated to contribute their skills because, through the organization, they could finally hope to fulfill, rather than reject, vocational aspirations that the earlier movement experience had often led them to question.

By "alternative institutions" we refer to such organizations as alternative weekly papers (which proliferated by the hundreds in this period), film collectives, and radio stations; legal collectives (offering legal help to both middle-class political and cultural "offenders" and economically disadvantaged victims of the criminal justice system); medical clinics (providing health services in ethnic and youth ghetto communities with an emphasis on critical perspectives that were not welcomed by the medical establishment); food and other consumer co-ops; psychotherapy collectives (emphasizing perspectives flowing out of the burgeoning human potential movement and/or offering assistance to disadvantaged sectors of the community); "free" schools (governed by pedagogical practices derived from Summerhill and other egalitarian traditions of educational reform); child care collectives; street theater groups; rape crisis centers; and a legion of other politico-cultural programs, projects, and enterprises.

These were "alternative" by virtue, first of all, of their structure, which was typically nonhierarchical, self-managed, nonprofit, collectivist. (For descriptions, see the studies by Case and Taylor 1979; Mansbridge 1980; Rothschild and Whitt 1986.) Second, they shared openly critical political stances, typically seeking to change or challenge the established sources of information, dominant cultural forms, and established professional practices, and to provide services and voice to constituencies poorly served by established institutions.

In addition to serving these public functions, alternative institutions were usually designed to enable participants to derive immediate satisfaction and meaning in their work, and to develop their skills as professional practitioners. At the outset, such personal gratification seemed worth the income and career opportunities forgone by those participants who did not take advantage of opportunities that might have been available in the mainstream occupational structure. At first, these organizations were most heavily concentrated in the university towns and youth neighborhoods that had been the setting for the student revolt. Efforts to turn Isla Vista into a "liberated territory," detailed in the previous chapter, represent this early stage of alternative institution-building, which was typically seen as but one part of the preparation for the impending revolution. At the outset, little, if any, thought was given to reaching out to middle America or integrating the daily lives of New Leftists with those of the nonrevolutionary (perhaps even counterrevolutionary) masses. But as apocalyptic expectations waned, many such projects were instituted in communities outside of youth enclaves as activists came to see these organizations as important vehicles for breaking out of their political and personal isolation.

Thus, five respondents in our sample moved into the city of Santa Barbara (a fair distance, both geographically and psychologically, from Isla Vista) to work on alternative projects. One group helped to establish a legal collective, working as paralegals alongside several radical lawyers to serve the needs of low-income and politically dissident constituencies. Another group established an alternative weekly newspaper (innocuously named the *Santa Barbara News and Review*), collectively owned by its staff and consciously aimed at reaching a broad audience with alternative political and cultural perspectives. Several activists participated in Santa Barbara election campaigns (defeating the district attorney, who was seen as responsible for the bank-burning arrests and the hard line taken by county authorities during the riots, was a top priority), abandoning the view of electoral politics as hopelessly reformist. For some of the builders of these institutional frameworks, then, ending activists' isolation meant that the movement not only had to reach beyond the student environment, but also had to modify what they perceived to be its often self-righteous tone and totalistic revolutionary style. Explicit calls for a renewed "localism" were heard as well, with political efforts now tied to the practical politics of community development.

Roger Wade recalls the details of this process: "The idea was that all radicals that could, should concentrate on working with people who don't relate to the universities—older people, the non-youth-culture type of people. And here the most fundamental change was seeing that we didn't have to come right out at the start and say, 'Look, we believe this, this, this, and this, and this is the solution.' Finally, we could talk about problems, individual problems; not aiming at creating a confrontation, but at creating a forum for discussion, based on focusing on one immediate and local issue. There could be a relation of trust developed between radicals, liberals, and moderates who share, to a certain extent, a viewpoint on that one issue, a sense of trust that can be extended over to other issues." "Being understandable and American, nonrhetorical and nondogmatic," was the goal. From this perspective, the newspaper's task was "base building." "The thinking behind the *News and Review*," Wade states, "was that it was necessary to build a base in Santa Barbara, to get outside the student community, without neglecting students, but to build beyond the student community, among regular Americans. To see if it would be possible to build a base of progressive-thinking people —not revolutionaries, but people who could identify with the need for social change."

These "moderated" views did not go unchallenged. As was noted above, it was not as if New Leftists forswore all talk of revolution. The newly formed legal collective, for example, was considerably more radical in its public stance than the *News and Review*. Moreover, there was a heated debate within the newspaper collective over, in Wade's words, "how much radical and socialist politics" could be openly presented in the paper's pages. Wade saw his position as a pragmatic one. "This whole idea of building a base was very much of a strategic one. It wasn't a commitment out of, 'This is the kind of politics I like.' It was very much strategic thinking, the sense that we need to reach lots of people in order to create an underlying level of support. The question of whether the paper should tone down its politics or not was a matter of expediency, a [question of] 'which strategy is more effective?'" "Reaching lots of people" and "being effective" were important for reasons other than these more obvious political ones, however; if activists were going to support themselves by working on the paper, then the paper had to become financially stable, had to attract advertisers and increase circulation. All this put pressure on the staff to produce work that would be acceptable to the public.

Other staffers attacked this position as unrealistic, and as politically dishonest and ultimately corrupting. "I and others felt that it was necessary from the very beginning to be explicitly political, to deal with political issues all the time," Sheila Barressi remembers. "And I felt, and others did too, that we shouldn't try to depend too much on advertising, that if we depended too much on advertising the content of the paper would be affected." What was justified by expediency would eventually become institutionalized values, these individuals declared.

Meanwhile, street demonstrations during the 1971–72 period (particularly the mass protests sparked by the 1972 Christmas bombing of North Vietnam) periodically revived hopes for a mass uprising and encouraged some of the activists to keep alive the flame of militancy and personal risk-taking. Several Radical Union alumni were arrested in these actions, including Barressi, who served forty-five days in the county jail for her efforts. Radical study groups flourished as post-student activists reevaluated the successes and failures of their movement, seeking guidance in the works of major revolutionary thinkers and attempting to provide the kind of theoretical analysis they felt the New Left had sorely lacked. (Most of the members of the legal collective played an active role in these groups.) Secret "cadre" actions and military preparation did not cease overnight, when Isla Vista III was not followed by Isla Vista IV. Even as commitment to this strategy waned, and even as activists debated how much radicalism the masses could tolerate or embrace, a few individuals continued to train and plan for guerrilla warfare. Eventually, however, such activities "kind of fizzled out," as one participant put it. "We started refining our views about the correctness of our point. Then we finally made a conscious decision to stop." Thereafter, full attention was directed toward experimenting with less-desperate forms of political action.

"We Weren't Gonna Let Medical School Turn Us Into Pigs"

A second type of effort to mesh vocation and politics, summarized by the phrase "radicals in the professions," involved the reconstitution of professional careers and identities along morally accountable and politically engaged lines. Thus, in the early seventies, radical caucuses, alternative professional associations, newsletters, journals, and informal networks sprang up in social work, medicine, law, journalism, city planning, and a number of other academic disciplines, as former student activists attempted to address professional issues in activist and critical ways. These efforts were often plagued with self-doubt, however; the question of whether one could indeed become a professional and remain "political"—faithful to the values of the movement—haunted those who followed this path. The radical caucuses tended to express the conviction that professional work offered radicals opportunities to use their skills and knowledge in unselfish, nonelitist, socially responsible ways, reshaping the meaning of "professionalism" in our society and joining lifelong vocational involvement with moral purpose.

Martha Koch's experiences reveal something of both these doubts and these convictions. After starting medical school in 1971, Koch reports, she and other students "who had been real active in politics in college" found that they needed to establish a "political support group" (later re-defined as a study group) to cope with a "totally different milieu than what we had been accustomed to. . . . We all felt tremendously pres-sured and alienated from the people in our class who had been straight premeds, who had oriented themselves entirely toward going to medi-cal school, where we had devoted all our time to politics. And we felt tremendously alienated from the fact that we were, in fact, in medical school. I mean, I think for all of us that were in the group it was really hard to know that we were in medical school and that we were profes-sionals, especially given all of the negative background of becoming a member of the bourgeoisie. So it was kind of a difficult transition, and the group focused on what was happening to us on a day-to-day basis in medical school. We were all determined we weren't gonna let medical school turn us into pigs."

The group soon found itself embroiled in the "politics of medical school education." "We started looking at how it is that medical school makes people into pigs, and to whose benefit it is to do medical edu-cation the way it's done, and who funds medical education, and what kinds of propaganda you get bombarded with as you go through med school. It started [from] the drug companies right away, and it was so blatant to those of us who were political that it wasn't like we had to go searching it out." Yet the most important contribution of the study group continued to be the emotional support of its participants: "It helped me to feel that if I wasn't like the rest of the doctors that I saw and the rest of the medical students in my class and didn't have the same goals and the same orientation as they did, it didn't mean that I couldn't be a doctor. There were other people who were going to be the same kind of doctor that I was."

This kind of support proved to be not enough. Few of the people in Koch's group remained active in politics over the four years of medi-cal school. "Many of them, in fact, became very self-centered, in terms of focusing their careers around what they can get for themselves and falling into what I view as some of the traps of medical education: getting real involved in super-specialization, working in academic medical centers, and, basically, becoming very private and feeling that they have no public or political obligations and that they'll just go into private practice."

In contrast, Koch was able to sustain her political involvement and activist stance through school and her internship, working in San Quentin "and setting up a program so that medical students could go there and work during their fourth year," spending six months in Peru working in isolated rural areas among the peasants, and participating in a women's group made up of both nursing and medical students that was active in raising consciousness of the problem of sexism in medicine. After receiving her M.D., she went into emergency medicine and pediatrics, working only in public hospitals and city clinics, rejecting private practice as fundamentally immoral and even avoiding alternative medical projects like collectivist "free" or "people's" clinics. "Setting up alternative structures," she felt, "left mainstream structures intact, and people that were being the most oppressed by the mainstream structures continued to use them while people that always had options away from being really oppressed by the system were using the alternative structures. . . . My preference was to work in public hospitals where the people I'm serving are the people that are getting screwed over."

In addition to these commitments, Koch continued to support a broad range of leftist causes and participated in organizations of radical health care workers and professionals, as well as a study group devoted to a more rigorous analysis of the economics of health care and the relationship between capitalism and medicine in the United States. Still, she was undecided about the direction her career should take. To a certain extent, Koch, like those respondents who resisted vocational commitments during the early seventies, was also "drifting," unable to make any long-term plans or commitments within her own vocation. And behind this uncertainty lay the same troubling concerns that she had faced since first expressing an interest in becoming a doctor: the issue, as she put it, of "what are we going to exactly do with medicine that will be consistent with our political motivations," the problem of "not knowing how to combine what I'm doing on my everyday personal work level with politics, within medicine." Perhaps, she felt at that time, these problems would never be completely resolved.

"We Need a Party—Something to Lead Things Forward"

Another form of collective experiment that emerged during this period was the establishment of disciplined cadre organizations—the effort to build what is sometimes described as a "new communist movement" (O'Brien 1978). This effort had its origins in the same criticisms of the movement's student and youth orientation that spawned projects like the *News and Review* and the Santa Barbara Legal Collective. But instead of a rather diffuse focus on reaching "older people" and "regular Americans," the neocommunist activists were attracted to an orthodox, explicitly working-class, Marxist analysis. Radicals should abandon their futile strategy of creating liberated zones in places like I.V. They should ally themselves with the workers, reject the self-indulgent lifestyle of the counterculture, transcend their class position, and repudiate their privileged origins. The following statement, taken from a letter published in the UCSB student newspaper in the winter of 1971, is a representative expression of this point of view:

> The dominant movement currently enjoying popularity in I.V. is the desire to make I.V. the showplace of the counter-culture. That is, to make I.V. an island of freedom and love by creating institutions and attitudes of a little utopia. Sponsored by the B of A's money as much as by anything else, this "constructive" approach is hailed by liberals and merchants, yippies and local officials, as the panacea for strife-torn I.V.'s problems. Nonsense.
>
> Although developing institutions to counter the existing exploitative and ecologically unsound ones is certainly part of any fundamental social change, we must face the fact that I.V. is hardly the center of exploitation and oppression. In fact, let's face it, virtually everyone in the world would change places with most I.V. residents, because the "counter-culture" is composed of the most affluent children in the history of the world. The counter-culture has another unique feature—nobody works. And because I.V. produces nothing it lives off the proceeds of people who do make the material things

which, like it or not, even people in I.V. need. Thus, this "new" lifestyle must end when working people are no longer willing to sustain it.

And since control of the means of production is the central conflict to be resolved in ending Imperialism and exploitation, those who feel that their efforts to create a counter-culture in I.V. are furthering the fight for social justice, or the fight against poverty, racism, and exploitation, or are doing anything except living off other peoples' work—the same as most of their parents—are only fooling themselves. The counter-culture is a dead end street, so do not be co-opted into ethnocentric Isla Vista Cultural Nationalism. The struggle is among the people of America, not among the privileged, elitist, however alienated, bourgeois youth. ALL POWER TO THE PEOPLE! FACTORIES TO THE WORKERS! (*Daily Nexus*, 15 January 1971.)

These same activists argued that the New Left had reached an impasse because it lacked a coherent doctrine, strong discipline, firm leadership, and the clear direction that comes from well-defined ideological and organizational structure. These new "party formations," drawing on the classic Leninist tradition (which the New Left had abandoned), on Maoist principles, and on the Old Left Stalinist and Trotskyist organizational models, contributed to the splintering of the New Left in the late sixties. By the early seventies, several new "parties" were competing for the title of America's vanguard.

The revival of interest in the doctrinal, Leninist-style party revolved around the assumption that the disorientation of the post-apocalyptic period could be overcome through party structure, party discipline, and party line. The party promised explanations for past failure, and assurances about history's course, that helped members cope with political frustration and uncertainty. Its hierarchical structure offered the promise of a political leadership capable of special wisdom that could effectively distill collective experience. In addition to political stability and direction, such parties implicitly promised personal solutions. All provided members a chance to embark on stable—and even conventional—everyday lives, while simultaneously assuring them that their activity, however mundane it might appear, had revolutionary historical significance. For all of the new parties, despite their apparent differences, advocated as a high priority that members participate fully in the everyday world of the working class, preferably by becoming factory workers. To be effective in such a role depended, it was believed, on members' living conventionally, in normal households, and abandoning the "petit-bourgeois" bohemianism of the counterculture in favor of marriage, family, a tract house in an industrial suburb.

Members of Maoist parties were required to abandon any residual aspirations for professional careers. They were expected to enter a full-time work world that their upbringing and prior socialization had typically encouraged them to avoid. Such a move may have been welcomed by some recruits, given the repugnance that many sixties activists felt for the middle-class rat race, and their doubts about either their objective opportunities or their emotional readiness to pursue professional careers. The party's emphasis on joining the working class resonated deeply with the revulsion many felt toward their own privileged upbringing and channeled their strong moral yearning to serve the disadvantaged and the oppressed.

In this sense, the Maoism of the early 1970s was of a piece with the fervent commitment of white students in the early sixties to work in poverty areas and slum neighborhoods. But the Maoist groups were recruiting, not for a summer in the ghetto, but for members who would become "working class." Taking such a dramatic personal step was facilitated by the social support members found in the party and by the doctrinal assurance it tried to project. Consequently, the party member, facing the daily meaninglessness and strain of factory work, could interpret his or her situation not as a mark of dead-end failure but as a real contribution to a worldwide revolutionary process. Whereas other post-sixties activists tried to resolve the tension between history and everyday life through "alternative" activity, the Maoist-influenced activist achieved a resolution largely at the level of belief. One's life might actually be mundane, and one's politics objectively ineffectual, but one's commitment to a political sect provided a highly coherent intellectual and moral framework.

Barney Thompson, the RU member who fervently described the I.V. riots as a "festival of the oppressed," was also the respondent most attracted to such a political framework. "In 1971," he explains, "it was obvious that the sixties had petered out." The revolutionary movement of that period had degenerated, he felt, into "reformism" and "anarchist terrorism." The *Santa Barbara News and Review* was a prime example of the reformist tendency. "I thought they were going to put out a real newspaper when they started talking about the *News and Review*—till I found out what their ideas were. All these people were saying at the same time, you know, that the problem is that we're just not being decent God-fearing Americans enough. I didn't find anything interesting about the paper. I was wondering why people were wasting their time on it."

As for the furtive, "exemplary" actions of those who "blamed the masses for their own lack of political direction, and didn't really trust in convincing people of things," they were miserable failures as well. "It obviously didn't work, because, in fact, as people tried to practice it in Isla Vista they became more isolated. You know, like when people tried to set up a few flaming barricades and thereby rouse the population of Isla Vista in the spring of 1971, and it just didn't work. People, instead of opening their doors for you—instead of running down an alley and having somebody open up a door and jerk you in their door and slam their door, you know—people would be up there on their balconies shouting, 'Don't come up here, we'll call the police.'"

It was at that time, Thompson recalls, that he "read [Lenin's] *What Is to Be Done?* And it was like it was . . . this mist was clearing away. It talks about the two poles of economism. One is saying, 'Look, all the masses of people can do is get involved in something that's like something they can see in front of their noses,' like getting ten cents an hour more. The other pole says, 'Look, man, all the masses of people can do is sit back and act like sheep and wait for a few dedicated revolutionaries to pull off something fancy.' And that's the two poles between the just disgusting pinkish pap of the *News and Review* and this urban guerrilla warfare crap."

This experience led to more reading, often in the context of a Marxist study group, and eventually to contacts with a Leninist/Maoist party. "I started reading this stuff and it seemed logical to me. Look, we'd gone through the sixties, right? And as I looked back on it, I felt we really didn't have any guidance or leadership, we had to rely on ourselves. There was nothing that represented the whole legacy of the struggle that people had been engaged in for over a hundred years on this planet. So people were saying we need a party, something to lead things forward. The struggles that were going on out there were something that couldn't be ignored." Consequently, in addition to his membership in the legal collective, Thompson began working with the party on a fairly regular basis: selling papers, attending demonstrations, occasionally helping to organize local activities. (The party was based largely in Los Angeles and San Francisco, and Thompson was one of a dozen or so Santa Barbara–area supporters.) Unlike many of his friends in the larger cities who went to work in factories and lived in suburban factory towns, Barney chose to remain in Santa Barbara, uneasily keeping one foot in the countercultural movement, while identifying with but not totally committed to a disciplined party organization.

"A Lot of the Anger That Came Out Was Directed at Men"

The largest and most self-aware group of New Left activists to embark on political post-student paths in the early seventies came from the ranks of movement women. Numerous feminist groups and communes were started during this period, in deliberate opposition to many of the practices of the New Left. The frustrations and criticisms that were expressed in several of the female activists' narratives—criticisms directed against the domineering style of male leadership and the macho enthusiasm for armed struggle, frustrations with the lack of sensitivity to personal needs—moved large numbers of movement women to create their own, often exclusive, circles. These circles offered a haven from the totalistic revolutionary posture and apocalyptic vision of late sixties, promoting therapeutic discussion of the personal stress people had endured during that period. At the same time, the groups also encouraged the discovery of the emotional costs of male domination and the search for alternative routes of personal development. In this way, feminist groups helped to provide new issues for focusing activist commitment to replace those that had animated the student movement.

Since the issues were connected to fundamental concerns of daily living, such as childcare, health care, abortion, gender identity, and economic discrimination, feminist groups and the larger movement of which they were part enabled members to see ways in which their personal, everyday choices and actions were connected to historical processes. Thus, activist women could view their vocational decisions as aspects of the struggle for equality in the workplace; their relations with the opposite sex as consequential for the transformation of cultural definitions of sex roles; their very appearance and demeanor as expressive of the drive for female emancipation. For many post-student activist women, then, the women's movement provided means to live by their activist commitments in ways that were far more fulfilling, both personally and politically, than those provided by the student, antiwar, New Left framework within which their activist identities had first crystallized.

In the early seventies, quite a few former student radicals and counterculturalists were attracted to religious and therapeutic communities for "healing." Feminist collectives bore some similarity to these, but with the crucial difference that feminist groups often enabled members to continue working for social change, allowing them to make a collectively supported transition to new forms of commitment and vocation.

Sarah Glenn's story offers us a close look at some of the dimensions of the feminist reaction to the movement. Sarah was Terry Lennox's lover, and some of her story, including their brief marriage in 1970 and 1971, was told in his narrative. The child of middle-class parents who were generally conservative in both their political and cultural views, Glenn decided to become a philosophy major in college because, in her words, "I had a very searching mind. I read a lot of philosophy in high school— a lot of existentialism, a lot of things like that—and I wanted to find the basic answers to life. I was always plagued by thinking about the basic issues in life, and that's what I figured school was for."

Glenn's explanation of how she got involved in the student movement affirms Lennox's account of their initial encounters with Radical Union activists through their work on the student paper and their desire to become part of the activist circle, to become part of an "interesting group" of people. But she makes a point of stating that she took a more active role: "I was the one who wanted to go to Radical Union meetings and all that. It was a big attraction to me. I felt the options of becoming just a regular middle-class person looked very superficial, and I was learning about socialism and communism and different ways of organizing society. I wanted to put that into practice. I went after it, and I think I did bring Terry along as a kind of security and kind of something to make it easier."

Once she became a regular participant in RU activities and movement gatherings, Glenn underwent a steady process of radicalization that was sparked by "the reaction of the police coming in and the steps they took as far as trying to quell any demonstration. I guess, slowly, I did come to the point where I thought violence was necessary in order to make change." Consequently, like many other students who were shocked by what they felt was a brutal and unjustified police occupation of their community, Glenn found herself becoming more intensely committed to militant politics and an activist career. At that point in her life, she believed "the revolution was going to be forever." This ebullience also infused her relationship with Lennox: "Terry was going to be forever—everything seemed like it was going to be forever." In this case, "forever" was a very short time, with their marriage falling apart at the same time that the hoped-for revolution started to look as if it was in serious trouble.

After that difficult period was over, Glenn states, "Things really looked up for me. I kind of threw myself back into a lot of social relationships and personal relationships." She became involved with women's groups in the Santa Barbara area and began to identify strongly with that aspect of the New Left. During 1971 she also became active in an Isla Vista cadre group, living with the other members, preparing for militant actions, hoping to follow in the footsteps of the Weather Underground. Now she tried to be as tough and brave as the more outspoken male participants in the group: "I felt that in order to be liberated I had to be more macho than the men, and I have to say that I got into it." Like almost all the other activists who were involved in these kinds of activities, however, Glenn reports that she "slowly began to see that wasn't the direction that the movement was going in, and things started to calm down." Motivated by the "realization that there was the rest of the country and they aren't at the same stage we are as far as the revolution, and that we have to go back to grass-roots organizing and dispersing information," she moved into Santa Barbara and began working on the *News and Review*.

For two and a half years, Glenn was part of the newspaper collective, covering city council meetings and other local political matters and trying to eke out a living on the thirty-five-dollar-a-week *News and Review* "salary" and food stamps. Toward the end of that period, the nearly insolvent paper decided that it could not afford to support staff members anymore (although some staffers, Glenn included, suggested that the economic rationale was a cover for a political purge by the paper's leadership); so Glenn went to work in a factory in Goleta. Later, she took a job in a nearby city's public information office. Her work on the paper continued without remuneration.

These were not pleasant times for Glenn, particularly in the final months when political debates within the newspaper collective were often acrimonious. This controversy was only a small part of the story, however. More significantly, she was experiencing a great deal of personal strain. Like other respondents whose stories have been reported, Glenn describes a growing sense of estrangement from the activist circle. "I was feeling real burned out and trapped," she recalls. In her case, these feelings were grounded in the reemergence of personal desires and needs that had long been suppressed, that had no place—or so she once believed—in the life of a truly committed New Left activist. "I started to rediscover parts of myself that had been pushed down and ignored for years, and I started to remember that I was interested in music and gardening and spirituality and other things [besides politics]. I guess I began to see that I had gotten down this real narrow path and it wasn't everything that was me. I wanted to break out of it."

These feelings, Glenn states, found little support among her fellow activists. Again, like our other respondents, she insists that there was no possibility of really expressing herself in that setting "because all these people, all my political friends, were so narrow and down on me when I started to talk about other things, when I showed interest in gardening, in spirituality, things like that. It wasn't cool, it didn't fit into the whole political thing. And they began to let me know that it was wrong, that I was off course and it was unacceptable." In response, Glenn "stopped relating to those people and changed friends. It was a very difficult time for me. It was real hard to let go of all that, and there was that guilt thing too. I was supposed to be a revolutionary and dedicate my life to that, and I wasn't going to, 'cause I was deciding that wasn't right, that wasn't me. I felt real put down by my old friends." (A lot of this pressure was self-inflicted, she admits, "probably because I was aware that there were contradictions in my life that I had ignored for a long time.") Once again, a wedge had been driven between the personal and the political.

Finally, Glenn left Santa Barbara, moving to rural Northern California. She lived with a man who was attending graduate school at UC Berkeley and devoted most of her time to writing short stories. "I turned into kind of this 'earth mother,' where I baked and wrote and we had this nice little place out in the country. In a way, it was a real healing time for me, to be with myself a lot. And the guy I was living with was into a lot of spiritual things and he got me into meditating."

The "earth mother" phase did not last long. She started to feel isolated and began traveling into Berkeley on a regular basis. The healing process went on, though. Glenn soon joined a therapy group—a "radical therapy group," she calls it—with other "burned out" former activists, both men and women. "I worked through a lot of my anger about the movement in that group. I had a lot of anger, not about any particular person, but that, you know, the movement was supposed to solve all my problems and be my life, and it wasn't. I think that was the point where I really became aware that while people were talking about collectivism and being together and working together, that we really weren't. There was very little caring and sharing, and I realized that there were people on real ego trips, and leaders and followers, just like everything else. And many people in that group had faced the same problems I had, and they were very supportive of me."

Following the therapy group, Glenn broke up with her partner and moved into Berkeley. Her anger and pain found a more definite focus: "I went through a period of total separation from men and got totally involved in the women's movement for a long time. I guess a lot of the anger that came out was directed at men and the whole male movement." It was not only these hostile feelings that drove Glenn away from men. "Choosing to relate [only] to women was for me more of a positive thing. I felt I had a lot to learn from women. The past several years I had learned a whole lot from men—I had learned how to get up in front of a microphone and talk to people, I had learned about politics, I had learned about guns—and I had ignored women a lot. Even though there was some of that going on, as far as women's groups, it was more of us getting together to figure out how to deal with the men, and what I saw in Berkeley for the first time in my life was just a whole lot of positive energy among the women, in how they related to one another, in how they worked together, how they thought about things."

Glenn quickly immersed herself in this feminist community. She supported herself by working in a women's publishing collective, which allowed her to continue pursuing her journalistic and literary interests. In addition, she joined a political study group ("reading Marx and Engels again, only this time from the feminist perspective, kind of reinterpreting things") and, at the same time, "started getting into the more spiritual aspects of women, how women are psychic and powerful in a spiritual way and how it was important for women to find that they had that power within them. There was a whole lot of spirituality to it that was very attractive and exciting to me. So I was going back and forth between these two factions, the political and the spiritual, in the women's community, trying to rethink the political and learn more about the spiritual."

THE FATE OF SIXTIES COMMITMENT: TAKE THREE

The stories told by our former student activist respondents about their experiences in the early 1970s provide us with important pieces for filling out the puzzle of the sixties generation. The first important conclusion is that the fate of that generation of activists cannot be properly interpreted without grasping the fact that its members faced, at the beginning of the seventies, a vacuum with respect to opportunities and models for morally coherent and practically relevant adulthood. The death of the Old Left in the sixties meant that there were no well-established Left structures to provide jobs for activists or to direct the energies of intellectuals. There was no party on the Left, only a few political campaigns such as the George McGovern effort, and few openings in the unions, only a sprinkling of jobs that rarely welcomed political creativity or involved frontline organizing. In short, unlike, say, their counterparts in the 1930s, sixties activists had to make their own roles, since neither the political parties nor the political vocations that matched their values existed, ready made, in the early seventies.

To some extent, this vacuum was a consequence of the student movement itself, as we have seen. For it seems characteristic of student and youth revolts that questions of the long pull and adult life are ignored, disdained, buried under the intoxicating romantic vision of a youth that lasts forever. Thus, through much of the sixties, young activists avoided the question of long-term vocation, and, then, in the late sixties, were caught up in the dark vision of a revolutionary solution to both society's problems and their own. By the end of the sixties, the atmosphere of the movement prevented free discussion of personal hopes and fears and required members to aspire to revolutionary selflessness and total dedication, effectively blocking serious consideration of how individual interests and potentials might find appropriate political expression.

As the movement lost touch with both social and personal reality, the seeds of disaffection were sown. By the early seventies, many of our activist respondents had left Isla Vista, some to find other political

connections, most to search out nonpolitical pathways for personal development. At the same time, instead of simply dying, the movement
in the early seventies began to be reconstituted, as remaining activists
(including the majority of our activist respondents) reevaluated their
revolutionism and began to redefine their political engagement in ways
compatible with the everyday and the long haul.

It is not surprising that large numbers of post-student activists put
much energy into forming and sustaining collective and communal
frameworks in those years. The vacuum they faced had to be filled by
self-created structures of support if they were to have any chance to
live in terms of the identities crystallized in the movement. Those who
were able to find an institutional basis for expressing their commitment
vocationally or who participated in self-organized collectives of shared
commitment were most likely to sustain political engagement into later
life.

The paths taken by former student activists varied considerably in
the degree to which they involved continued commitment to political
activism. For many, as we have seen, the late sixties climate produced
a revulsion against politics, burn out, and involvement in spiritual or
therapeutic quests. At the same time, no one in our sample expressed
complete disillusionment with, or rejection of, the movement experience
or Left politics as such. None had fundamentally changed his or her
ideological position, or had come to accept conventional values and institutions, or deeply regretted participating in the movement. Indeed, until
recently it was hard to find any public expressions of disillusionment or
conversion to conservatism among former sixties activists. There is, so
far, a considerable contrast between the situation in the aftermath of the
sixties and the aftermath of the earlier wave of radical activism in the
1930s, when a large number of former communists and socialists ended
up renouncing their past, denouncing former comrades, and celebrating the virtues of capitalism and American global hegemony. Indeed, it
was not until the "Second Thoughts" conference in Washington, D.C.,
in 1987 that one found a significant number of former New Leftists embracing the political right, and even that event turned out to be less a
renunciation of the sixties than initial press reports seemed to suggest.
(For a report on that conference detailing the nuances of disaffection, see
Gitlin and Kazin 1988.)

The contrasts between the fates of 1930s and 1960s radicalism should not be overemphasized; indeed, there are striking similarities as well. But the contrast helps highlight some of the distinctive character of the sixties experience as a factor in the personal development of participants. For example, compared with former thirties' activists, our respondents typically held to the belief that they had not changed, that they remained contributors to social change even when they withdrew from political involvement. How was this belief in one's persistence sustained?

We observed in Chapter 1 that the sixties youth revolt revolved around two intertwined but opposing orientations: on the one hand, emphasis on social responsibility (a life of service to humanity, a commitment to justice and equality), on the other, emphasis on personal liberation and autonomy (resisting authority, fostering self-expression). One of the myths of the New Left was that there was no contradiction between these ideals. But one way to interpret the stories we have been telling is to see them as efforts to respond to the difficulty of reconciling these perspectives. One method of reconciling them, however, is to come to believe that loss of commitment to one can be compensated for by long-term commitment to the other. As a result, we have a Maoist condemning the self-indulgence of the youth culture; a religious seeker becoming isolated from urban society; a founder of an alternative paper anxious about reaching "regular Americans"; a physician condemning her "self-centered" colleagues who go into private practice. All of them claim that they are continuing in some way to fulfill the ideals they set when they were at the high pitch of their activist youths, because all continued to follow the logic of at least one dimension of movement ideology, and all feel a connection to historical change in the way they are trying to live.

The New Left at its peak seemed to be a fusion of socialism and anarchism, of collectivism and individualism, of politics and culture as terrains for social transformation. What its adherents found in trying to make lives for themselves was that such fusions were not practical. But the movement's embrace of these ideological polarities provided sufficient material for what Bennett Berger (1981) has called "ideological work"—the elaboration of beliefs that allowed them to feel a sense of moral consistency. Development required pluralism rather than totalism, an abandonment of seemingly "pure" revolutionism. Most of our respondents seemed to feel in the first few years after the sixties that their maturing did not require the abandonment of "idealism" and "principle" as such.

By the early 1970s, the sixties movement was over, but it had been reconstituted as a host of locally based projects, alternative institutions, communes, collectives, and community organizations. Instead of a single embracing revolutionary force, activists were now engaged in a diversity of causes including such distinctive new movements as feminism, environmentalism, new therapy, new spirituality, radical professionalism, local democracy, and new communism. The proliferation of forms and ideologies on the left was a consequence of the historical and political context. It was also, if our analysis is correct, the result of a multiplicity of small-scale collective efforts by groups of activists to define their own personal futures by experimenting with vocation, lifestyle, politics, and ideology.

If the 1960s had been a time when the developmental needs of large numbers of young people made possible a historically potent mass movement, the 1970s were a period when these same people, moving into adulthood, were creating continuing social and cultural ferment as they continued to make themselves. These later personal and historical developments were less dramatized in the mass media, less likely to be seen either by participants or the larger public as a single wave of action. So for many in the generation, having grown used to the media spotlight as the primary indicator of their historical importance, the period was a letdown, an ending. Yet for most of our respondents, especially those who remained involved in collective projects, it was a time recalled as quite promising both for themselves and for the country.

INCREASING INDIVIDUATION

The collective experiments of the early seventies grew out of a hope for long-term vehicles for integrating personal needs and political commitment. Over the next five years, however, many participants began to find them inadequate. Tensions between collective demands and personal identity resurfaced, and a new phase of "post-movement development" emerged: a turning toward more individualized forms of activity and the taking up of more stable vocations and career paths.

One reason for this shift was economic. Most young radicals, in their early twenties, were willing, even eager, to live with low income and high uncertainty. They were willing to trade economic insecurity for a chance to live autonomously, engage in creative work, and have time for personal expression and self-development or for full-time political involvement. Working in an alternative institution for a subsistence wage, being a free-lance writer or artist, taking a low-skill job in order to have the wherewithal for self-defined pursuits—all these options were chosen by members of the liberated generation in the first half of the seventies. Such choices seemed preferable to more secure and well-paying jobs in corporate or governmental bureaucracies. Although, as we have seen, some former student activists entered graduate or professional training, larger numbers who were equally qualified academically did not. As the seventies wore on, however, vocational insecurity became an important preoccupation for most of these men and women; the economic and emotional costs of subsistence living were increasingly difficult to tolerate.

"Everybody Got Tired of Being Poor"

The experience of the Santa Barbara Legal Collective, drawn largely from the account of Paul Little, a founding member of that group, illustrates this problem. Born in Los Angeles, Little spent most of his teenage years in the Midwest, where his father worked as a book salesman. Both of his parents were college-educated liberal Democrats. Little was active in Young Democrats as a freshman at UCSB and helped organize a "McCarthy for President" group, but his politics quickly shifted leftward after he witnessed the police violence at the 1968 Chicago convention. By his sophomore year, Little had become a founding member of Santa Barbara's short-lived SDS chapter. In the spring of 1969, he ran as a successful candidate for a leading position in student government. Little was frequently interviewed on radio and television as a "radical spokesman," particularly during the riots, but this high visibility had its risks: in the fall of 1969, he was one of those charged with inciting a riot in the Santa Barbara 19 case and, a few months later, was indicted for the burning of the Bank of America.

After his acquittal in the bank-burning trial, Little was elected to the first Isla Vista community council, again as part of a radical slate. Then, in the fall of 1970, he enrolled in law school at UCLA. "I had always planned on going to law school," he notes. "I wanted to be a politician at that time—I was always running for office, it seems. I liked the role, and I did a good job too!" The Left "had to use institutions that people legitimized," Little figured, and activists should not dismiss electoral politics out of hand. And an activist who wanted to run for political office would be wise to become a lawyer: "Most politicians were lawyers, and I was always facile with words, so it really was a natural thing."

Little lived with a radical collective in Santa Monica during the first year of law school and continued to be active in politics, but in the summer of 1971 he decided to return to Santa Barbara to work with a group of former student activists (including Denise Saal and Barney Thompson) and radical lawyers who were planning to start a community-oriented legal collective. The guiding idea behind the legal collective was that it could serve the legal needs of poor people and also take on large-scale, politically important cases, particularly those involving labor unions. The collective hoped to help broaden the base of the movement, reaching out to those sectors of the population to which the New Left was ideologically committed but with which it had yet to build any real ties. Additionally, they would seek to eliminate the "bourgeois" professional distinctions between paralegals and lawyers in their everyday legal practice, remaining true to the movement's antihierarchical stance. Political organizing was to be given top priority. Denise Saal sums up the project's underlying philosophy: "We saw ourselves as socialists trying to create a socialist enclave, at least with socialist relationships within the structure, if not in terms of the structure's relationship with the rest of the world. We saw the collective as one way to earn a living while we could still do political work."

Little worked as a member of the legal collective from 1971 to 1976. These were, he reports, "exciting times," and the legal center did indeed reach out to the disadvantaged of Santa Barbara, helping to overcome some of the radicals' isolation. Financially, however, the collective was barely able to keep its head above water. Collective members were, in Little's words, "always living from hand to mouth. We did all the tough law that doesn't pay, and our clients were broke and never paid us. After five years of this, I never made enough money. We were always living on the edge." Consequently, Little reports, "I [got] tired of it . . . everybody got tired of being poor—it was always a struggle."

Barney Thompson adds to Little's account: "Economically, we were pretty much killed in the '74–'75 recession. We never recovered from that." But economic insecurity was not the only problem. Its demoralizing effects were compounded by tensions that were endemic to this type of political activity. Each client helped, each hard-won legal victory provided some immediate satisfaction but seemed to make no dent in the "system's" armor. Defeats simply reminded them of their weaknesses and the enormous task ahead. One especially difficult project involved a long, sometimes violent strike by garbage collectors (the majority of whom were Latino) against Browning Ferris Industries. The outcome was a crushing defeat: almost all the workers lost their jobs. "We took all the tough cases," Little concludes, "and the work—the work was so emotionally draining, I was getting burned out."

Such demoralization was, for some, intensified by the localized, marginalized quality of alternative institutions. In the absence of a national movement or organizational structure capable of linking these local efforts to larger political strategies, resources, and a sense of historical impact, many participants were increasingly hard pressed to justify the great personal sacrifices they were making to achieve such limited political success. Sometimes, bewildered by their failure to spark a new mass movement, activists called for more disciplined ideological study—as if yet another close reading of the revolutionary texts would finally provide the answers. Bitter internal debate destroyed much of the élan needed to go on living activist lives.

Thus, the organizational and psychological supports for collective efforts to construct new forms of adulthood were undermined. For many individuals, the time had come to look beyond the movement for self-definition and direction.

"I Just Lost Some Confidence in the Things I Had Believed in Quite Confidently"

The Santa Barbara Legal Collective was a victim, in part, of this demoralization. The collective dissolved, the law center closed, and most of the members moved on to more individualized lives and more promising economic circumstances. But these breaks were not experienced as sharp or fundamental, for the individual paths people followed were typically more or less continuous with their earlier collective activity or were based on skills and interests that first developed within a movement framework. Some collective members were led to law school and the pursuit of full-time legal careers; others moved away from whatever professional identification they may have developed to experiment with more personally satisfying possibilities.

Other collective experiments continued to develop, but they were not robust. The *News and Review* collective, for example, managed to survive and grow, but it had difficultly sustaining the members' commitment. Roger Wade was one of many who left, feeling much the same demoralization that beset people like Paul Little. "The two years at the *News and Review* marked [a] big political transformation for me," Wade states. "The movement as the sort of defining feature of my life gradually, just imperceptibly but steadily, declined. And my political beliefs, they changed too. I think they became more confused, as opposed to change. I just lost some confidence in the things I had believed in quite confidently, and the idea of a socialist revolution seemed much more nebulous, much less possible, and much, much more of an abstraction than it had been before."

Like many respondents, Wade began to look outside the framework of the New Left for direction. "I began, for the first time that I'm aware of, to think about making some sort of career for myself," he recalls. Wade, like others, pursued a career that was an extension of skills he had developed within the movement. "The idea of becoming a journalist, which had never entered into my original calculations, became more and more an interest and a possibility." Wade came up with a scheme for publishing a magazine for students that would be distributed as an insert to student newspapers and would have a countercultural, politically progressive orientation. He spent a year seeking financial backing, and a large publishing company offered support, but after one issue he dropped the project. "I had to pretty much negotiate all of the politics out of the thing. I was having real troubles justifying this publication to myself, or even legitimizing it to any of my friends as being halfway socially redeeming. Mostly it was just a lot of fluff—the kinds of things you find in *Rolling Stone*."

At this time Wade started thinking about going to graduate school. The academy was one of the few institutional settings where former student activists could expect a degree of career and economic stability yet feel relatively uncompromised. "I had always been interested in history, and I had been impressed by certain radical faculty people at Santa Barbara. I was impressed by the potential for 'molding young minds.' The prospect of doing that for the rest of my life seemed very nice, and the idea of exploring questions raised by my radical experience in American history seemed very good too. And as I contemplated the possibility of going to graduate school it was very much so that I could do this kind of personal thinking about the New Left and other Left movements in history, and also play some sort of role in developing a social consciousness in young people. It seemed to offer opportunities that would enable me to feel good about myself, and it was also a comfortable, secure, fairly high-status kind of occupation."

Other *News and Review* members began to pursue personal interests that had previously been in the background as the poverty and political frustration of working on the paper eroded their commitment to it. Sheila Barressi, for instance, whose left-wing parents had worked in the film industry, left the newspaper to take a job as a cab driver and then, after two years of driving and periodic union-organizing efforts, enrolled in film school at UCLA. Barressi hoped to be able eventually to make her own political documentaries. And Paul Little, who started playing guitar in a politically oriented reggae/rock band while still a member of the law collective, decided to give up his plans for a career as a lawyer and commit his life to music. He and the band went on the road, playing in towns up and down the Pacific coast, hoping to land a record contract.

Cynthia Spivak, who remained active in movement collectives for several years after returning from her travels to Asia and India, went back to school to get her teaching credentials. Spivak had tried to earn a living as a dedicated, politically committed staffer for a community organization that counseled and assisted young women with pregnancy and birth control problems, but the wages were simply too low. Further, the collective living arrangement she was in had grown "too complicated, too heavy, both emotionally and sexually," and she felt she "just had to run." After earning her credentials, Spivak left for Australia to teach, intrigued once again by the possibilities of living outside the "destructive" climate of the United States. Kristen Van Duinen took a similar route out of the I.V. radical circle, and had a similar personal need to get away. She moved to southern Greece and found a job teaching English. The stories of Little, Wade, Barressi, Spivak, and Van Duinen are typical in their descriptions of growing disaffection with collective living, alternative institutions, and other post-sixties experiments. These people were becoming increasingly individuated in their goals, but they continued to try to infuse their personal quests with some political meaning.

Sarah Glenn's story offers another view of this shift from collective to more individual commitments, one that expresses vocational ambitions and the desire for financial security more directly. After two years of involvement with the feminist community in Berkeley, the restlessness and psychological turmoil that had characterized her life through the early seventies began to resurface. Once again, Glenn felt that she "had outgrown the political groups" she was in; once again she "wanted to break away." Still relating only to women, she left for New England, moving with an intimate female friend. What she found there, however, was not "that separatist feminist environment I had known in Berkeley. Here I was forced to relate to men, and I wanted to become part of what was going on here. There was a while when I did try to relate to the feminist community here, but people were going through a lot of things I had gone through already, so I was very peripherally involved, and then I got out of it."

Instead of continuing on the path taken in Berkeley, Glenn entered another period of drifting and self-exploration; she left feminism as an entire and separate way of life behind. In fact, while living on unemployment compensation for almost a year, Glenn began writing a novel that represented "a working through of everything from California," a science-fiction-style story of "a women's revolution that takes place in the future, intermingling spiritualism with politics." Although she worked diligently on the novel for some ten months, she never finished it. "It was never intended to be published. It was a learning experience for me, a cathartic thing for me to write and express a lot of things."

When the novel-writing ended, she took a job as a reporter for a muckraking weekly paper, drawing on the journalistic skills she had acquired at *El Gaucho* and the *News and Review*. Things then began to move very fast. In a few months Glenn took a job with a daily paper in a nearby small town and within another year was working as a reporter for one of the largest and most prestigious papers in the state. She set her sights on a career in the newspaper business. Although she says that she "felt better politically working for the weekly," she could not turn her back on the financial benefits and professional opportunities of working for the major daily. And after years of erratic experimentation with various nonconventional lifestyles and political commitments—from existentialist philosophy to student radicalism to preparation for armed struggle to alternative journalism to rural pastoralism to radical therapy to feminist separatism to literary self-analysis—Sarah Glenn was ready to try what looked like a more stable way of living. "It was challenging, a real ego trip, and I could get a lot of the things I wanted by moving up."

Even those who much earlier in the decade had withdrawn from politics and had been drifting were, by the second half of the decade, showing signs of a more concerted search for lasting vocational commitments. David Carroll, for example, after two unsatisfying years of working as an unemployment claims clerk, decided to apply to graduate school in religious studies. "I basically couldn't stand it [anymore]," Carroll states. "It got to be a real drain, and, well, I had a lot of other questions and concerns in my life. I had religious questions that I wanted to resolve, and I wanted to do something with my life that was more meaningful, that would use my skills and affect things where my concerns were at." He wanted "to meet people on a very real level," to become involved in the community rather than remain primarily concerned with "intellectual" issues. This led him to enroll in a Methodist seminary, to "try the church system" as a vehicle for pursuing his religious concerns. The ministry, he hoped, was a way of life that would enable him to "translate feelings into action." Why the Methodists? Partly, he says, it was his alienation from "the Baptists and the rest of the Protestant tradition that I was raised with," but he was also attracted to that denomination because "they don't have the hierarchy or authoritarian structure." He and his wife had begun attending a small Methodist church in their community and had "become deeply involved in the life of the congregation," team-teaching Sunday school classes, reading the lessons in worship services, and serving on the church council.

"Sort of a Free-Floating Person Who's Walking Around Just Experiencing Things"

Still, not everyone in the group was ready to abandon experimentation for stability. Some of those feeling economic pressures sought regular employment, but their jobs did not offer the opportunities for creativity or the intellectual challenges they desired and needed. These were people who saw themselves as simply trying to earn a living, rather than finding a lasting vocational commitment. For them, a subsistence income might provide the freedom to pursue their real interests, interests that were hard to convert into livelihood.

Terry Lennox, for example, after moving to rural northern California and working at low-wage, part-time jobs for almost two years while continuing to pursue a writing career, decided to move to San Francisco and take a position as counselor in a city drug program so that he could support himself more adequately. After two years in the city, Lennox moved back to the countryside and got a job as an intake worker in the local office of the Department of Social Services' food stamp program. He viewed this position as a temporary one, however. He was still intent on becoming a writer, and spent most of his free time working on his short stories and poems. "Community, being part of the community, [being] very much a member of the community," was also still important to him. He had not given up on his search for that elusive ideal.

Joyce Weston's story provides another example. When Weston received her bachelor's degree in humanistic psychology in 1974 and moved away from her close-knit community of friends in Mendocino, taking a secretarial job with a small advertising agency in San Francisco, she was admittedly "getting a job because I had bills to pay." Although she tried to put off her job search as long as possible—spending nine months traveling around the country immediately after graduating—she did not have the resources for a life of wandering. "I had thirty dollars in my pocket, and I didn't have any goals of becoming a hobo and going up to the wilds of Alaska, and so I had to look for some ways of making money." An employment agency, discovering she could type, told her she should become a secretary. They offered her a job at an advertising agency. Desperate for work and thinking that a job at an ad agency "sounded kind of interesting," she took it.

Weston worked at the agency for three years, and was able to learn some typesetting and copywriting, but her main concern at work, she says, was trying to develop the kind of "closeness, that tribal, communal spirit" she had been looking for since her days in Santa Barbara. In this sense, Joyce Weston had changed very little. "I looked at the agency as a family, I tried to make a family out of that group, but that didn't work," Weston ruefully recalls. "You can't do it with business because people are there for business, and I spent a lot of time crying in the ladies' room because all the men out there didn't understand how it was more important that we cared about each other than all this business bullshit.

My bosses were just really unenlightened people. It was the hierarchy again, and I really resent hierarchies."

Weston finally decided to quit. She moved out of her apartment, sold or stored most of her possessions, and "lived out of the trunk" of her car. She then became, she says, a "sort of free-floating person who's walking around just experiencing things, not really involved in any kind of 'social definition system,' not somebody's wife or the things my parents would like me to be." A "peripatetic" one of her friends called her, and that pleased her. "I looked it up in the dictionary and it means 'walking around.' I like it. I was gonna get business cards made up. I thought it was classier than just 'itinerant.' And the cards would have a back side where I'd have to fill in wherever I was staying at the moment. There's no permanent address."

THREE PHASES OF POST-MOVEMENT LIFE: A SUMMING UP OF THE SEVENTIES

Looking at each of these people close-up, in isolation from the others, it is difficult to discern a pattern. In fact, the most striking thing about them in comparison with our nonactivists, is the seeming formlessness of their lives through the 1970s, or rather the apparent unpredictability of their choices. At the same time, when one looks at them as a group moving through time, narrative threads connect individual stories and clear patterns emerge. All of the former student protesters tried, through the decade, to organize their lives in relation to the principles embodied in the movement and the counterculture. None of the people we interviewed were drawn into "conventional" styles of living, "traditional" frameworks of morality, or "mainstream" forms of political participation.

Because movement and counterculture were constituted by contradictory emphases on both collective responsibility and personal freedom, and because participants in the youth revolt tended to avoid examining how such values could be expressed in adulthood, participants lacked coherent models or frameworks within which to define their post-student direction. In this chapter and the preceding one, we have traced the generational struggle to find a synthesis between principled commitment and personal fulfillment through three phases in the seventies, and it will be useful to review the main features of this sequence. The first phase we described as "Waiting for Apocalypse." For a brief time

in the late sixties and early seventies young radicals were almost universally convinced that the breakdown of the social order was imminent
and that "revolution" defined both the historical and personal future.
Such beliefs solved the problem of personal choice by obliterating it,
and defined commitment as total absorption in self-sacrificing collective
action. Do not worry about becoming an adult, the argument went, with
all the moral ambiguities and problematic decisions that would entail—
for there would be no possibility of normal life in an apocalypse.

The second phase was "Collective Experiments in Everyday Living."
The fading of apocalypse brought young radicals face-to-face with the
problem they had so far evaded: how to make principled lives in the
long haul. Through much of the seventies, former student activists self-
consciously experimented with vocation and lifestyle. Some pursued the
quest for meaning and coherence in relative isolation; most, however, did
so in the context of collectives: alternative institutions, feminist projects,
communal households, rural communes, neocommunist party formations. Some of these projects and living arrangements formed the basis
for permanent ways of life. Most of our respondents, however, came
to find their involvement problematic. The economic marginality and
insecurity of trying to live outside established institutions became increasingly wearing. The political frustrations of working in small, highly
localized projects with little evident historical impact proved frustrating
for some.

In addition, enthusiasm for collective living was eroded by the difficulties such living entailed. Studies of collective experiments (see especially
Kanter 1973; Case and Taylor 1979; Berger 1981) have closely detailed
these problems. The time and energy required for making and enforcing
rules and dealing with interpersonal tensions, the absence of privacy, the
difficulties of developing alternatives to established marriage and family
relationships—all took their toll on communal enthusiasm. Work and
household collectives often survived and grew during the seventies, but
turnover within them was high. Some of our respondents worked for as
long as five years in alternative work collectives; several lived for many
years in some kind of communal household. But by the time we first
encountered them (during the first round of interviews in 1979, almost
ten years after the bank burning), most had moved on.

The third phase we termed "Increasing Individuation." At the moment we initially encountered them, most of the former student activ-

ists, who were all about thirty, had embarked on life courses that were both more individuated and more settled than had been typical in the preceding decade. Few were by then involved in alternative institutions or collectives; most were beginning to define their vocational directions more in terms of personal interests than movement-defined priorities. Moreover, most were hoping to find a career or job that would provide at least a modicum of economic security and comfort, and some were thinking about marriage and children. Nevertheless, it is worth noting that some continued to want to live outside established institutional and household frameworks, pursuing visions of life based on artistic expression, revolutionary politics, or deliberate rootlessness. What all had in common was a new resistance to having their goals defined by either a small-scale collective or a large-scale movement. Many continued to expect that the careers they were entering would permit them to make a political contribution, but it would be political work that they themselves would choose.

The individuation common to virtually all our respondents in 1980 represented the culmination of a decade during which, their stories tell us, there had been a gradual departure from collective involvement and movement commitment. As we have seen, some exited during the apocalyptic phase, or in its immediate aftermath, because they were unable to reconcile the totalism of the movement collectives with strongly felt personal interests or needs, and because these collectives provided no space for free discussion of the personal. After their experimental phase, revolutionary collectives were replaced by the diversity of projects we have described. Despite the fact that these were typically far more responsive to members' needs, and were constructed out of members' interests, they ultimately proved inadequate for assisting further personal development.

Throughout the seventies, then, those who had been socialized by movement and counterculture, although seeming to go down separate paths, nevertheless shared a continuing resistance to involvement in established institutions. They were, as Kenneth Keniston (1968; 1971) had predicted at the height of student protest, prolonging their youth, extending that time of life in which role-experimentation and the quest for coherent meaning takes precedence over role-obligation and career. As the eighties began, these people were entering their thirties, and, for the most part, were ready to enter adulthood. How would their commitment to youthful idealism fare? Have those individuals who remained politically active through that decade been able to sustain their commitments in the eighties? For those who withdrew from political life, has depoliticization proved to be a temporary phase or a permanent condition? And what of the men and women of Delta Omega, the football team, and Kappa Phi? Are their political attitudes, cultural values, and lifestyles still markedly more conventional than those of the activists? These questions will be taken up in the next two chapters.

5

Where Are They Now?
Case Studies in Persistence
and Disengagement

A COLLECTIVE PORTRAIT

Let us look at a collective portrait of our respondents as they appeared in our most recent contacts with them. Such an overview provides a map of the terrain that we will examine in some detail in the pages that follow, helping us define the main paths our interviewees have followed in the years since we first made contact.

We start with political beliefs and behavior. Nearly twenty years after the burning of the Bank of America, the political attitudes of the former Radical Union activists are, on the average, well to the left of those of the nonactivists. Many of the activists describe themselves as radicals, socialists, or progressives, and the rest use terms like "left-liberal" and "liberal" to identify their views. Whereas most of the nonactivists now describe themselves as "conservative" (and, with one or two exceptions, the remainder use the term "moderate" to describe their positions), few of the activists embrace any positions that might be termed "conservative."

The contrasting political convictions of the activist and nonactivist cohorts are evident in their attitudes toward Ronald Reagan. Most of the nonactivists have been favorable toward Reagan, with several of them expressing ardent support. Only two of the former activists displayed even a qualified respect for Reagan. None voted for Reagan in 1980 or 1984, while nine nonactivists did so in both elections.

The two groups also differ greatly in the level of their political involvement. The activists remain, as a group, relatively active, although the overall level of activity is, of course, considerably lower than it was when they were students.

Because these two groups were selected to highlight their political differences, the fact that the political contrasts between them continue to be strong is not extraordinary news (except, perhaps, to those who assume that sixties activists have become conservative as adults). More dramatic are the continuing sharp contrasts in vocation and lifestyle. We saw that student movement veterans overwhelmingly avoided conventional marital and family arrangements in the early seventies. For example, during the riots and the "apocalyptic" period that followed, Terry Lennox and Sarah Glenn were the only ones who were married among the activists, and their marriage lasted only a short time. By the middle of the decade, only two other activists were married. In contrast, many of the nonactivists married within a year or two of graduation; by the mid-1970s the total had reached twelve out of fourteen. Within the past few years, nine additional activists have married, bringing the total to eleven. The fourteen nonactivists have produced twenty-one children among them; at this writing the seventeen activists on whom we have data have produced eight children.

These comparisons demonstrate both the degree to which sixties activists sought to resist the conventional demands of adulthood and the tendency of some, as they reached age thirty and beyond, to begin to settle down. Thus, not only "increased individuation," but a considerable degree of what might be called "postponed conventionalization," is an important theme in the post-movement development of the activist cohort.

Despite such drift toward the mainstream, however, the activist and nonactivist cohorts remain very different in terms of their occupational choices and income. Of the twelve nonactivists who are currently employed, nine are pursuing careers in the private sector, primarily in corporate management or, in a few cases, as owners of large, multimillion dollar businesses (the tenth is a football coach at one of the military academies, and two are school teachers). In all but two cases, these careers are the same ones they entered in the years immediately following graduation. The average annual individual gross income in 1984 of these twelve men and women was approximately $50,000. Three had incomes well in excess of $100,000.

In contrast, of the fourteen former I.V. activists who are currently employed, only four currently hold jobs in the private sector. One works for an advertising agency as a production supervisor, one is a newspaper journalist, and two are self-employed. Most activists have been working at their current job for less than five years, and several have recently started careers. Their average gross individual income in 1984 was about $25,000 a year.

To what extent are the Isla Vista "bank burners" representative of veterans of the New Left as a whole in this regard? Some data from other studies allow us to make interesting comparisons with respect to marriage, number of children, and income. Nassi (1981) studied former Berkeley Free Speech Movement activists. When she compared them both to former student government members and other former students (a representative cross section of Berkeley alumni from that period), she found that marital status and number of children were independent of the level of activism in college. The FSM arrestees had married at about the same rate as the student government and "cross section" groups, and the average number of children born to the former student activists, student government members, and the university cross section were similar (an average of one child). The only dimension that showed significant differences was income: the average annual gross income for the FSM alumni was approximately $17,900 (very close, in 1980 dollars, to that of the former UCSB activists), while the former student government officers averaged slightly more than $28,000, and the cross section over $26,000 (Nassi 1981: 758).

Nassi's findings suggest that FSM participants were somewhat more ready for conventional family commitments than our sample of UCSB activists. Such a difference may have something to do with the fact that the Isla Vista experience involved a blending of youth culture with New Left politics that was less evident in the early sixties. And we have seen how the aftershocks of apocalyptic rumblings that swept over Isla Vista in 1970 almost certainly contributed to the turmoil and flux of UCSB activists' post-riot careers. It is also possible that Nassi's respondents were somewhat older when contacted than our activists were. In any event, when and how one participated in the movement certainly has something to do with the nature and meaning of its legacy.

Thus, despite a significant reduction in the level of political activity and some evidence of settling down, the former "bank burners" do not lead strictly conventional middle-class lives. Our findings, consistent with previous research on former activists, indicate that veterans of the sixties have tended to remain oriented in career and lifestyle to core values and perspectives that derive from movement and countercultural experience.[1]

This conclusion, however, masks the variations and ambiguities in political commitment that are evident in the life-history materials. When we take a closer look at the current lives of the former "bank burners," several types of political orientation and levels of political involvement become visible. For discussion purposes, we have divided the activists into four subgroups. The first is made up of those individuals who are still radical or left-liberal in their political attitudes and still very active politically. We will call these respondents "persisters" (see Abramowitz and Nassi 1981). Five former RU activists fall into this group.

A second subgroup, consisting of three people, can be described as "disengaged radicals." They remain leftist in their political convictions but no longer see themselves as active in politics. A third cluster consists of seven individuals who have experienced more tempering of their radical political beliefs and their political involvement and who might be described as "left-liberals." The final activist subgroup contains three people, all of whom show a willingness to embrace at least some conservative political and economic views. As would be expected, none are active in leftist causes. These individuals can be called "nonpersisters," since they seem to have made a considerable break with their radical past. (However, one of the nonpersisters is Kenneth Essian, who was never active in the movement, and had no real activist commitment to abandon.)

It is much more difficult to identify subgroups in the nonactivist cohort. Although there is certainly some variation in political philosophy (and, to a lesser extent, involvement in politics) among the nonactivists, no well-defined clusters emerge. Except for one person whose political beliefs are left-liberal, the nonactivists describe themselves as "moderates" or "conservatives." There have, however, been some interesting patterns of change in this group, and some traces of "sixties thinking" remain.

Beneath these broad-brush depictions of "persistence" and "disengagement," of "conservatism" and "leftism," are the details of people's everyday lives, the social contexts within which values and beliefs are expressed, struggled over, and reassessed. All the people we interviewed have had to make fundamental reevaluations of their youthful assumptions, yet those who are most persistent have developed in ways that

would surprise their younger selves, while those who have broken away
the most retain considerable fealty to their youthful identities. The central question about where the "bank burners" are now is not really
whether they are still as they once were, but how the principles and
commitments that bound them together in their youth now mesh with
their lives nearly twenty years later. We look now at some representative
stories from each of the subgroups we have identified. In the remainder
of this chapter, we focus on the persisters and disengaged radicals; in
the following chapter, the left-liberals, nonpersisters, and nonactivists.

PERSISTERS

Several of the Isla Vista "bank burners" are as active in leftist politics today as they were in 1970, or more so. Their current involvement
is much more varied, with their commitments reflecting nearly every
political tendency on the Left today: the peace movement, grass-roots
community organizing, "democratic socialist" efforts to work within the
Democratic party, the labor movement, environmental politics, Maoist
"party-building," and progressive professional work. The case studies
in this chapter highlight those features of persisters' lives that differ-
entiate them from others in the activist cohort who are no longer (or
rarely) involved in public political activities. We are particularly interested in understanding what, in a national political climate of conservative retrenchment, keeps these men and women going. The man who
talked of a "bloodbath" while these individuals prepared for the Revolution had occupied the White House for eight years at the time of our
final interviews. How do they manage to sustain a radical faith? What
ways have these persisters found to join "making life" with "making history," to continue (where others have faltered) the New Left's quest for
a personal-political synthesis?

Our interviews reveal that the persisters often hold back from the
political sphere, harboring doubts about their own effectiveness and the
eventual success of their cause, yet they continue to find direction and
definition in political commitment. Each person accomplishes this, in
part, by integrating commitment with a larger moral or political vision.
Moreover, each has found practical, vocational means of achieving this
synthesis by using one of two somewhat different strategies. Two have
pursued careers that are tied to leftist political practice. These people ap-

pear to be telling us that professional commitments do not have to lead to complicity with oppressive institutions, that we can turn such vocations into vehicles of social change. Three rejected or were much more skeptical about their ability to resist co-optation in such careers, and tended to seek explicitly unconventional livelihoods. Only through ongoing acts of moral resistance, these individuals seem to be saying, can one remain uncorrupted and politically effective. (By the late eighties, however, one of those who had taken this path, resisting the very idea of a career, had moved to a professional occupation, albeit in a limited and hesitant manner.) But while numerous ambiguities and complicating factors underlie such generalizations about strategies for sustaining commitment, the details of individual lives say quite a bit about the possibilities for and barriers to everyday political involvement in these times.

"One of My Moral Choices Is to Contribute as Little as Possible to the Machine"

Warren Newhouser went underground rather than go to jail, and we had little hope of finding a man who had changed his name, assumed a new identity, and contacted no former friends for close to thirteen years. But Newhouser called Whalen late one night in the winter of 1983, saying he had heard that we were trying to get in touch with him. While he sounded wary—as well he might—he was also very interested in the project. We arranged to meet in one month in a mutually convenient town, in the lobby of an old hotel. Waiting in front of the building's antique stairway, Whalen had no trouble recognizing Newhouser. Even without a description, he was easy to identify: sporting a thick beard, his long hair spilling out from under a black wool cap, and wearing an army fatigue jacket and old blue jeans, Newhouser looked like an inveterate sixties radical.

Newhouser seemed to enjoy the opportunity to talk about his experiences in Isla Vista, as well as the kind of life he leads today. "I work now as a writer–editor–outreach person, kind of, for an environmental organization in New England," he began. "Gathering memberships, that kind of low-level, practical aspect. But it's also a matter of issue orientation—talking about issues, organizing around issues. I do community organization work as part of this, and writing a newsletter. I also do a lot of writing in national magazines on the side, on my own, for money. Just a lot of issue orientation. Spreading the gospel. A missionary to the heathen."

The money is not much; Newhouser earns, on the average, five thousand dollars a year. Married, with a six-year-old son, he lives sparely. He and his wife grow almost all their own food, keep goats and chickens for milk and eggs, and live in the mountains in a small, unelectrified cabin that they built themselves. His income is the only outside source of support for the family. "Gardens, raising your own animals, not having to pay rent, not having to pay utilities: you put those things together and you don't need much money," he explains. "Just plain don't spend money. I think it's perfectly fine. I approve of that and I enjoy it. It's no hardship. No hardship."

Writing, he says, fits in well with his lifestyle. "Writing has been and will take up most of my time. It's a kind of cottage industry that's possible, that can be done anywhere, right? And things like electricity aren't required. I mean, if I were a computer programmer, for example, I don't know how I could live where I live!" Not having electricity has other implications: "We don't have a television and all that," he notes with a smile. "So what fun we have we make on our own, kind of. You know, have neighbors over and have parties and visit people and have potluck dinners. It's the normal kind of trip, if you understand how people live in that kind of rural subculture. It's fairly typical of that. I can say that with some authority because I travel around and visit other little subcultural areas very similar to [ours]. And they're doing the same sort of things. And that's basically the way I live. Except I travel around and visit with them, and share information, and tell them, 'Well, I should tell you about what these guys did over here because they were facing the same sort of trip,' in whatever kind of issue they were involved in."

Newhouser believes that his "approval" of this style of living represents a resolute moral stance, not just a ratification of his family's circumstances. "It's absolutely one of the important ingredients of my life, making moral choices about things. And one of my moral choices is to contribute as little as possible to the machine that operates all around us. I mean, every time I hear about something like the B-1 bomber or the Federal Emergency Management's plans to evacuate major cities into the country or any one of several million obnoxiously gross details of modern life, I always think to myself, or we say to each other, 'At least we're not helping this business, at least we're not paying taxes, at least we don't have a job that contributes to this kind of stuff.' I mean, we have much better control of what we're doing than somebody who has a regular street job and functions in his own little way to perpetuate this madness." Questions like where to have a baby (he and his wife chose home birth under the care of a midwife rather than going to a hospital) and how to educate a child (they are using an alternative school and home study rather than sending their son to public school) also involve important moral choices, Newhouser suggests. "Watershed kinds of issues," he calls them. "It's part of practicing what you preach."

Making such choices, Newhouser says, "gives me some kind of purpose to my life. My opinion is that me, especially, but people generally, need purposes, they need reasons to carry on. I mean, I think it would be a simpler, easier lifestyle—in terms of effort to put out, right?—to have a regular straight job and have a television and hang out and become catatonic every night with my Manhattans and my television. I don't want to do that, because I think it would be wrong, with a capital R!"

"It would be wrong because to do that is to not think, to not really know yourself and not know your situation and to purposefully, or accidentally I suppose in some cases, just not make any choices. Or just go the easy path and do what you're supposed to do. What you're 'supposed to do,' in my opinion, is not the best for the planet, and it's not the best for the sanity and health and safety of the citizens of the United States, and it certainly isn't best for the people in the world. Because that kind of lifestyle requires sacrifices by billions of people for the good of a very small, elite group, who by pure chance happen to be born white Americans. And so tough shit for everybody else, and you get to do what you want. And I don't approve of it; I don't think that's right. I don't think that's a morally correct position. It may be easy, it may be simple, but it's not right."

The only solution, he feels, is to create alternatives to conventional ways of living, to refuse to become ensnared in mainstream institutions. "If I'm not gonna do 'what you're supposed to do,' then I have to think of some other way to live, to survive. [And that's] on the fringes, because you can't involve yourself in the mainstream and still expect to have that handle on the moral issues. And if you're involved in the mainstream, you lose that moral sense immediately, because you have to make all these compromises to keep your job or befriend your boss or whatever bullshit comes down the line."

Asked whether this stance made it difficult to communicate with all the people in the mainstream, Newhouser replied that he understood that there were "millions of people [who were] not willing to make a giant sacrifice," to give up their entire lifestyle, "but [who still] want to do something. That's what environmental organizations—the one that I'm related to—have going for them. They can tap into that kind of energy." He sees his life and commitments in relation to others as unified by the theme of raising consciousness by example: "I understand how other people don't have the same viewpoint I do. And I don't try to tell them this is the only way to live. But I feel that. And I do feel that my life is an example for other people. I don't know if anyone's ever reevaluated their own position because of my example, but I think that it's the best way to tell people something, by example. I mean, I don't really feel that the choice I make is right for everyone. Or even adequate for everyone. [But] if somebody asks me how I live and how I support myself, I'll tell them. Or if they ask me when was the last time I paid taxes, or something like that, then I can tell them. The truth. And it might, you know, kick them in the pants a little."

The very act of making moral choices and setting an example for others, the struggle itself, is as important for him as the broader social or political results. Newhouser quotes an old Wobbly—a member of the Industrial Workers of the World—who told him, "God damn, it doesn't matter if you win or lose in this kind of struggle, at least you kept your own act together, and that's really important. If you can really sow [those seeds], then that's worth something."

The path that led him to this position was, at least in the years immediately following his flight from California, a thorny one. Newhouser had not been part of the activist circle at UCSB; his affiliation was more with the movement's "cultural revolt" side. Although he shared many of the radical activists' views on matters like Vietnam and the draft, it was a combination of bad luck and bad judgment, more than political commitment, that put him in the position of having to choose between jail and the underground. And as we have seen, few people could assist or advise him in making that decision. On his own after leaving Santa Barbara, Newhouser moved frequently; his paranoia was such, he recalls, "that I would leave an area at the slightest provocation. And I still to this day don't know whether some of the places I left that I basically had a good future at and would have enjoyed staying at—whether I left them for a good reason or not."

Typically, his jobs during this period were temporary, part-time ones involving manual labor. For most of the 1970s, then, he lived provisionally, always looking over his shoulder. Over time, however, as the paranoia faded and he became more confident of his capacity to live "normally" within the framework of his delicate circumstances, Newhouser took up writing and then environmentalist outreach work as vocations and settled in to his present situation. Looking back, he insists that despite the initial emotional pain and confusion it was all worth it, that he feels no regrets for his decision to flee. "It's just real important to have left Santa Barbara. That was like leaving childhood behind or striking out on your own or becoming an adult or something like that. It was just too easy, too simple to stay there. I probably would have stayed there, and I never would have really come to grips with some of the things that I've learned or the experiences that I've had. I've had some incredibly incredible experiences and had some marvelous things happen to me as a result of needing to go, having to leave. So, philosophically, it's been a very positive kind of trip to have actually gotten what I got out of it."

Although he could probably return to California and receive a suspended sentence or probation (with a community service assignment) for what was, after all, only a misdemeanor conviction, Newhouser has no immediate plans to do so. In this sense, he seemed reluctant to resurrect that part of his past. It took him many years to rebuild his life. He is comfortable now in the life he leads and, we think, more than a little worried about the personal disruption that would certainly result from any effort to recover his old identity.

Given that Newhouser was not a political activist in college, his recent high level of political involvement represents a dramatic increase from his days in Isla Vista, a fact he clearly recognizes: "I'm more involved now with issue-oriented organizing, speaking, et cetera. I was more concerned then with myself, and less with convincing others. I used to be a 'not give a shit' anarchist. I mean, I was content to think in terms of, 'Well, I'll stay way out in the woods, and those fuckers can blow themselves up.' I don't feel that way anymore. I think it's more important to involve myself and care, and so that means I'm rearranging my philosophy. I've started voting. I do care about the elections. I'm not necessarily convinced that it always works, and the candidates I've supported haven't necessarily turned out to be worth half a shit. But I still care enough about it and I tell other people to vote. I'm thinking of joining the Democratic party to infiltrate it."

Both his increased political activity and this shift in views are due, he feels, to the recent stability of his home and family. "Having a son, depending on the future, understanding how generations work, how time passes in human history from generation to generation, seeing a place in it, feeling older, becoming more stable—it all has a part to play. I can't really pin it down to any one of those things, but I think together —maybe it's called maturity, I'm not sure. Maybe it's losing something. I don't know. I mean, there's definitely an edge to my beliefs that I try to think of as losing irrationality, gaining rationality, but I'm not really positive." It is not that he repudiates his former views or his actions— "What I did was right, and I was proud of it"—but rather that he feels that conditions have changed: "That's a different world. The world is not the same." Views considered radical then are more widely accepted now, and "there's a lot of people who are in it for the duration, they're committed, they care."

His politics, he states, are currently torn between what he calls "moderate anarchism," born during his countercultural/New Left experience and based on a deep suspicion of any type of state authority, and "democratic socialism" (again, his terminology), based on his belief that, "unfortunately," some form of state apparatus is necessary to "control, change, alter, redirect, whatever you want to say, the mega-corporations that are in charge." Newhouser's sense of the future is equally torn between two ideas: he feels that society is "tottering on the edge, that [there's] a fifty-fifty chance of having either a serious realignment of the social and political forces in this country or a crash, economic chaos." Thus, the worst case would be a national collapse where personal and community survival are threatened, whereas in the best case "the new attitudes that are surfacing in the [nuclear] freeze movement will grow," and people will recognize that "Reagan has taken money and power away from the people and given it to a very few." If collapse does occur, however, Newhouser notes that he "probably would have been much more welcome [in 1970] to a chaotic indestructible madness to occur than I am now. I'm not very willing to see that happen. I've been through it, I've been there. I've been under the helicopters and I'm not as anxious to do it, 'cause I know what it would mean."

For Warren Newhouser, then, maturity and marriage and child-rearing responsibilities did not mean withdrawal from politics or the adoption of conservative beliefs. Instead, they convinced him of the importance of digging in for the long haul, and of trying to ensure that there will be a world to pass on to his son and later generations. There is no doubt that some of his views have changed in the years since the I.V. riots. He is less convinced that change occurs outside the established political system, but his basic principles are similar to those enunciated by the New Left and counterculture two decades earlier. Most important, he has tried to integrate these principles into family life and everyday decision making, tried to avoid compromising.

We were not able to contact Warren Newhouser in 1987, so our report will have to end with these remarks from 1983. Our memory of New-houser will thus remain that of a friendly, quiet man in his late thirties who, in a hand-built cabin in the mountains, is living a radically uncon-ventional adulthood, continuing to pursue the pastoral, romantic vision of the youth revolt, resisting incorporation into "the machine."

"I've Sort of Chosen This Downward Mobility"

In the summer of 1981 we received an interesting letter from another of our respondents. "Announcement of a creative dislocation," it was cap-tioned. The letterhead sketch of Isla Vista's coastline was overlaid with Ed Pines's name and address. It was photocopied, and our names were penned in where Pines had left space for the salutation—a combination form letter to his friends and press release. After eleven years of living in the same Isla Vista apartment (the one he was living in the night the bank burned), Pines was moving out—out of Isla Vista, out of southern California, and into his parents' home up north.

While a large rent increase was a factor in his decision, Pines's let-ter stated that the principal reason for moving was that he could not afford to live in I.V. and pursue the project he had set his mind on com-pleting: a book on child psychiatrist Robert Coles, author of the multi-volume chronicle of poor children and their families, *Children of Crisis*. He planned to take a cross-country trip, visiting all the places, and some of the people, Coles had written about, and culminating in a meeting with Coles himself. Moving in with his parents, he felt, would free him from financial worries so that he could make a "concentrated effort" to finish the project. A short pitch for funds to help pay for the trip was included in the letter.

The project, Pines emphasized, was closely connected with his long-standing political commitments, an extension of his radical identity. Highly active in the nuclear disarmament and peace movements for the past several years, and recently holding a staff position in a family violence program, Pines said that this latest project was "an attempt to integrate my concern for the personal with the political, for the poor, for the hungry, for social justice with the larger threat to us all of nuclear war." In closing, he alluded to these underlying themes and suggested an even deeper personal significance to the move. He wrote of a friend who "has shared with me . . . the need for 'creative dislocation' and 'downward mobility' (in her case moving to New York for six months to work on the U.N. disarmament session). . . . I'd like to think these terms apply to me in their positive sense," Pines concluded. "We'll see." It is a good idea to make changes in your life once in a while, he appeared to be suggesting. At the same time, the reference to "downward mobility" hinted at a particular kind of change.

When we talked to Pines several months later, he provided a much fuller account, both of his absorption with Robert Coles's work (including the relationship between this concern and his own activist career) and of his expressed need for "downward mobility." This account reveals a great deal about the "inner qualities" and ideological convictions that have given Pines the strength to sustain his political commitment over the years, as well as the self-doubts that remind him of the continual need to reexamine and renew this commitment.

Pines's interest in Coles began when he read the first volume of *Children of Crisis* shortly after his VISTA hitch in the mid-sixties. Its moral appeal strongly resonated with his own values: "[These] are stories of the ones who would otherwise never be heard from," he explains. "They are the stories of children like those I worked with during VISTA; Coles touches this side of me." Pines stresses that he was attracted to a humanistic spirit in Coles's work, similar to his own. This "real genuine humanism" calls attention to both the suffering and resiliency of the poor by "telling people's life stories, [without] social scientific or psychoanalytic or even moral judgments." Here "the personal," without any imposition of meaning, tells us a great deal about our culture, its "forgotten" people, and our all-too-frequent practice of condemning the victims of injustice instead of challenging the institutions that are responsible for their plight. "If society could humanize itself on the institutional level in the same way," he wrote in his journal on Coles, "if society could keep that spirit and apply it, then we would not have the injustices that we do."

Yet Pines was also critical of Coles's approach and his role as a teller of tales. Listening to him, we came to realize that his examination of Coles's contribution to social change was also a self-examination. Coles, like himself, projects the image of a sympathetic and compassionate person, but perhaps he is actually more like a "sympathy machine," wanting to change deplorable conditions but never going beyond his middle-class writer's stance. Pines seemed to wonder whether he was more than a compassionate observer, whether he was accomplishing anything.

These doubts suggest a man who is burned out, but the level and variety of political activity that involved Ed Pines for the ten years between the I.V. riots and these comments create a different picture: working on the problem of violence in the family and the predicament of battered women, fund raising and organizing for the nuclear freeze campaign, helping to organize teach-ins on disarmament, joining in the struggle against the Diablo Canyon nuclear power plant, making occasional forays into local and statewide Democratic party politics, traveling on a study tour of Nicaragua, membership in the Democratic Socialist Organizing Committee. While other activists were turning to more individualized pursuits in the late seventies, Pines continued his political work on prison reform. He was even able to find ways to turn "straight" jobs into meaningful social experiences. He took a job with the Census Bureau because it seemed as if it would be an interesting experience. It "gave me reasons to go 'neighborhooding,' sort of, just go around to all types of neighborhoods. I think it got me in better touch with more aspects of the community than before." And as a field supervisor, he was able to hire many of his political friends as "crew leaders."

Why did he feel so discouraged then, even if only in his more private moments? With respect to the moral values and political beliefs of his youth, he had changed little since 1970, pointing only to a greater commitment to nonviolence when pressed for comparisons. But he no longer believed significant change would occur. "In the sixties," he tells us, "I thought my actions could make a difference; I had more hopes then. But [now] I don't believe that there will be the sort of socialist, humanist revolution that I would like. That's just not gonna happen, it's not gonna happen the way I would like, the path I would like to happen."

These feelings did not drive Pines out of political life, because he believes that political activism is valid for its own sake, as both a moral necessity and a source of personal gratification. Consider Pines's reasons for refusing induction during the Vietnam War: "It was the right thing to do, for its own sake, regardless of what its impact was." This conviction, he insists, never left him; it is what kept him going. "You do it because you enjoy the process, you enjoy planning something, strategy. You enjoy painting posters, distributing leaflets, doing news releases, organizing, reaching out to people. The events themselves, they're satisfying in themselves, even if they only raise consciousness an eighth of a point or something. The stuff has meaning beyond the impact of it."

But it is not enough, Pines feels, to rely on such "existential" beliefs (as he terms them); it is necessary, he argues, to constantly resist the "slippage" of commitment, and to wage "holding actions" against the disillusionment and frustration and co-optive pressures that undermine radical consciousness. Indeed, he suggests that "holding actions" are all that is possible in these times. In the face of political discouragement, and in the midst of a hostile political climate, Pines persists by openly confronting those pressures. His self-doubts clarify what needs to be confronted. Heightened self-awareness, he seems to be suggesting, can sustain activism.

Admitting to some envy and resentment of those in the activist cohort who have made lasting vocational commitments or achieved some level of economic security, Pines rejects what he calls an "economic rationale for compromising. The economic justification—I think people are gonna have to watch that. It's become a subtle rationalization for compromising. 'I have to do it for economic reasons, I have to do it for survival reasons.' That's just one of the words. I just react. When people do things for 'survival,' I think they're really talking about survival of their [middle-class] lifestyle."

Pines made a conscious effort to lower his economic needs. "I've sort of chosen this downward mobility. I've been influenced by Dorothy Day. If I was not living at home, I'd live in a Catholic Worker hospitality house or something. It's not like I don't have my contradictions—[I'm all for] self-denial, but if I can just get some popcorn, right?—and I'm not into a vow of poverty, [but] I have cut back quite a bit. I think I'm working toward modest living." Staying at his parents, Pines reports, "freed me to not be in the economic struggle." His housing expenses are zero, a drastic reduction from the five-hundred-dollar rent on his I.V. apartment, and his parents—both "moderate Republicans," but supportive of their son's commitments—help with the food bills. "I can't say that I'm totally happy with it, it gives me freedom but there's also a loss of freedom . . . but I guess it goes against the grain. And occasionally I feel this pride thing. If I'm with really straight people, it's hard to explain that I'm living at home because their whole life has been up and up toward independence and making it. It's almost like I've [already] had my independence in a way."

Given this orientation, even routine decisions about spending money —for instance, replacing the flash on his camera before his cross-country trip—can assume a degree of ethical significance. Moreover, the Catholic Worker/Dorothy Day influence, as well as Coles's focus on "moral engagement with poverty," can be seen in his decision (just before our 1982 interview) to volunteer as a truck driver, maintenance man, and general laborer for a local hunger project—"doing the shit work, not trying to be director or social worker," he emphasizes. He was very conscious of refraining from any kind of leadership role: "I find that it keeps me grounded. I've almost evolved [into] not needing to be the organizer. [I'm] alienated so much from the role, it's become much more professional, and mechanical, and all this organizing technology, from computerized mailing lists to fund-raising techniques, alienates me." While Pines sees this volunteer work as part of his "downward mobility thing," it also appears to be an effort to reanimate his "idealistic VISTA self." "It's real . . . grass-rootsy," Ed Pines states, groping for a way to describe its appeal. "And it feels good."

As for the future, Pines was then rather unsure. "I worry about after the [research] trip, you know. I think if I ever finish this Coles project, then I'm gonna have this void. I may have to go do a shit job or something like that." He was seriously considering becoming an organizer of domestic workers, but he was not sure that he could balance his commitment to downward mobility with his need for involvement in vocational and political activities that encourage creativity and autonomy. Pines recognizes that such moral dilemmas are ever-present, and his "political identity" remains stable. "That never has left me. It never has. I don't know if I just have it in my blood or something, but I just can't drop out. I go through retreats, but I don't drop."

In late 1987, Ed Pines was still active in local, community politics. He certainly had not dropped out or changed his political views or moral values. But he had made three significant changes in his life. He decided to abandon the Robert Coles project. After meeting with Coles and pulling together a large amount of material, Pines saw the project evolving into a massive social and political critique, something he never really wanted or intended to do. Having put the project aside, Pines decided to work toward a teaching credential, and has done some substitute and student teaching at local high schools during the past year.

As he takes his first step toward a professional career, "downward mobility" and excruciating internal debates over every economic decision have given way to increasing stability and balance in his personal life. Pines still expresses some uncertainty and self-doubt about what kind of teacher he will be if and when he finally gets a teaching position. Moral accountability to his New Left past remains a central theme in his life, and he is likely to elaborate on that theme in the classroom. Indeed, he has tried to use his classroom teaching of economics to foster a critical, questioning attitude toward capitalism.

Pines now lives with a woman and her two children (ages ten and fourteen), whom he met in 1983 when he was still staying with his parents. Also a teacher, she shares Pines's values and politics. All in all, Ed Pines is moving toward a more settled existence while continuing political commitments that began more than two decades ago.

"I Will Be Responsible for the Course of Our History"

Warren Newhouser and Ed Pines find strength to carry on in the very act of making "moral choices," regardless of their historical impact. The intense satisfaction and personal meaning they find in taking such a stance helps them to avoid being politically crippled by the defeats and disappointments that burden the history of the New Left. Other sixties persisters, however, have found moral sustenance in the ideological framework of "scientific Marxism," firm in their conviction that despite setbacks and defeats in the revolutionary struggle, history is on their side. Their own political actions, however limited or ineffectual they may seem at the time, are contributing to the forward surge of history. They are less vulnerable to feelings of being "marginalized" in local enclaves or to the self-doubts that plague "humanistic" activists like Ed Pines, confident that the same historical forces are shaping the struggle in each locale, unifying the cause, sweeping it onward.

Barney Thompson expressed these sentiments time and time again in our many conversations during the past eight years, and in a poem:

I choose to participate in [the world's] future
It is no life and death choice,
But I will be responsible for the course of our history.
Does everyone see that these simple things take a long time?
I appropriate to myself a life of unease
And the long years of an unsatisfied class.
The world may have a future of very big mistakes,
But bigger victories follow each setback.
The wrong side may win again and again
But not ultimately.

For most of the past decade, Thompson worked as a postal clerk and lived alone in various one-bedroom apartments. His 1982 marriage ended after six months when his wife returned to her native France. In 1987, he moved to Los Angeles and took a job in a bookstore run by the small "new Communist movement" group that attracted him while he was an active member of the legal collective. Thompson was also employed during 1987 as a substitute teacher in an inner-city school and currently teaches adult education classes four nights a week.

Thompson's decisions about work hinge on politics, recalling the choices of other persisters. When the legal collective disbanded, he briefly considered training to be a lawyer, but realized that he did not want to make any kind of middle-class career commitment: "I made motions, I looked to the future, but as far as having a career goes—God, you know, you run into people at a high school reunion or something that are insurance agents in Fresno. And you think nothing could be worse." An equally significant factor was the feeling that he should merge his life as much as possible into the working class rather than take up a higher-status vocation. Having passed the post office test, he started sorting mail on the night shift in 1976. Eight years later, he had worked his way into a day shift, counter clerk position. Although he was dedicated to his job and proud of doing it well, the move to Los Angeles seemed worthwhile and politically important.

"I'm a supporter of [the Party]," he says: "That's how you should classify me. I read their paper, and I help sell and distribute the paper." Prior to moving to Los Angeles, he participated in a few political projects in the Isla Vista/Santa Barbara area that were not related to the Party. His move was primarily motivated by his desire to be closer to the center of Party activities. His work in support of the Party also involves attending meetings or conferences and occasionally helping to organize local activities.

The relationship between this persistent political involvement over the past twenty years and his thinking on historical continuity and purpose are especially evident when Thompson reflects on the lessons of the sixties. He argues that "the fact that the sixties actually happened" disproves the common view that "people are happy, people are satisfied, nobody's ever gonna rebel because of what they've got in this country. In the sixties people had more of what they've got now, and they still rebelled. And that's a tremendous lesson—that people can say, 'Fuck this shit, this life is dead and boring, and I want something that's a little more exciting, even if I get my head bashed in at the end of the night.'" Thompson still finds great revolutionary inspiration in those events. Perhaps even more important, he sees similarities between that period and contemporary rumblings among young people. "Why couldn't the same thing happen again? New forces are arising, are coming into being. There's a lot of similarities between the punk riots that are happening now and some of the early riots and early demonstrations in the sixties," he insists. He acknowledges "a real contrast culturally," but he believes the underlying motivations are the same. "The reason I got involved was because it was more exciting, it was more fun. It was not because I read Marx and a bunch of books and decided that's what I had to do. The one big thing we and the punks have in common is this whole attitude of 'this whole system that we live in is fucked up.'" Over the past few years, Thompson has demonstrated his attraction to the punk movement by dying his hair orange (only for a few months, however) and occasionally donning punk styles of dress. He also avidly collects new wave and punk rock music.

Barney Thompson's recent lifestyle is a curious mixture of conventional and unconventional practices. Rejecting a middle-class career, he has formed affiliations with two vehemently rebellious groups: the punk subculture and a hard-line Maoist sect (wildly dissimilar but for their shared preoccupation with violence and social decay). He worked steadily for years in a very traditional and relatively well paid working-class occupation, but now teaches in settings most of his colleagues would avoid. Thus, his current occupation and penchant for culturally "deviant" expression link him to the recent lives of Ed Pines and Warren Newhouser, while his greater vocational stability over the past decade sets him somewhat apart from these other persisters. Unlike them, Thompson feels little moral obligation to live at a subsistence level or refrain from taking advantage of any of the opportunities a steady income allows. For example, a certain elegance of taste characterizes his free-time activities: he owns an expensive bicycle; is a connoisseur of French wines; is a gourmet cook; is studying Latin, Greek, Italian, and Spanish (in fact, he now teaches Spanish); and has become quite fluent in French, facilitating his recent travels through Europe.

The difference is more than a superficial one. Thompson does not depend on "making moral choices" in his daily life to give him a sense of purpose, in the same way that Pines and Newhouser do. Instead, his affiliation with a democratic-centralist, revolutionary party (and adoption of an orthodox Marxist-Leninist perspective) allows him to define his daily life in political terms. His life has revolutionary relevance by virtue of his participation in this historical enterprise. Thus, his ready acknowledgment of "bourgeois habits" entails no obligation to purge his life of them. The difference lies, then, in the place in which people find their political and moral sustenance: in history or within themselves.

Moreover, Thompson's occupations as a postal clerk and a teacher provide him with the kind of close contact with the working class that his political identity suggests is important, but fewer opportunities for the autonomy and creativity that are so important to Newhouser and Pines. While the teaching is very demanding emotionally, the scarcity of resources and the enormousness of the task allow for little free experimentation. Newhouser uses writing as a form of creative expression in his daily round, and Pines' project on Robert Coles was similarly oriented; but Thompson has not structured this option into his everyday activity. Further, Thompson has less creative freedom in his political life, confined as it is within the strictly drawn ideological lines of a Maoist sect. In this light, Thompson's choices for spending his free time reveal a generally creative and intellectual orientation. Rather than a wholehearted embrace of consumer culture, those choices mark efforts at self-development, attempts at self-expression that have no outlet in his occupational or political activities. His interest in the punk movement can also be interpreted in this way.

To say that Barney Thompson is able to interpret his political commitment in terms of a clear-cut historical purpose is not to say that he is free of doubts about his own capacity to fulfill the role of a historical actor or that he is always comfortable in it. For example, he sometimes questions his own effectiveness in reaching people with a political message and criticizes his reluctance to be a leader. "In some ways I'd rather let other people take the heat and the responsibility." He frequently worries about the considerable amount of time he does not spend on politics. "Ambiguity is endemic to me. I suspect myself, and reasonably so." But at the same time he feels isolated from those who are not political. "When you actually become politically active, it takes more than doing what feels good. You have to make a rational choice, a conscious choice. And there's problems when you make that conscious choice; it sort of puts you in a different place than everybody else; it sort of alienates you from everyone. It's like you have the mark of Cain on your brain." However, his revolutionary faith counters these doubts and anxieties, providing meaning and purpose at times when his personal experiences in political life offer little comfort. "They say no rose has ever seen a gardener die. You know, people don't live as long as social systems; they live very short times compared to social systems. I have the feeling of being part of these great spirals—historical spirals. Being a materialist is great because it sort of gives you a feeling of immortality or something."

"I'm Still Optimistic That Things Can Change, Every Day, Little by Little"

Martha Koch and Denise Saal are two persisters who have successfully combined professional careers and leftist activism. Koch, after several years of working in emergency medicine and pediatrics, is now a specialist in environmental and occupational health. From 1980 to 1984, she was employed by a large, relatively progressive labor union; since that time, she has been the director of a state program on occupational health and safety. Her job with the union primarily involved evaluations of work sites for health hazards; she visited the plants and spoke to workers about their concerns, reviewed their medical records, and, if necessary, examined them. Her job with the state involves many of the same responsibilities. Koch is also a member of Democratic Socialists of America and very active in community politics. Married to a man who is equally active in leftist politics and works as an urban planner, she owns a home in an integrated urban neighborhood and is the mother of two young children.

From 1974 until 1984, Denise Saal was a paralegal worker in a large western city. After the Santa Barbara Legal Collective dissolved, she first worked in a law office for a team of leftist lawyers and then helped to form another, smaller collective with three other activists who worked side by side with lawyers in preparing defenses and selecting juries for capital punishment cases (and an occasional political case). She entered law school in 1985 and graduated in June of 1988. She has served as an officer in a national association of radicals in the legal profession, heading up an information and education project on the Palestinian cause, and is active in protest and electoral politics on a community level and with Jesse Jackson's "Rainbow Coalition." Saal is single.

This integration of vocation and radical politics has not been without its difficulties. Koch, for example, when we interviewed her in 1982, emphasized that she was very excited about her job with the union because "it's the first time I've really seen my way clear to 'What am I going to do with my medical skills that will be a good thing to do with them?' And all the other things I've done, I sort of grope around and say, 'Well, I don't really know about this—I don't know.'" In large part, she says, the problem lies with the fact that medicine in this country is focused on the individual, divorced from the social and political processes that give rise to so many of the problems doctors treat. "I mean, you can work in a public hospital or work in a community clinic and pick the population that you're going to work with, but, basically, for your sixty-hour week, you're working with individuals. And you can teach people about medicine and health care and stuff, but while I'm into breaking down professionalism and teaching people about their own health care and everything, I'm not into this 'consumer, heal thyself' nonsense—that if you just take proper care of yourself, take vitamin C, do breast exams every month, stop smoking, stop eating fat, you'll be healthy. Because that's like a liberal, blaming-the-victim approach to medical problems that I can't really go for. Everybody knows just as well that if you work with asbestos or have a high-stress job you are also going to die of lung cancer or have a heart attack.

"And the other problem that I've found extremely frustrating, both in the emergency room and in pediatrics, is that 80 percent of what you deal with, or even more, aren't medical problems. Taking care of the people that are drunks and addicts and stuff that come in to have their abscesses drained, or come in to have their heads sewn up after they've fallen down a flight of stairs, or come in to have themselves taken care of after they've gotten shot or stabbed with a knife—those are all social problems. And pediatrics is the same: trying to take care of kids that have been abused, trying to teach parents about adequate nutrition. And so most of the clinical medicine, at least most of the clinical medicine I've done, either has its roots in social and economic ills, or [means] taking care of the one-in-a-million kid that has a rare brain tumor. And that's real medicine, but it's pretty irrelevant to me. I mean, it's relevant on an individual level, but it's not politically relevant. It's so hard to know how to put into practice what your politics are, when medicine, clinical medicine, is basically an individual thing. So what do you do, if you're working individual to individual, within the confines of the medical system as it exists?"

What you do, she decided, is find a way to steer your medical practice toward dealing with those socioeconomic ills, attacking them directly. "The thing about doing occupational health, and especially working with the union," Koch stated, "is that all the power relations of the society just stand out, and it's like you can take a political analysis and say, 'Look at this—look at the power relations between the workers and the state, and industry and capital.' And it's all clearly laid out, you know? And the value of collective bargaining and organizing around issues is real clear, because the only workers who have made any strides whatso-ever in terms of occupational health and safety are unionized workers. And it's a real good educational tool in terms of, 'What are the hazards that they're facing and what can they do about them?' And why get-ting together is the only way that they'll be able to deal with issues that are literally life-and-death issues. So it's an incredible organizing issue." While bureaucratic in-fighting and factional disputes within the union often detract from or undermine this political potential, Koch was still secure in her feeling that she had finally found an area of medicine where her training had political relevance: "Occupational health is something where medical skills play a real role," she concludes.

Yet bureaucratic in-fighting, and internal union politics in general, played a significant role in Koch's decision to leave the union and work for the state. The program she now runs is responsible for investigating work-related illnesses and injuries, which involves regular visits to and inspections of work sites, as well as surveillance of occupational disease cases. The pay is very similar to that for the union position (the full-time salary rate is about $60,000 a year), and the work is similar. While Koch makes it clear that she "doesn't enjoy working for the state," the satisfaction that she receives from being able to do her medical work in this politically conscious, socially aware fashion more than makes up for whatever problems the government affiliation creates.

Denise Saal's concentration on capital punishment cases in her paralegal work also reflects a desire to tie her job directly to political issues. Capital punishment is used primarily against the poor, particularly racial minorities, Saal argues, and assisting the defense in these cases was an important part of the struggle for equal justice under the law. By focusing their efforts on this issue, the collective was able to give their work more political purpose and avoid the feelings of futility and isolation to which groups like the Santa Barbara Legal Collective were prone.

This solution did not go far enough for her, however, and Saal's decision to go to law school marked a change in the form of her political commitment, even if the underlying values and beliefs, and the commitment to legal work as a "social change vocation," remained fairly stable. Since "the jury project was, in some ways, an extension—it was very, very different, but in some ways an extension"—of her political activities during the years in Isla Vista and Santa Barbara, becoming a lawyer involved a shift to a much more individualized, professional style of working and living. She explains this shift as an effort at self-development: "I spent ten years helping to build that jury project. It was very exciting! And I'm very proud of it, very proud of the role that I played—and could be there still, you know? But somehow, for me . . . I don't even know exactly how to word it but it has—it has something to do with wanting to step into the mainstream. I really do want that. I mean I could have gotten a 'Bar card' [to practice law] without going to law school. I chose to go to law school. And I want to go through the same socialization experience that other people have gone through. I mean, it's sort of an ethnological experience, or something. And I made that choice. [It didn't involve] a lot of internal turmoil. In fact, very little. When I figured out that I wanted to do something—as opposed to what I was doing, I mean—I almost felt like I woke up. I had started to feel dissatisfied. And I began to explore why. And to go through that whole process. And the more I tried to sort it out, it just felt like a reason, among many reasons that I felt dissatisfied, was that I felt as though I stopped developing at some point. And even though I was helping to break ground in a new field and start a new organization, I didn't feel that I was developing personally. With the jury project, I had written, and lectured, and trained people, and all these things that had given me a lot of recognition and personal validation, but I was uncomfortable as a trainer and helper, in this sort of para or ancillary role. For a lot of people that's fine. For me it wasn't. I wanted to do what I was training people to do. So I did it to kind of consolidate myself, professionally and politically."

Saal's account recalls remarks by other respondents that were presented in our earlier examination of the phase we called "increasing individuation." She was experiencing many of the same feelings that led other "bank burners," in the late seventies, to leave their collective, experimental institutions and groups and follow more conventional career paths. These career paths were often a continuation of prior commitments and experiences, however; rather than representing a sharp break from the past, such changes could be interpreted as efforts to find more personally satisfying ways of remaining accountable to it.

Saal plans to work for a large law firm for two or three years after graduation, to "put in a couple of years paying my dues, getting that on-the-job polish. . . . The work that I really want to do is work in a small law office, a small collective-ish kind of practice, working with people that do a general practice—some criminal defense, some small business, some just general small cases—and also with an emphasis on civil rights. But in order to do that—I mean, that's what everybody wants to. It's very, very hard to do that. To do that you have to position yourself. And that's kind of where my energy is now."

Saal talks openly—and with a touch of humor—about the compromises and risks that this strategy entails. "I figured out that the thing that hooks people is the mortgage. That's what I've figured out. What happens is that people go and they work in this big firm, and they get a lot of money. They have a lot of cash. Then they start going, 'Oh my God, the tax problem!' Well, how do you avoid the tax problem? You buy property. And then you have like this thousand-dollar-a-month or this fifteen-hundred-dollar-a-month mortgage payment to make each month. And then you can't go anywhere else. And that's that. It's just that simple. So to me, the secret is not to get the mortgage!"

For both Koch and Saal, professional commitments are coupled with a hope that their work is part of a gradual, long-term process of social transformation, that their efforts at working within mainstream institutions are, in fact, making a difference. Instead of seeing limited gains and small victories as evidence of the futility of activism, they see them as more steps along the road to social justice. Both women have "adjusted," then, to the political limitations of their work and the current political weakness of the Left; they continue to see their lives as having political relevance. Koch, for example, states that while she's "very pessimistic on one level—I see more famine, more disease, more death, more destruction, more war, more waste in the future of the world—on another level I'm very optimistic. I'm still optimistic that things can change, every day, little by little. And my everyday politics is the way I express my optimism. I mean, continued involvement in efforts to seek social, political, and economic change is the way I express optimism, because if I don't think there's any hope, then there's no point in me doing anything."

Both women look to other people who are making the same kind of "everyday" contributions for radical renewal. The movement has to rebuild itself "from the grass roots up," Koch feels, developing this same kind of incremental approach: "I don't think there's going to be any kind of unified Left movement in the next couple of years, and I'm not sure that that's important. I think stuff that's happening on a local level is more important. I really think things have to develop, models have to develop, on a local level. I don't think you can make like this giant big bang without some kind of infrastructure; we've been remiss in building infrastructure." Saal offers a similar judgment. The activists who are doing the most important work, she suggests, are "people that are sort of fish in the ocean, who are taking a radical line in their workplace and their community, who are teaching in the schools or working as civil servants, who are sort of immersed in the mainstream and have clear sociopolitical lines and put that out in a nonrhetorical way and educate people and point things out to people. I think that's what really has to be done."

Saal and Koch recognize that this stance represents a "scaling-down" of their former expectations. "I have a better perspective now on how slow things go," Koch explains. "I guess what keeps me going is the optimism that it can happen, but I don't think that it will happen—that there will be a socialist, democratic society in America—in my lifetime."

While Saal emphasizes, "I still see myself as a socialist, I still see myself as a revolutionary, someone who wants, who expects, revolution will come at some point, and wants to be part of creating it, participating in it," she too has come to believe that the path to that distant revolution will be an extraordinarily difficult one: "But you just don't win overnight. You just don't fold up your tents and go home. You remain committed to the idea and, while the circumstances may change, the idea remains the same."

Finally, and most important, their commitments to a more daily-life-oriented politics and their lowered expectations have been paralleled in recent years by increased attention to their personal lives and renewed efforts to find a more workable balance between personal development and politics than the New Left was able to create. Koch's marriage and the births of her children are obviously significant events in this regard. The decision to have children, she reports, was made easier when she took up occupational health work. "I sort of felt like a lot of things in my life were more and more settled than they had been. I found an area in medicine I was interested in working in, and that had taken me a long time." Having a baby would have been tremendously disruptive ten years ago, Koch notes ("I don't think people had a sense of balance between sort of living your life on a long-term basis and doing politics at the same time"), but she and her husband have so far been able to work out the time and energy conflicts between politics, work, and personal life. Cutting back on their work hours so as to have more time together as a family (Koch now works only part-time in her state job) and sharing child care responsibilities equally have helped. Some decisions have required compromising New Left political principles, as when they decided to send their older daughter to a private school because they felt that the public schools were academically inadequate.

Similarly, Saal's mid-1980s interview related her personal life and her political commitment to a critique of what she calls the New Left's "all or nothing." "Political work has become less of a time commitment, but not less of a priority," she begins. "It is one of a number of things that are important in my life now: I enjoy having fun much more than I used to. I consciously try to do things that are fun, that have no political significance, like fishing and hiking and all that kind of stuff. I do that much more than I used to, which I think is a positive and healthy development. And also another thing that is going on is that I'm beginning to look down the line, at the years in the future, which I never have [done] in the past. The last few years are the first time in my life where I've thought, 'Where will I be when I'm forty or fifty?' Which is a real unique thing. So my life is an interwoven mesh of a variety of different things, politics being one of them, and will always be one of them, but not the only thing. I just think people have somehow gone astray in terms of figuring out what 'political' is and what 'political' isn't. I feel like in a lot of ways people think being political is giving up a personal life and that, in and of itself, is political. I disagree with that."

Last year, only a few months before she finished law school, she placed many of these ideas in a more biographical context, trying to connect the changes in her thinking about personal life and politics over the past two decades. "I remember back when I was eighteen years old, looking at people who were thirty-five and saying, 'Why do they sell out, with cars and houses and mortgages and children?' And asking, 'What happened to them?' And saying, 'That should never happen; we should remain true to our ideals.' That was really the question for us: what happens as you grow up and life changes and as you mature? What happens to you that has an impact on what you do? Spoken from an eighteen-year-old's perspective, it's pretty easy to say, 'Nothing should affect your commitment.' But for me it was . . . I mean the war was over in 1974, or whatever. And that period of my life was over. And, at least for me, a period of incredible emotional commitment ended with that. I've never felt that way again. And I don't expect to. Because I . . . I think that there was an enormous confluence of factors that caused us to be how we were at that point in time. You know, frankly, I feel incredibly grateful that I got to live through that, and feel those feelings, and do those things, and learn and 'be,' and those kinds of things. But I also have to recognize that doesn't happen for your whole life. And so, what does happen? Other things become important, certainly. You just kind of think to yourself, 'When I'm fifty years old, am I gonna want more than three pairs of Levis?' I mean, that crosses your mind from time to time! And you start to realize that you have to think about yourself and your future."

DISENGAGED RADICALS

The stories of the persisters dramatize the continuing effort by veterans of the student movement to find a balance between living a plausible life and living in history. It is against these cases, then, that the experiences of the less politically involved members of the activist cohort can be compared. Research on former student activists (our own included) has charted a sharp decline in the political activism that was their hallmark, while revealing a resiliency of leftist convictions in their post-movement careers. This tension between values and action is the subject of the following case studies, which underscore the analysis presented in the sketches of the persisters' lives. Where people lack confidence in the political significance of their individual actions or are unable to link their vocational commitment and their round of daily life to political commitment, they find it exceedingly difficult to practice their radical values publicly. The following case studies demonstrate that disengaged radicals are disillusioned, but not with the values espoused by the movement; rather, they have lost faith in the possibility of changing society so that those values can be fully realized. At the same time, the studies reveal how individuals can be moved to defend such values and moral sensibilities when they are threatened (as with the conservative assault on the social and cultural legacy of the sixties), leading at times to a reawakening of political commitment.

"Semi-Passive Radicalism—I Sort of Find Myself There"

In an earlier chapter, Roger Wade described his decision to become a professional historian in terms of the possibilities for developing, through his teaching, a radical consciousness in young people. The story of how his hopes changed reflects a disillusionment with "making history" and a lost historical purpose that has affected many former student protesters; most of their radical convictions are intact, but they are much less committed to the activist stance. The ebb and flow of political involvement among former New Leftists in the 1980s can be understood in just these terms.

In our first interview, which took place during his fourth year of graduate school, Wade spoke about the aspirations of earlier years: "Now I have few illusions about academics doing those things I thought I would do. The university definitely could be, if one had tenure, a secure place [to be], but as for 'molding young minds,' or doing much that I think is politically viable, I don't think that it's really possible." Ironically, this disillusionment was a consequence of his own historical inquiry, an effort to explore historical questions raised by his New Left experience.

"The study of history has solidified certain understandings that make it hard for me to have a lot of faith in radical action," he explained. "In studying and reading about one Left movement after another that failed, and in thinking about social processes, I come away with just very little sense that man has been capable of consciously directing events to shape their destiny. People can make history, but they can't necessarily shape it. It seems to me that most revolutionary movements have failed outright, and the few that have managed to succeed have taken courses that are generally not at all intended—they haven't lived up to the ideals and initial goals and directions. I guess I'm impressed with the evidence that despite the fact that people, even in all kinds of circumstances, try to make one kind of historical event, something else most always results.

"I became cynical—not about the possibility of making an impact, but the possibility of that impact being a desired one. I stopped believing in theories [that projected] the inexorable amelioration of society and man's condition; I stopped believing [in] historical inevitabilities. So without either a concept of historical inevitability or a belief that man can create institutions that will function relatively in accordance with the ideals and purposes that they've been designed to fulfill, there's nothing left. I mean, there's really no way to act if you can't come up with either of those, except just, sort of, blind existential commitment without any sense of faith in the utility of those actions, and I'm not existential, so I was left without the ideal. I think the more I thought about it, and about history, the more confused I got."

This confusion carried over to his graduate school teaching: "I found it impossible to really say much or do much that could contribute to an activist or radical sense of society. I was unable to do anything that felt like I was contributing to even social criticism of American society. I thought I [could] really contribute to a sense that one could . . . that there was a radical critique of American society and there was a place for, was a need for, a radical movement to restructure society. And even that sort of limited role I was not capable of playing, 'cause I couldn't feel it enough; I couldn't feel positive about anything."

In addition to the debilitating effect of his pessimism, there was also the moderating influence of professional, scientific canons, standards that were an essential part of his graduate school training. "In large part, I clearly ingested the ethics of a historical profession, which is to seek some kind of honesty, if not truth, in your description and understanding of processes and events. And so I found it impossible to kind of fudge my explanations in order to make the Industrial Workers of the World more glamorous, or more of an ideal, for these students. And so, in effect, I realized that I was teaching a class in a way that I never thought I would when I [first] thought of going to graduate school. When it came down to it, all I could be was a straight historian."

Confusion also became the defining feature of his political views. "It's mostly that I have only questions now, and almost no answers, about what should be done," Wade said in that first interview. "I have no answers about what a model society would be, and also how anybody or any movement can go about creating change. Primarily what I feel is not something that I would call apathy, but rather a lack of energy and direction. And with a real sense of frustration with *that* feeling—frustration with my own self, my own inability to feel the way I did, to feel sure and directed." Political paralysis had set in.

Clearly, Wade was self-conscious about this change of direction and troubled by what he saw happening to himself. "I didn't like the idea that I was losing the radicalism," he stated, "giving up radical ideals and lapsing back into my middle-class heritage." Finally, Wade often felt guilty and defensive about being in graduate school, even though he does not remember anyone else being very critical. "I would sort of put graduate school off as a frivolous thing to do. It was as if I suspected that people would be thinking I was just wasting my time."

These frustrations, disappointments, and self-doubts were expressed in the early 1980s. In retrospect, they seem to be a product of a difficult period of transition, a time that marked "an attempt to kind of adjust out of the view of myself as a political warrior, whose self-conception revolved around some sort of larger attempt to change the world, into a more personal set of goals and motivations." A lengthy interview in 1984 reveals significant changes in his thinking, about both himself and politics. In the intervening years he became "better and better adjusted" to the political limitations of both his career and the movement that once defined his identity—and realized that he was not alone in his plight. "I think what has happened is that my senses are just more reconciled to it," he remarks. "It has just become clearer to me that I'm very much a product of what has been going on on a very large scale. I feel more 'normal' than I really felt three years ago. I feel more readjusted."

Most important, "readjustment" did not mean the cessation of all political activity; for the most part, coming to terms with his disappointments and frustrations enabled him to participate to some extent in leftist and liberal causes. "I feel better about the different kind of political role that I'm in now—a different kind of activism. It's sort of a passive radicalism. It's a very low level of involvement in anything. It's sort of more like audience participation in social change. I really don't feel like a leader anymore. I don't feel like I have the energy to lead the charge and put together the plans or whatever it requires. But I do feel like supporting—some moral support above all. And in the last couple of years I've taken an increased interest in, and am excited about, local politics. I don't feel any inclination to go out and become intensely involved, but I am very happy to walk the precincts, to be one of the 'army.' I've worked on the rent control campaign, and the election campaigns of this leftist congressman. It's fascinating to go on election morning to the community organization's headquarters and see all these old radicals. I think that there are a lot of people that somehow or another came to the same level of passive or semi-passive radicalism—I sort of find myself there."

In addition to local activities, Wade became a "passive member" of a radical/Marxian historians' organization and occasionally attended demonstrations addressing national or international issues. Everyday manifestations of this attenuated commitment—"tiny political statements," as he puts it—include avoiding shopping the conglomerate-owned supermarket and patronizing the cooperative grocery store. "It's owned by the members. It was started by a bunch of leftists in the thirties, kind of an 'Owenism' organization," he explains. Although the co-op's size and supermarket decor make it look "like a model of Safeway," Wade also suggests that more is involved: "In principle and spirit and theory, somehow, it really is an alternative to Safeway. There's actually some, you know, very intangible, but different feeling. Maybe it's the people who shop there; there's a nice sense of socializing. And there's a lot of buyer information, and the membership votes periodically to exclude certain products, boycotted items like Nestlés. It's a political thing to shop there —one of the tiniest political statements that I've made in my life, but it is there, so it feels right."

Wade nevertheless expresses a yearning for the days when the "infectious optimism" of the movement prevailed, even though he feels that he is no longer able to make that kind of commitment. "I still look back on the level of commitment and activism of my adolescence, my early adulthood, as a vital and extraordinarily valuable kind of experience. If there were some way that I could feel right about being that way today, I would very much want to do so. But I have made other choices." Partly, he said, these choices have to do with his more settled, established style of life: "I'm more used to the comfortable style of existence and more alarmed at the prospect of losing it. I have become more security conscious—timid, I suppose, is really another way of putting it. I'm timid about taking those kinds of risks and making those kinds of commitments."

A recent event "really brought this all home": "I watched the news about these nineteen-year-old kids that are facing trial for refusing to register for the draft. I think of this kid down in San Diego, this kid going on trial and facing five years, and I marvel at it. I have a very hard time coming to grips with the fact that I did that. I did exactly that. I was willing and mentally prepared to go through with that and into prison on exactly the same issue. I didn't think very much of it at all. Now it seems like a horrendous sacrifice. Going to prison for five years! Laying everything on the line like that. I marvel at it. That's because I have a whole different orientation toward security and sacrifice that I did then. As a nineteen- or twenty-year-old, risks and sacrifices of that nature were no big deal. It was somehow part of the process. I didn't take it as seriously as I do now. That's what I mean by being timid. I don't, and I'm not willing to, take the same kinds of risks for the same kinds of purposes."

Nor has Wade rediscovered his faith in radical action. His belief that radical struggles to forge a more humane and just society, no matter how well-intentioned, are fated to go amiss still exerts a powerful hold on his thinking. While, "in spirit," he remains a socialist, he "tries to distinguish between spirit and program. I like so much about the socialist tradition, about the whole concept, that there's a part of me that wants to be a socialist, but on a practical level, any time that I can look at the programmatic choices that I can make, I can no longer see a grand scheme. I would be not telling the truth if I said that I haven't lost a lot of steam, because I don't feel that faith in conscious struggle or in the ability to control events—not as much as I used to. I don't have any faith that the ideals—although I believe that the dream of a Marxist society is the most wonderful dream that man has ever had—I don't have any faith that it can be worked out in practice or it can be executed in this world. So I don't have the dreams right here in front of me, ready to push with all my might. And having been burned once—I guess that's the way to put it—having seen it fall apart once, I would be hard pressed to believe in the magic again. It's not real. The dream isn't real."

To deal with this loss of faith, Wade has made "adjustments" in his expectations. Where he once felt that "differences between the capitalist parties, the two parties, was not a concern for socialists," Wade now found that "the little points, the little differences are much more important. The idea of defending certain civil rights, [political] gains, and the prospect of hanging on to a slightly less belligerent foreign policy seems to me to be quite important." The election of Reagan, he told us, made "defensive actions"—"preserving what's left of the civil rights gains of the sixties and fighting this conservative mass"—the focus of his political thinking. "The right-wing agenda is so powerful, you don't have time to be confused. So my heart is still there."

Roger Wade has not resolved the tension between his leftist values and his political passivity, between the longing for a sense of historical purpose and efficacy that characterized his past and his current doubt that purposeful struggle will bring about a progressive social order. Marriage to a historian who also has leftist ideals, home ownership, and a faculty position at a prestigious university increases the tension. In this new setting, he periodically shows some reluctance to engage in activities that might jeopardize his established life and career. In the 1984 interview, when asked about his personal hopes for the next five years, he replied that "almost all of them would be phrased in terms of career and family." But he did not discount his moral and political resiliency. "Given all my doubts, my lack of faith, I still think that once you struggle, just having the dream is enough. So I am not saying that I am totally incapacitated by my doubts or concerns."

Three years later, Wade's feelings and political involvement remain fairly stable: he continues to volunteer in local election campaigns, gives small donations to progressive community and national organizations, and has maintained his membership in the radical historians' group. His academic career remains his primary concern. His first book is scheduled for publication next year, and his tenure situation looks promising. He and his wife have been unable to find full-time positions in the same place, and they have had to live hundreds of miles apart for much of the past three years. They hope to solve this problem soon, but Wade notes that leaving the university where he now works will not be easy.

Wade's current enthusiasm about teaching stands in sharp contrast to his despair about reaching students some nine years ago, when just beginning his academic career. Speaking about the political significance of his work, he restates many of the themes from earlier interviews. "I think those who want to do something effective in terms of making social change wouldn't do it in the historical profession; they wouldn't do it through scholarship. There's much more to be done through direct political action. But what I *do* do that's political is teach and convey my view of the world, my values. I use historical lessons in American history, labor history, teach what's good and what's bad about the past, give students suggestions about what's important about the future. So the role of teacher, I think, lends itself to political concerns; the role of scholar seems to be less significant politically. For instance, I'm putting so much energy into this book, which has some thoughts and some useful, I think, bits of understanding about American culture today. But I've put ten years of my life into that, and it's going to be read by a few thousand people, and I could have used those ten years much more efficiently if I'd been interested primarily in making political change."

Cynthia Spivak withdrew from activism in the early seventies but, like Wade, still feels a connection with her movement past: "I don't really think I've changed a lot." In Chapter 4, we saw Spivak leave the United States to take a teaching job in Australia. She made friends there with "many people who were out of the radical movement in Sydney." Like her, they felt that the movement "had become too destructive," and they sought refuge in the remoteness of the island. In Spivak's second year in Australia, she fell in love with a local auto mechanic, and the two of them decided to return to the United States. This meant, Spivak says, that they would have to marry. As she recalls, "I didn't think I'd ever live in a nuclear family. I'd lived in collectives all the time in Santa Barbara. I was once an idealist about living simply in a commune, and I wasn't a monogamous person until I married, but we had to do it so that he could work in the U.S."

Her family helped them with the down payment on a small house in Northern California, and their first child was born a year later. Two years after that, a second child arrived. While Roger Wade was struggling with the problems of an academic career, Spivak was settling in—without any major reservations, she says—to "being a full-time mother," a very different kind of life. "The most important thing in my life is my children," she told us in 1982. "I'd rather not have a job; I don't want to put my children in the care of other adults. I'd rather spend time with them." This leaves her, she emphasizes, "no time to be involved" in politics. It is not at all clear, however, that even if she did have the time, Spivak would choose to use it in politics. While she expressed some enthusiasm for involvement "on a local level"—"I've given up on radical change on a national level, but there *has* been a lot of radical change in small places" —she also feels that political life is, for her, "a complete drain emotionally, with very little back. A lot of what you get back is real cynicism and real downers. If I devoted my free time to politics, I wouldn't have anything left for my children."

As with Wade, Spivak's disillusionment has not significantly tempered the beliefs and values she developed in the movement; her views remain considerably to the left of all but a handful of respondents. She spoke of "wanting to see the guerrillas win in El Salvador," expressed bitter opposition to the Reagan administration's policies in the Third World, and articulated heartfelt concern over racism, sexism, and economic exploitation here at home. But without confidence in political activism as a vehicle for change or, perhaps more important, in her ability to integrate activism into her life, these convictions do not provide enough motivation to act. Moreover, her definition of political commitment is one of full-time, complete engagement. It is not certain that she even recognizes the barrier this view creates. How can there be any role for a dedicated mother of two young children in that kind of political world? Thus, when she talks about those who are "still committed activists," and says, "I'm glad they're doing it," she uses individuals who are organizing factory workers as an example. And when she states, without prompting, "There's a lot of guilt in me" about not staying active, she goes on to say, "I wouldn't be any good at organizing workers. I don't think I'd help anyone."

Spivak locates her commitment to "doing something for people" in teaching: "I want to do something that has value, and if I can do that well, and influence people that way, then that's what I want to do. Right now my kids take precedence, but after they're old enough to go to school, I'll go back to teaching," probably health care education. Politics can be found, she says, in this work and in these concerns. Spivak had been employed by a women's medical project while living in Isla Vista: "A political thing that really got me is something like doctors dispensing the Dalkon Shield, and doctors handing out sedatives to the elderly—*that's* political, it really is."

This commitment to expressing her convictions in a practical manner can also be seen in her emphasis on "daily decision-making" as the focus of her life and the place where the values she adopted during her activist youth—especially those emphasizing the refusal of middle-class privileges—might still, in small ways, be visible. "We do everything in cash," she notes. "We don't drive new cars. I haven't lived up at all to the expectations of my parents. They wanted me to have a career," maybe to get a doctorate. "They didn't want me to have kids. And the last thing they wanted me to do was marry a mechanic." At the same time, she recognizes that the changes in her life since her Isla Vista days make the context of those actions and decisions very different; her account nicely captures one person's experience in separating "making history" from "making daily life." Talking once again about her commitment to her children, she recalls the difficulties of finding an acceptable kindergarten. "I inspected nine places, and I chose a Catholic school because they *didn't* push academics, and they had a good ratio of adults to children, not thirty-five to one like public schools. Now these are decisions —not political decisions, but important decisions. Maybe the decisions I had to make in 1970 were political decisions: whether you go and sit down, or you bail someone out of jail, or you throw a rock. These were the decisions you had to make daily. And the decisions I have to make daily now are not political."

"We're Caught Between Two Worlds"

Sheila Barressi lives alone in a small one-bedroom apartment. Barressi is an associate producer at a public television station in Northern California, earning approximately $25,000 a year. She has worked there for the two years since she graduated from film school at UCLA. While in school she worked part-time as a video editor. Her enrollment in film school is the key to understanding her current lack of involvement in "political work." In some respects, Barressi's story is like Roger Wade's: her efforts to find a "meaningful," morally acceptable vocation and to join her personal life—her economic needs and her creative impulses—to political commitment have been fraught with difficulty. She also feels that she has made significant adjustments and compromises, but, unlike Wade, she has not lost her faith in people's ability to create a more humane and just social order. She continues to hold out hope for revolutionary change, for democratic socialism. Her story, then, involves a temporary withdrawal from activism.

Barressi moved from Santa Barbara to Los Angeles and began her studies at UCLA in 1976. She had grown up in a family that was deeply involved in both leftist politics and the film industry, but not until she helped her father with a script he was writing one summer did she begin to think seriously about the film business as one she might enjoy. When a friend of her father's put her in touch with a collective in Los Angeles that was making a film on Vietnam, she decided to move to the city and "give it a try." She did not work on the Vietnam film, but instead helped with a fund-raising film for Tom Hayden's senate campaign. "I just started getting involved with film down there [in Los Angeles]. I started going to City College, took film courses there, got involved with the Socialist Media Group, which was a progressive group of film and media people who met once a week and was connected with the New American Movement. Then I decided to apply to UCLA. I didn't really know what I wanted to do, but I thought, 'Just in case.' And I completely forgot about it and then in August I got this letter of acceptance. And so I went."

The transition from almost full-time political commitment to school was not easy. The intense political pressure that she had felt within movement collectives during the early seventies in Santa Barbara—the pressure to live an exemplary political life, to devote all of her efforts to authentic political work, preferably with the working class—still haunted her. "The first couple of years I spent at UCLA I really didn't get much done. I was still suffering from feeling that it wasn't legitimate for me to be in school at all, that I should be working in a factory. I was still judging myself in that narrow way, on the basis of relationships I wasn't even still having with people! I wasn't even relating to these people [in Santa Barbara] and yet I still hung on."

Trying to remain accountable to her political conscience while in school, Barressi found the going tough. "I was in a study group with some people I'd met through the Lawyers Guild and at the same time not doing very good in school, 'cause I was so distracted by this political stuff, and just distracted emotionally. I felt very judgmental of the other students and their films. I thought, 'There's no political film makers here at all; they're all into building their careers.' So I felt very isolated; I felt socially alienated." This sense of isolation was intensified by her father's death two years into her schooling. "I was considering dropping out at that time, and his death really made the decision for me." Her first attempt at linking politics and career had ended in failure, a victim, in large part, of the same forces that had short-circuited similar efforts in others.

For the next four years, Barressi moved from job to job, mostly within the film industry: working with a film collective on a documentary about Peru, a "shit job" with a large company "splicing film together all day long," grant-proposal writing for an educational company, and an aborted film project on black activist Frederick Douglass. Then, six years ago, she enrolled in film school again, determined to make a better go of it. She "really enjoyed school this time, very much," she recalls. "All the confusion, the hangover about politics and personal life" no longer plagued her thinking. In 1983, in her third year of school, she told us: "I feel happier than I've felt in a long time. And I think it's because I'm finally learning some skills that I feel good about and actually seeing the results of using those skills." She was particularly excited about a video-tape documentary on the draft that she "ended up doing everything on —directing it, producing it, and editing it."

This new-found stability involved some definite changes in her approach to having a career: "I really tried for a long time to find work that I could do that would be personally satisfying and would satisfy my desire to do politically useful work, and I guess I'm at the point now where I'm willing to compromise more than I was in the past."

Today, Barressi regrets the time that she spent struggling with the morality of having a career. Film professionals her own age who "started earlier [now] have their foot in the door." She wishes that she had started earlier: "I've only been seriously pursuing a career for the past few years. Until then I was really in the fog; I was floundering. My own willingness to spend a lot of time trying to figure out how I can be a correct Marxist-Leninist kept me from realizing a lot of my creative potential." Her intense drive to build her career leaves little time for political work. "I'm working my ass off now; I've become practically a workaholic," she notes. "I'm too busy. I've become, really for the first time, really focused. It's like I'm finally catching up. I finally have a direction in my life at this point, and it's enough just to focus on that."

Although she has gone to several demonstrations, Barressi does not count that as "political work," which she defines as commitment to put a great deal of time and energy into organizational matters. She would not go to meetings, "even if I did have time." Recently a young woman, perhaps twenty-four or twenty-five years old, came to ask her to support a local political project. The encounter reveals Sheila Barressi's feelings about continuities and discontinuities between her present life and her activist past. "She came over and she told me this long story about how she'd gone to Nicaragua and El Salvador and how incredible the experience was. And it reminded me so much of how I felt when I got back from Vietnam. It touched me. I listened to her for a long time, and she had so much enthusiasm and passion, it was kind of encouraging. But I got into an argument with her, because I said, 'Why aren't you out there on campus, trying to get young people involved with this?' Then I said, 'I just really don't have time. I mean, I care a lot, but I really feel as though I just don't have time to get involved in a lot of organizational stuff. I'll be a warm body. And I'll give you some money, but . . .' And I guess I took some pleasure in telling her what I thought some of the lessons of the [New Left] movement were, and what they could learn from it. And she was real interested in my experience. But it made me feel kind of old, though. I mean, especially, when I heard myself saying, 'I just really don't have time.' I have postponed a career for fifteen years and I'm finally getting into it—that's where I want to focus. But it was just funny hearing myself saying it. I felt a little bit guilty, but not a lot. I was telling her, 'You know, it's not just because people my age don't have the energy. It's literally what daily life is like when you're an adult!' "

Living as an "adult," combined with the difficulties of finding work in a depressed, highly competitive business, has, of course, generated other adjustments and compromises in Barressi's life over the past decade. She may not feel much guilt, but she is concerned about the moral effects of her decisions, and has resolved not to compromise too much. In 1983 she analyzed the film industry: "You have to prostitute yourself. That's probably what I'll end up doing. . . . For example, I'll probably end up, for a while at least, being willing to work on commercials, which I thought in the past I would *never* do, not in a million years! But now I don't really have much of a choice. . . . If you're a craftsperson or a technician in film, if you don't practice your craft you're never gonna be good at it. And the way you practice it is by making a living at it. And the way to make a living at it is to be willing to work where there's money, and that's commercials. Not just commercials, but schlock of various kinds. I'd still draw the line: I would not work in a creative capacity on a commercial. I'll be a technician, an editor, or a production assistant, [but] I won't be a director of a commercial or a producer of a commercial." The opportunity to work in public-affairs programming or public television has in fact enabled Barressi to avoid most of the compromises she worried about while still in film school.

Barressi sees her withdrawal from politics as temporary. "I don't see myself as being real active organizationally until I'm more secure financially and until I feel that I'm really using my skills in the way I want to use them." Her need to "be in a formal atmosphere with people who are trying to think politically about what needs to be done" is moderated by her reluctance to become involved in organizations. "I don't want to get involved with just any organization, because I just have this view of myself that I wasted too much time already in organizations and study groups. I have zero patience with narrow-minded, mechanical Marxist theoretical discussions, discussions that seem to be still centering on how do we make sure the American Left is pure in a Marxist-Leninist sense. Some years ago I just threw up my hands. I was just sick; I couldn't follow it anymore, all this shit." When she does become active, Barressi asserts, it will be through using her film and television skills "in a political way" and through what she sees as the "natural" process of working with others in her workplace. "Wherever I am, I'm willing to be fighting for my own rights and the rights of others." She appears to be making good on this promise: almost all of her film projects in graduate school and many of the documentaries she has worked on at the station have had political overtones and were framed by a progressive perspective. Her first "solo" project at the station, a documentary about prison life which aired in January 1988, was a technical and professional success, and clearly the product of heartfelt social concern.

Like almost all the respondents in the activist cohort, Barressi has lowered her expectations of revolutionary change without changing her values and is keenly aware of this shift in her thinking. "In 1970 I saw

America as a very sick society, which a growing mass-movement was going to transform. Today I see America as a very sick society, which is going to get much sicker and more life-threatening to the whole planet before it gets better. Revolution seems much less likely to me now than it did in 1970; I have less hope now than I did then that socialism is an achievable goal in the next fifty years. In fact, I think there's almost no hope of seeing even the beginnings of socialist revolution in the next fifty years." We have lost "the kind of vision we had in the old days," she feels. "We have no models anymore, no clear way of knowing what approaches 'true' socialism, and no clearly defined revolutionary group-ings in the U.S. at all anymore."

However, this lack of models or clear-cut visions provides "an incred-ible opportunity—if we aren't destroyed, before we have a chance, by a nuclear holocaust—to build an entirely new kind of revolutionary move-ment. Being cut adrift is, in some ways, a very healthy turn of events." In contrast to what she views as the narrow focus of the student move-ment and New Left, Barressi believes this new movement must involve change "on many levels in society—people can influence others at what-ever level of society they live and work in. This influence will operate slowly, in subtle ways through daily relationships, relationships over long periods of time, over generations." Like Martha Koch and Denise Saal, Barressi seeks political hope and the personal strength to go on in the promise of incremental change. As we have seen in previous cases, this perspective can function to sustain radical commitment when radical social transformation appears to be a lost cause, at least for the foreseeable future.

It makes sense that Sheila Barressi strives to justify and give meaning to her life, particularly her career concerns, within this perspective. "I can take advantage of my own social privileges," she says, "to make the small changes that, added to the small changes of millions of others, can make a difference in the long run. I've decided I have to adapt, in some sense, to the 'success' values which I so despised years ago, to use every possible advantage and privilege of being a middle-class, overeducated white American, and to use my skills for change *and* per-sonal fulfillment." Still, even as she expresses these feelings, she finds it impossible to feel completely comfortable with them. "I don't know— is it all a question of growing older, of adaptation, and rationalization for one's accommodation?" she asks. Barressi tried, at the end of one interview, to describe her ambivalence and indecisiveness. Her words provide a fitting conclusion to this chapter. "I think we are somewhat of a lost generation. We're caught between two worlds: a world that we thought we were about to create that never came about, and a world that really is that we're not quite adjusted to. That makes it difficult. It's not easy for us to know what we want."

6

Where Are They Now?
Case Studies in Withdrawal,
Reversal, and Continuity

The previous chapter focused on former activists whose present lives display considerable continuity with their past. Thus, even members of the "disengaged radicals" subgroup continue to hold radical political beliefs. But the largest group of our respondents, while remaining true to many of their youthful convictions, would no longer define themselves as radicals. This third cluster of individuals we have called "left-liberals."

LEFT-LIBERALS

All members of the left-liberal group ceased their political activity in the years immediately following the riots. As we observed in Chapters 3 and 4, when the apocalyptic expectations of 1970 faded and the level of student protest dramatically declined, some individuals came to experience politics and political organization as increasingly alienating, pervaded with risks and tensions that seemed unnecessary in light of a growing belief that little was being accomplished. Such withdrawal was motivated not only by perceptions of futility, but also by a feeling that the movement's demands for self-sacrifice were now blocking aspirations for self-fulfillment. Several were unnerved by the intensity of the street battles of 1970 and the "preparing for revolution" period that followed. Their alienation from political involvement was marked by a personal effort to rediscover, outside the political arena, the movement's lost spiritual and communal promise.

Alienated from radical commitment and shunning politically moored settings, most of those men and women who withdrew from active participation in the New Left in the early seventies have, not surprisingly, changed many of their political views. Nevertheless, their attitudes are still considerably to the left of all but one of the nonactivists; they show little attraction to conservative ideology. In what ways have they changed? How do their current vocational commitments and daily lives reflect the continuing influence of their participation in the student movement and counterculture?

Although a majority are no longer active participants in political life, many are trying to practice personalized versions of the values they once expressed through intense political commitment. We begin with Bill McNaughton, who is now teaching chemistry in central Oklahoma.

"I Refuse to Spend My Life Working So That Someone Else Can Make Huge Profits off the People"

"This is the flattest land you're ever gonna see," Bill McNaughton said when he met us at the airport. He was right. We got on the highway that ran outside of town, where the dry Oklahoma plain stretched to the horizon, its even contours broken occasionally by an oil well, an isolated building, or a barbed wire fence. We searched in vain for a small hill, a low rise, even a dip in the road. As we reached the outskirts of the town, a single tumbleweed rolled past.

A position as an assistant professor of chemistry at the state university brought Bill McNaughton from Santa Barbara (where he continued to reside while a graduate and postdoctoral student at UCSB) to this southwestern city in the fall of 1980. He bought a small two-bedroom ranch house that same year. Unmarried, he lives now alone, although he lived with a woman friend for two of the past seven years. His academic career has been very successful, and he is known and respected in his field. He received tenure and was promoted to associate professor in 1986.

McNaughton has slowly adjusted, he says, to the climate and geography of Oklahoma, coming to appreciate the distinctiveness of its unsullied expanse. He has had a good deal more trouble adjusting to its culture. "There's nothing to be positive about, really! The politics here are very conservative. Like, if you look up *churches* in the yellow pages of the phone book, you'll see more than five pages of entries. I'm sitting here and I see this town of 150,000 people and out of them, 80 percent refuse to use their native intellectual ability. Every year, every day, that I've lived here I get a little more alienated. I had been alienated for a while after the sixties, but I've lived here so long—living in the heart of the beast, as someone once said—and the environment, it's too overwhelming."

He is also bothered by the prevailing attitudes toward women. "People here think women should have two kids, no career, and stay in the house all their life. Men here cannot handle women who show that they might have some kind of intelligence, who are willing to speak their own mind. I met this woman because she had gone through a lot of men, because either they couldn't tolerate her because she's a very intelligent person, or she couldn't tolerate them because of what they expected of her. They expected her to be a traditional woman who would shut up when she was told to shut up. Attitudes here are extremely sexist. This part of the country is really disappointing at times, or it's just depressing. I don't know—it's just bizarre!"

Isolation, McNaughton says, contributes to these "backward, ingrown attitudes." The university's more varied, multiracial environment alleviates the problem to some extent, and he is grateful to have his tenured appointment at a time when the academic job market is very poor. In sum, he says, "I can live here. The honest-to-God truth is I don't care too much for it. But I can live with it. I just figure there aren't that many places I could go where I would be that happy, 'cause there aren't that many university jobs."

Although it would have improved his job prospects (and his earning potential) considerably, at no time did McNaughton consider working for private industry. While the vast majority of his fellow graduate students in chemistry pursued careers in the private sector and now earn, he states, double his salary, McNaughton valued the greater freedom of university research and the opportunity to pursue his interest in theoretical problems (his specialty is chemical reactions in the gas sphere, and his recent work is focused on problems of interest to both chemists and astronomers). But there were moral considerations as well. "In part, my decision has to do with this being a capitalist society. By definition, industries are there to make profits; that is how they work in this society. I refuse to spend my life working so that someone else can make huge profits off the people. I don't want to go work for General Motors, because I can see what they do. I wouldn't want to work for a company that was composed of a bunch of liars and thieves. And I avoid science that could be directly or indirectly harmful."

These beliefs about sexism and industrial capitalism are traceable to McNaughton's involvement in the student movement—indeed, that is the source he himself identifies—but are no longer connected to political action. McNaughton belongs to no political organization and has very little interest in participating in political activities. The residue of student protest lies beneath the surface. McNaughton admits that he does not routinely raise political questions in the course of daily conversations with his colleagues and friends or even in his private life. "Inside me, it's still there," he declares. "It's on the edge, but it's part of me." "On the edge?" he is asked. "Maybe someday," he muses, "when the time is right . . ."

McNaughton tends to draw a sharp line between the world of political life and the world of everyday life, and does not seem to believe that he is capable of crossing it. Nor does he want to at present. "I'm really concerned now with trying to do things with my own life," he states. Although he takes an interest in politics, keeps up on current affairs, and has definite opinions on political issues, he cannot see himself as the kind of person who would go beyond this realm of limited participation. He puts it this way: "I'm sure if you just went to Vietnam or China, you wouldn't find everyone devoting all their days, every hour of every day, to politics. I mean, some people just aren't political, that's what I'm saying—or only political in certain ways. I'm in between. I'm more of a scientist than a political activist. There's different ways to be political, there's different ways to be anything. Do you like music? Do you like music enough that you want to make your living cutting records, and live your life that way, or do you just like listening to it every night?"

When pressed, he searches for a stance that will allow him to be true to himself while remaining accountable to his past. "I think that I am political. I think that being political in my own life [is] what I should be doing. That's what I want to do. I'm going to be fairly political as a scientist, but *as a scientist*. It's within the context of what I do best. What I can't do best is be a true social activist, an organizer in the streets. Which you know I tried. But it's not me. It's just that it's not me."

McNaughton's political views are similar, he feels, to those he held twenty years ago. Aid to the Nicaraguan Contras sparks particular anger.

"I hope you don't think that I could possibly be for them. Aren't they mostly former national guardsmen for Somoza? The only aid that I think they should get is that I hope they all get rounded up and shot. I have not changed at all on those things. Of course, I don't say that to people who live here. It's interesting how people around here believe that jerk in the White House when he says that they're 'freedom fighters.' Sure, right!" The Iran-Contra scandal and Oliver North generate a similar response. "Ollie for dictator! I am really disappointed in the American public, and how they are falling head over heels for someone who just came right out and said that he's a liar. And I sit here and think, my God, we have a nation of people who just take their ethics—you know, our moral values and moral standards—and can just put them away when they want to. This is just really hurting me." On both issues, McNaughton's alienation from the public realm and his strongly negative feelings about his fellow citizens reinforce his withdrawal from political life even as they help to sustain his leftist beliefs.

He has changed his views in one area, however. "I've made a complete reversal on the question of how to accomplish things as an individual in this society. Independently of your own political, moral, or economic persuasion, the only way you are going to propagate your own beliefs is to work your ass off. And the only good people of any society are those who work their asses off. I don't believe that the average member of any society is going to do this unless she or he has the incentive." The threat of economic deprivation can serve as such an incentive, he believes. He makes it clear that he is not advocating laissez-faire capitalism or the dismantling of the welfare state. In fact, McNaughton believes in a more socialistic system, in which the government meets the public's need for housing and other basic necessities, operates public utilities, exerts more control over corporations, and sets an upper limit on how much one person can earn. He also is a strong supporter of the labor movement. His views, then, lean in a left direction but contain a strong work-ethic component.

Perhaps this attitude is explained by his own devotion to hard work and long hours. His passion for science—and "passion" is his word here —is a powerful, driving force in his life. He frequently launches into a long, detailed, but very enthusiastic account of some scientific problem he is working on or some puzzle that has him baffled. More than any of the other respondents, he seems genuinely excited about his vocation. The questioning spirit of his youth is still there, but instead of being employed within the political realm, it is now being directed at understanding the chemistry of the stars.

"I Feel I'm Leading a Very Schizophrenic Existence"

"I feel guilty because I'm not politically active because the world is so totally fucked up. I play video games, I'm smoking a lot of dope, and being nice to my friends—and I feel guilty about it." The speaker is Joyce Weston. It is 1983. We are seated on the floor of her room in a large Victorian-style house that she shares with two other people. Weston laughs when she finishes this statement, but she does that often in our conversations. It is her way of emphasizing the hopelessness or absurdity of something. Then she continues: "It's not something I think about much, but every once in awhile I go, 'God, what are people doing to each other out there?' Then I keep thinking, 'Well, my life is so easy.' Then I keep thinking, 'You arrogant bitch. You must be concerned about other people's lives too.' I say, 'Okay, I'll be concerned about the people I like.' That's as far as I've gotten. I'm not doing anything for humanity."

This vignette seems to capture much of Joyce Weston's recent life and its relationship to her past. Although the guilt is significant, Weston is not heavily burdened by these feelings. Faced with the seemingly insurmountable problem of changing the world, she finds meaning and significance in caring for her friends. Alienated from much of her environment, she seeks relief in the small pleasures of Space Invaders and cannabis. As she puts it, "I have a lot of escape mechanisms."

Prior to this 1983 interview, Weston had quit her job and was "wandering" without any particular itinerary or destination. Eventually, however, she had to go back to work, and she found a job as a secretary, once again, with a large communications corporation. The company ran itself into the ground within a year, however, so a few more months of unemployment followed. Her next job had more positive consequences. It was with a small advertising agency, and although she was hired as an office manager, she was able to begin learning print production. The firm sent her to school for a year of training—"accomplishing the visual sensation of ideas with paper and ink"—and she found the work interesting. Then came a major opportunity: the largest advertising agency in the city had an opening in its production department. Offered a chance to be second in command, she took the job.

In the mid-eighties, Weston still felt torn between what she needed and wanted to do for her personal development and what she had to sacrifice to achieve those goals. While she was excited about finally having "a legitimate thing, a skill," several things about her situation troubled her. The larger firm, she said, was "emotionally barren," and she had to "relate to it completely differently" than the jobs she had held in the past. There could be no "community" there, no "tribal spirit." Even the people her own age who worked there were "shallow and superficial." "They aren't my contemporaries," Weston concluded, because they "haven't had the same experiences" and are not "coming from the same place."

The experience focused her attention, she says, on the entire practice of advertising. "The administrators are all sleazy. They're dishonest, lying on personal as well as business levels. Just lying people. And there are a lot of alienated values at that agency. It frightens me, every time I meet someone that is twenty-five years old and they have been studying marketing and advertising since they were in high school. I'm suspicious of those people, because basically advertising is extremely immoral in this country. The American capitalistic culture lives off of selling trash to the people that live there. If it was information to send the nation, that is one thing. That's okay. But basically they are just trying to sell people things that people don't need."

How does she reconcile these attitudes, we asked her, with working there? She tried to explain how her own personal involvement did not necessarily involve her in the "sleaze." "I'm not selling any of those [trash] products. The energy that I put in, is to sell video games, which I think are just fine. I think that is part of it. I am selling Chevron Oil, but I did the [Chevron] advertising for [public television's] 'Creativity,' with Bill Moyers, so I didn't mind putting energy into that. That's not too bad. And I don't buy a lot of that trash. I tell my friends not to buy it. I'm very honest with people. If there is a product that my advertising agency is selling and somebody asks me about it, I'll tell you the truth." Further, she sharply distinguished the role of the "media" people at the agency, the "prima donnas" who come up with the selling strategies and design the ads, from "down to earth" production people like herself.

Weston separated her identity as a moral, sensitive person from the alienating nature of certain aspects of her work. "I go in to work in the morning, and I leave, come home and smoke a joint, and talk to my friends. It's a different life, and I do put on a different facade when I'm there. The person that I am at work and the person that I am at home are different parts of me. I feel I'm leading a very schizophrenic existence."

Weston's alienation from the advertising industry is paralleled by her alienation from American society. "I just think it's sick. I think capitalism is in a state of decay. I think this whole society has lost control of itself. I think the materialism has warped values as to what's important. Greed runs rampant in America: give people a little bit and all they want is more, more, more." These feelings did not lead her to become involved in politics again, however; she holds out little hope for changing society. Instead, she dealt with this problem much in the same way that she coped with her alienation from work, which was to withdraw into her personal world and to focus her energies on making that very limited environment a better place. "I have not been living a political commitment. I see my personal life, my friends, as where my commitment is— putting some of the things that were theory in Santa Barbara into action, but on a very individual scale. My guilt about not getting involved in politics [isn't] enough that I would go out of my way for something to do. I would work on a personal thing," helping people, "being there for them."

"You don't have to be political to be radical. I don't think I've plugged into society. I think that is very radical. I think it is important to become desocialized as much as one can: you may decide to turn around and embrace the values that have been placed on you by society. You just have to keep reexamining, you just have to keep saying, 'Hey, am I feeling good about my life right now?' Now society is set up to dull people's senses. The society is not based on having to ask those questions to yourself. I do think it is important to ask those questions, and I do it from a personal level. When I have felt that I was starting to stagnate or when I was unhappy, I asked, 'Why? What can I do to change it?' Now, how to do that on a mass level, I don't know."

"I don't think my political beliefs that I had and was acting on in 1970 have changed. I'm not suddenly ready to register with the Republican party, and I'm not into the idea of getting a job at the top of the corporation. I still think the government is fucked and is ripping everybody off.

I don't trust any of them. I think that capitalism is collapsing right before our eyes. I think there are a lot of people out there having hard economic times, so they come in and they steal from you. And Ronald Reagan —it's a living nightmare! And I'm against nuclear war; I'm against the death penalty. I don't want to put up a new parking lot across the street. [But] I'm not doing anything to make those things happen. I know my life is very insular, but it's the one I'm living."

The explanation, she said, lies with changes in herself at a more basic level. "I was naive [in 1970]. I thought I could change it all, I think I really did. I was eighteen years old. I was very idealistic. Something happened, in between Santa Barbara and now." A disillusionment, not so much with political ideals "so much as [with] this whole concept of brotherhood and sisterhood, 'we're a family struggling together,'" kept her from going beyond her personal concerns.

Moreover, in reacting against what she sees as her youthful naivete, Weston tries to avoid viewing the world in an "all or nothing kind of framework." "Really political people still believe in the good guys and the bad guys," but Weston does not "think it's really that easy anymore." And although she feels the government is "fucked," she finds it hard to align herself with any organized political grouping or to feel comfortable participating in political activity. "I could walk around ten years ago and make claims as to 'this is the way things should be.' It's not so easy any more."

Contact with protest politics has tended to reinforce the distance she feels between her past and the present, between the exciting days of the sixties and the "nightmare" of the eighties: "Every once in a while there will be a peace march or something, and I'll go past it, but it's always so depressing. Because the spirit is gone. I remember I went to the big peace march in November of 1969 in San Francisco, and oh! that was the most incredible experience. I don't remember how many people, but thousands and thousands of people marching through the street, and all different kinds of people. And it was really very moving. Now, it's, you know, no one shows up. There was a demonstration down at the park not too long ago, Third World Liberation Week or something, and there was maybe 250 people. The vitality was gone. You know when not too many years ago you see thousands of people all chanting together and going through the street and having a beautiful, peaceful demonstration, and now you have to face 250 people, and it's just . . ." Here she pauses, searching for a way to describe the vast dissimilarity. Finally: "A comparison between the two is superfluous."

Her few positive experiences with contemporary radicalism have involved feminist music. She likes the music—but for the music, not the politics. "They've had a couple of political benefits that I've attended, and I sort of identify with the topics in the women's community, but primarily I went because I was interested in hearing them more than I was really supporting the cause, if the truth be known." And while she expresses strong support for feminism, she also states: "I don't consider myself firstly a feminist. I consider myself first a person." Once again, she is reluctant to define herself in political terms, preferring to find self-definition in personal life.

As for her future, Weston told us in 1983 that she would like to set up a small advertising agency "that was a little more low-key with more mature people" and promoted "products that people should really know about because they're good for you, or they are interesting." She also thought about getting married and having children, but these thoughts were more playful musings than indications of serious goals or plans. "I'm taking it as it comes," she declared. "I have no idea what the future is going to be like, but I'm looking around and going, 'Well shit, I haven't been doing too bad.' That's where I get my moral support."

Weston is still working in advertising, still specializing in print production, still single, and still living in the same city. In between 1983 and now, we discovered in our most recent conversation, there have been some not unexpected changes. Her goal of starting a small advertising agency with a few friends was achieved in 1984, but the effort lasted only one year. "We realized that we were not really emotionally suited to play advertising," she explains, "and so one night we got really angry and quit all our clients!" With the money that she earned through the business, Weston decided to travel for a year, visiting Europe and friends across the United States. It was as if she was reliving her earlier experiences as a young radical, "just kind of wandering around." Returning to her home city, she started doing free-lance print production work, and then got a job working for a large agency, in a position almost exactly like the one she had held before. Her wanderlust has not dissipated, however: she is now making plans to live in England for a year or more, although employment is a stumbling block. She insists, "If I had my way right now, I would end up with a big chunk of money and just wander. I just love going someplace and trying to make myself as invisible as possible and wander around and see how these people are living."

Her cynicism about advertising, her commitment to her friends, her alienation from the wider culture have not changed. Yet recent political events have had a noticeable impact. The Iran-Contra scandal brought her left-liberal views farther into the open. "I was ranting and raving around my office. There were too many people that I work with that were all whipped up—the Oliver North bit, you know? So I would sit down with them and tell them one thing that they really needed to learn was critical thinking!" And Weston reports that she does "lots of liberal things, like give money to the sanctuary movement and Live Aid, and [support] the Amnesty International tour when it went around." But this stirring has certainly not brought back any desire to become involved in political activities on a regular basis. In fact, her current passion is rock and roll history: collecting books, records, and other materials, and even doing research for a book she would like to write someday. As her comments make clear, her limited political involvement is closely tied to rock music. In these ways, then, the personal-liberation side of the counterculture continues to exert more influence on her life than the political and moral framework provided by the radical movement.

"I Guess I Didn't Want My Whole Life to Be Causes"

Joyce Weston's and Bill McNaughton's recent experiences illustrate how values and commitments that have their roots in the New Left experience may find expression in private life even where public political activity is avoided. For both, alienation is a central theme, and their personal values clash with their environment. Both have chosen to contend with this problem in an individualized and, for the most part, depoliticized manner. Indeed, they are alienated from politics as well. Yet, in these depoliticized ways, they continue to fulfill at least some of the aspirations of the New Left and counterculture: self-expression, autonomy, personal liberation, continue to be crucial issues in both their lives. Significantly, both Weston and McNaughton assert that in their private lives they are still "radical" or "political," and appeared to feel that they could make such assertions because they were, in fact, remaining true to the reasoning of this "personal liberation" dimension of movement philosophy. Further, their statements about what they will not do, either in their work or in other aspects of their lives—what they do not approve of, what they cannot bring themselves to support—appear to be motivated by the same kind of social responsibility that was applauded by the New Left. The imprinting of that movement may be largely hidden from public view, but it is most certainly there.

A similar pattern is evident in other stories. Ellen Hemmings still works as a nurse, and is still very committed to social responsibility and service, although she has moved from the Veterans Administration institution to a smaller public hospital in a Willamette Valley community in Oregon. After working in the critical-care unit for many years, she recently switched to pediatrics. Marriage (to a long-haul truck driver) and the birth of a daughter (now three years old) have contributed a sense of greater stability and "ordinariness" to her life, but she also reacts against the conventional nature of that situation. "I'm really feeling the effects of marriage. I'm really rebelling against it. I wish it could be different. You know, I really enjoy my daughter and I love my husband very, very much, but I don't like all the work that I have to do! Like, I enjoy child rearing, but there's a lot to it that's not a lot of fun; I don't have much free time."

Although Hemmings is not involved in organizations or public activities ("I guess I didn't want my whole life to be causes"), her political views can be characterized as left-liberal. When she does vote, she votes Democratic. She supports Jesse Jackson's campaign (but thinks he does not have a chance), and deplores President Reagan and his administration's policies. Indeed, she has a deep-seated antipathy to most forms of established, hierarchical authority and to what she describes as the ubiquitous racism and sexism in medical practice. This tendency sometimes leads her to criticize hospital authorities (both administrators and doctors) when she thinks their actions are wrong or unfair. Most important, she makes a point of explaining this behavior as guided by beliefs and commitments rooted in her student activist past.

Hemmings recalls that while working for the Veterans Administration, she "came into contact with a lot of very angry blacks," primarily nursing assistants, who "did not like white women if they have any kind of authority." The other nurses, almost all of whom were white, frequently clashed with the assistants they were supervising. Hemmings dealt with the situation differently. "I just tried to treat the nursing assistants with as much respect as possible, because I figured if you show them some respect, then they're not as angry at you. They're not angry with you as a person, they're angry at you as a symbol. I try to ignore [the hospital hierarchy] as much as possible; it's sort of a caste system, really, and I tend to ignore those kinds of castes. And some of my fellow nurses just can't understand why I don't get angry at my assistants, but I think you have to figure out a way that's going to best benefit the patients as well as have the personnel feel good about themselves. I just think you have to give people credit for being human beings." Hemmings does not use confrontational tactics; her strategy is to attack the problem by setting an example. "There is a lot of racism in our society, and a lot of white women do not like black people. It's been really difficult for me to accept that and not get angry at it when I see it [from the other nurses], but I don't think anger changes it. I just try not to be a racist myself, and I think just by acting differently, the other nurses can see there is an alternative."

Kristen Van Duinen and Paul Little are two other members of our activist group who can be categorized as left-liberals. Although we have lost touch with both of them in recent years (Van Duinen continues to live in Greece but several changes in address resulted in a loss of contact, while Little dropped from sight after his marriage of two years broke up in 1984 and he separated from his wife and young child), our last extended communication, in 1983, found them still expressing commitment to New Left principles such as social and economic justice, antiimperialism, and antiracism. Moreover, though we lack detailed information on their current lives, brief letters and occasional news received by mutual friends suggest that both continue to live in ways that reflect the vocational commitments they made in the late 1970s. Van Duinen still supports herself by teaching English in Athens, and her economic situation remains fairly marginal. Little apparently still hopes to build a career recording and producing rock and reggae music. In each case, then, alienation from political involvement is paralleled by orientation to a somewhat nonconventional lifestyle.

"I Am a White Person Sharing a Few Bits of Knowledge with Those Who Need So Much"

Terry Lennox and David Carroll also became depoliticized following the period of apocalyptic expectations, but, unlike the cases discussed above, their stories reveal a reemergence—even if on a very small scale

—of political commitments. First, David Carroll. In the aftermath of the riots, he was "drifting," deeply disturbed by the violence that he witnessed during those events and uncertain about what to do with his life. That period of confusion lasted only a year, however; the spiritual and religious concerns that developed in the wake of the Isla Vista rebellion (and in the emotional upheaval he experienced in reaction to its violence) motivated Carroll to enter a Methodist seminary to study for the ministry. While his fascination with Eastern religions remained strong, Carroll recognized that he had to find an American religious context for continuing his search for spiritual meaning. After completing his studies, he became an assistant pastor for a congregation in Southern California.

Carroll never completely forgot or rejected the political and moral values that he held in Isla Vista. His withdrawal from activism in the early 1970s represented only a temporary depoliticization; it was a response to the apocalyptic expectations of that time, and thus only one phase in a continuing struggle to find ways to integrate political commitment with daily life. Carroll had developed a deep interest in "liberation theology" while at the seminary, and was soon organizing educational meetings in his church on the suffering of people in Latin America. Moreover, although his congregation included many workers who were employed in the defense industry and he had to move cautiously on issues related to arms control (indeed, he is generally reluctant to be "too open" about his views), Carroll supported the 1983 nuclear freeze campaign. He was appointed pastor of his own congregation two years ago, and continues to seek practical, low-key ways to express his left-liberal politics through his religious faith and practice. Accordingly, while his political involvement in progressive organizations or in protest actions over the past decade has been minimal, Carroll's personal life and the approach he takes to his vocation are both characterized by orientations developed during his days as a New Left activist.

Finally, consider Terry Lennox's story. After leaving Isla Vista and moving to Northern California, Lennox spent almost eight years trying to establish a career as a writer and editor. He wrote short stories, poems, essays—he even tried his hand at a weekly column for a local newspaper. Several pieces were published in small literary journals, but his writing provided a very marginal living. He supported himself with odd jobs, such as working in restaurants, hardware stores, and (for two years) a social service agency. He was involved in political activity only when an issue emerged (such as the fate of the local library) that was of importance to the small Marin County communities where he made his home. The experience of Isla Vista in 1970 had shaken him so badly, Lennox explained, that political activism would never again be an important part of his life.

Then there were some dramatic changes in his life. In the summer of 1982 Lennox met and fell in love with a white South African woman who was vacationing in California. They were married a few months later. Because his wife, a medical technician, had difficulty finding suitable employment in the United States and Lennox still yearned for a position as an editor in a publishing house, they decided in early 1984 to move to South Africa to find work. They believed (correctly, as it turned out) that Lennox's writing and editing skills would be in demand there, and the trip would give him an opportunity to see his wife's hometown of Johannesburg. They planned to stay one year. Four years later, they are still living in Johannesburg. Their reasons for staying on, and Lennox's experiences as an American in South Africa, were detailed in a letter we received from him in the fall of 1987.

"We have stayed," the letter begins, "for various reasons; having good jobs has been a primary one, another is the contact I've begun to make with the 'other world' of blacks." This contact has become a central part of his life and work, and it developed, Lennox states, in several phases. First, there was his initial experience as a somewhat distanced "observer" (his term) of apartheid and its "horrible features"—conditions that were immediately apparent to him but, because of his (and his wife's) white skin and upper-middle-class status, did not fundamentally affect his life. He enjoyed his job as an editor, and his contact with blacks at this point was limited, consisting mainly of routine interactions with the service workers who attended to the predominantly white citizenry. This first phase was followed by an increased awareness of the inhuman, "unnatural" (again, his term) character of the South African system. When mass protests in the townships broke out and large numbers of blacks were killed by security forces, "I began to feel that these deaths were not just another isolated incident, seemingly of another country, divorced from where I was. I stopped viewing the uniformed gardeners and maids and gas station attendants and guards I passed every day as just a sad part of a unique foreign structure. . . . I decided to start volunteer-teaching English language skills once a week." He felt he had to make some personal commitment to addressing the situation there. He took a training course through a local literacy organization and soon was teaching his first students at a church near his apartment. These students were all service workers who had come to Johannesburg to find work and lived apart from their families back home in the rural areas. Lennox stresses the "personal satisfaction" he derived "from teaching some English to a few people who had missed earlier opportunities to learn it," although he recognizes that these efforts were largely symbolic: "Mostly, I valued the contact with blacks, who were becoming a bit less faceless to me." He developed a friendship with one student in particular, but the man had to return to the countryside when he dared to question his boss about his rights and was fired.

Lennox's third phase began in December of 1985, he states, when a number of whites were killed by landmines and bombs, and the "death toll from unrest in the black townships reached into the twenties and thirties on some days." The government declared a state of emergency and severe press censorship was instituted. Daily life for most South African whites, Lennox observes, continued much as it had before, but the spreading violence was frightening. Lennox and his wife considered moving to England.

They did not leave. Lennox decided to try to teach full time. He quit his editorial job and took a position in the English department of the black teacher-training college in Soweto. The pay is very low. He could not continue to work as an editor, because he "felt it was somewhat irrelevant to edit what most people can't read." Lennox has become strongly committed to education as part of the solution to his new nation's problems; teaching is his own way of contributing to the struggle to bring about a new South Africa, one where the black majority can take control of their lives and their land. He talks about his work with great passion and with a realistic understanding of its limitations. "The teaching is in many ways no more than a desperate attempt to partially rescue these teachers-to-be from twelve years of inferior education, and to provide them with their first opportunity to have English taught by an English-speaking teacher. The college for me is the only place I want to be working. I am a white person sharing a few bits of knowledge with those who need so much. Sometimes the class sings an African hymn to me. We have discussions about witchcraft and evolution. These daily interactions make South Africa a compelling place for me."

As was true of David Carroll, Lennox's withdrawal from political activism in the wake of the Isla Vista rebellion did not represent a permanent depoliticization or abandonment of the ideals embodied in the New Left. On the contrary, his resignation from his job as an editor (a job he had sought for close to nine years) and his related decision to teach full time, for very little pay, in a college for black South Africans exhibits a deep commitment to the New Left's vision of a selfless, socially responsible life of service.

NONPERSISTERS

Writing in 1965, one year after the Free Speech Movement upheaval at Berkeley and the Sproul Hall sit-in, Hal Draper (himself a veteran radical) had this to say about the activists who participated in that historic action: "Ten years from now, most of them will be rising in the world and in income, living in the suburbs, raising two or three babies, voting Democratic and wondering what on earth they were doing in Sproul Hall —trying to remember and failing" (Draper 1965:169). We have shown how inadequate this portrayal is for the vast majority of former student activists. The even more cynical assumption that these men and women "work on Wall Street these days, their inverted Y in a circle peace symbol . . . now a status symbol adorning the hoods of their Mercedes-Benzes" (Johnston 1982:3), has been shown to have little basis in fact. But might this image be accurate for that relatively small number of former activists who have, in fact, changed their political views considerably, who appear to have become political conservatives? Are these individuals now complacent suburbanites? Are they now unable to remember why they marched and sat in—and burned a bank? Even if most former activists remain relatively faithful to their youthful idealism, perhaps those who have given up on politics or on the Left have indeed "sold out."

The lives of these "nonpersisters" would seem to provide the testing ground for the radical-turned-stockbroker hypothesis. Steve Rubin's case suggests that even when veterans of the Isla Vista riots have moved well to the right of their youthful New Left radicalism, the change is quite a bit more complex than conventional wisdom supposes.

Eighteen years ago, when Rubin was released from the Chino State Correctional Institution after a ninety-day "diagnostic observation" stay (his second jail term for politically related offenses), he was, as we saw, a badly shaken young man. Fearful of being sent back to prison, he soon withdrew from all political activity. "If I kept doing what I was doing, I would have had a lot to fear. You know, you could go up the river for a long time." His means of escape from these fears was an old Boston whaler, and he did indeed become a fisherman, starting out as a deckhand on charter boats and then, after getting his one-hundred-ton captain's license in 1974, running charter boats himself. Finally, in 1976, he borrowed the money to buy his own boat. For the next seven years, he earned his living as a commercial fisherman, plying his trade along the south coast of California, often staying at sea for weeks at a time, usually sailing alone.

It was hard work, but it gave him, he said, "a feeling of self, a good healthy living." When we first interviewed him, in 1979, he tried to convey both the good and the bad sides to the job by telling a little story. "The other day I went up to Point Conception, and I got up in the morning and it was ground-zero fog; you couldn't see nothing in front of your face. So you have immediate stomach-churning anxiety at five A.M. And we got out to the fishing ground and I made one drop and the current was so bad—it was ripping. And the fog was just drizzle-wet. I had my glasses on and I couldn't see shit. I couldn't even find my gear after I put it in the water. I looked at the radar and there was four steamers coming, I looked in the water and there was sharks everywhere, and I just thought to myself, 'Fuck, this is the worst way to make a living in the world, it just sucks.' And then three hours later the sun was out, it was flat glassy calm, you could see for a hundred miles, the fish were biting like stink and there was no sharks in sight, and I thought, 'Boy, this has got to be the way to go.' There you have it, all in one day."

This tale provides a brief glimpse at the rather unique reality of Steve Rubin's life for most of the seventies, a life that was certainly very different from that experienced by the other respondents, all of whom at least kept their feet on dry land. Moreover, it makes more understandable the "rugged individualist" philosophy that has evolved out of his experiences. Having once believed, as he puts it, "that everything should be socialized and nationalized and everybody should have the same amount and everybody should love and live together, and competition in any field was abhorrent," Rubin became convinced that a laissez-faire economic system with unbridled competition was much more conducive to human betterment. "Left-liberals," he thinks, are "stuck in an intellectual rut. They've got blinders on, and they refuse to see the world as it really is. When Karl Marx was writing, he was looking at some fucking ugly sweatshops, and he was looking at fat cats who were making a lot of money, and terrible toiling conditions, and things were basically black and white. They're just not that way anymore; that's just not the way it is."

Rubin attributes these changes in his thinking directly to his experience as a fisherman, his experience "in the real world," experience that taught him the value of hard work, competition, and "hustling your ass off." In many ways, his attitudes came to resemble those of other small businessmen—for that is what he was, as an independent fisherman—who were constantly struggling to make ends meet (in a good year his income might have reached $20,000). A streak of anarchism ran through his politics, however, fueled by the continual clashes between fishermen and the government over such matters as protecting sea lions and porpoises. Regulations protecting these animals were perceived by fishermen as threats to their livelihood and by Rubin as an example of the "freedom-denying" character of the liberal state and the naiveté of liberal, guilt-ridden environmentalists. This anti-state position also came out of his student movement experience, however, an experience that was rooted "in a lifestyle that was not just politically motivated by a quest for freedom, but emotionally motivated toward freedom."

In sum, Rubin joined his New Left–style rebelliousness and emphasis on personal liberation with the self-protective views of the small independent producer. Rubin had moved to the right, but he was hardly the prototypical ex-radical gone straight: smoking dope every night as he sat on his boat in the anchorage while reading news magazines from cover to cover so he could keep up on world affairs, distinctly unconventional—at least by middle-class, status-conscious standards—he was following a more complicated path.

Further evidence for this judgment comes from Rubin's reflections on his student movement activities. While he was extremely bitter about what he believed were efforts by friends in the movement to make him feel guilty about "selling out," criticisms from people who had not had to pay the price he did for his actions and who therefore, he said, had no right to tell him how to live, he refused to repudiate or even distance himself from his past activist commitment. In fact, he took just the opposite stance toward his past. "I was young and I was bright and I was concerned, and I think it was a world-historical time that will be remembered in a positive kind of way forever, in terms of its impact on American society and its influence on the world," he told us in that first interview in the late seventies. "It was a very good experience. I think it helped me grow up tremendously, a tremendously maturing experience for me. And I'm very proud of everything we've done. I think we did the exact right thing."

Rubin was able to bring this stance into accord with the changes in his political views since those events by arguing that the actions of student protesters were made necessary, even dictated, by history. "I think it was just right for the times. History is a lot bigger than those events were. History said, 'Steve and Roger and Kristen—and all the people who are sympathetic—it's time to do something; it is time for a change.' Hegel called it a world-historical consciousness. There was a consciousness about the air, there was a world-historical feeling going on, that we were involved in a major type of change. Pot smoking and flowers and ending wars and being free and all kinds of things were to be, and we were to be part of that. There was a feeling about those times that we were doing something that was what we were supposed to do." In line with these feelings, Rubin was highly critical of those who wanted "people to go back to the way they were or admit that it was just a passing fancy and they never really meant it in the first place. Neither of those theses are viable as far as I'm concerned."

Such was Steve Rubin's political and cultural stance as he fished the Pacific coast during the 1970s. Recent years have brought some major changes in his life. Although these changes have not fundamentally altered the political perspective he expressed in that first interview, they have moved him in a new direction in other ways. By exploring these more recent experiences, we can gain a better understanding of the complexities of his "nonpersistence" and the inadequacies of assumptions about wholesale repudiation of the past by former activists who no longer identify with liberal or left politics.

In 1984, after seven years as a commercial fisherman, Rubin had to sell his boat and start a new career as a free-lance writer, concentrating on magazine articles that combined his fishing expertise with his still-intense interest in politics. "I want to get into writing [about] resource management issues," he states. "Investigative journalism: writing and

researching the current, hottest contemporary issues in resource management, because it holds all the political excitement that I've always
thrived on. I mean, it entails all these questions, right? It holds all of
the fun and ideology of politics about man's relationship to the universe
and things." With almost five years as a professional writer behind him,
Rubin has published several pieces in a national magazine for fishermen
on the relationship between the oil exploration business and commercial
fishing. He plans to try to market these pieces to the *New York Times*, the
Los Angeles Times, or some other widely circulated publication. He also
writes on a wide variety of other subjects, and here too his publication
record is successful enough to support him financially.

The initiative for this career change came from a combination of
factors. In 1980, Rubin was stricken with serious kidney disease and,
two years later, had to undergo a transplant. Although he was healthy
enough to fish by 1983, and did work his boat that season, the illness and
operation led him to reevaluate what he was doing with his life. He came
to the conclusion that "quality of life" was what was most important to
him and that he needed to make some changes. "I'll be thirty-six this
year," he explained to us at that time, "and I've been on the ocean for
twelve years now, and I don't want to be seventy-five and still on the
ocean. I love every now and then going out on the ocean and fishing,
but I want to write, [to] change my career and do some other things for
the next ten or twelve years." In addition, we believe his decision to take
up writing, rather than another occupation, reveals a desire to return to
the intellectually oriented life he led as a student, before he became a
fisherman. His vocation did not allow him many opportunities to express
that side of himself, but it always seemed to be lurking beneath the
surface. For example, he would condemn the pretensions of middle-
class intellectualism by constructing a detailed intellectual argument of
his own. He relished intellectual debate, and, as he himself stated, has
"always thrived" on political excitement. Writing gives him the chance
to meet that need.

Finally, Rubin decided to get married soon after his transplant, providing further incentive for cutting back on his sailing, both because it
would give him and his wife more time together and because she could
help support them while he worked to develop his writing to the point
where it could provide an adequate income. (He also talks of working

part time, captaining dive boats and fishing charters, until his writing career is established.) He hopes, he says, to earn a lot more money writing than he did fishing.

Rubin's approach to writing about resource management questions will be based, he says, on the same "individual rights philosophy" that he has held to for the past decade, but with "more of a libertarian than anarchist bent, maybe. I still consider myself a lover of freedom. And I would like to think that even in a libertarian or maybe anarchist vein that I react to current events still as a lover of freedom, and that is from whence the politics come." Accordingly, he is still highly critical of what he calls the "humanist save this, save that, movement" where the "good intentions of all the conservation groups actually beget a lot of pain and suffering in the ecological community." As an example, he cites the legislation protecting the California sea lion, legislation that he believes has led to overpopulation of the herd and consequent damage to the ecology of coastal islands and the halibut and sea bass populations.

Rubin intends, with his writing, to promote a more scientific analysis of these problems, countering the emotionalism of the environmentalists, using his investigative skills to dig out the necessary scientific information. At the same time, he thinks people like former Interior Secretary James Watt are equally bad. "The 'pave it' mentality is not a rational way to approach environmental questions either. Watt's a dangerous man. He's one of those guys that doesn't know where to draw the line. And the time is quickly coming when we can't pillage and rape as much as we want." The difference between Rubin's thinking and that of the environmentalists is that he "would like to see the regulation come from within [the person] and not from the state."

Rubin also makes a point of saying that his writing can serve as a voice for fishermen: "It gives me a chance to articulate for the thousands of guys who may not have had the benefit of a college education; it allows me to articulate their side of the coin for them. You know, some of these guys are poor Italian immigrants, you know, in their mid-sixties, and they know in their heart that [the arguments of the extreme environmentalists] are a lot of bull, but they don't know how to go about . . . it's very frustrating for them. They need a mouthpiece in Sacramento, and they need a mouthpiece in trade journals and what have you. So that's where I'm trying to fit in."

Although this noninterventionist approach to ecological questions bears a resemblance to the now dominant right-wing position, Rubin's anarchist/libertarian political philosophy leads him to take some decidedly "nonconservative" stands on other issues. "I still feel resisting the draft is a very individualistic and individualized act, and I salute that kid [Ben] Sasway. I salute anybody that fights conscription, for whatever reason they want," he emphasized in our 1984 conversation, referring to a young man who had recently been indicted for refusing to register for the draft. "Nobody should make any other person go off to war. I just have never believed that." On a broader scale, he suggested that "the common good" depends on the "individual freedoms obtained by society's members, whether it's not having to go to war, or being allowed to smoke pot, or being able to abort your baby, or whatever." Rubin admits to finding Reagan's "down-home individualism" attractive, but strongly opposes his conduct of foreign policy. "It reminds me of the policy of a very myopic, boneheaded conservative who wants to rattle the sabers and match missile for missile, and that worries me very much. I have problems with how I feel about the president, conflicts that I myself just haven't resolved. I mean, he frightens me. I'm a totally anti-nuke kind of person. Who needs to be able to destroy all the people in Russia forty times over? It's mindless."

In addition, Rubin has not lost his positive identification with his past or changed his positive assessment of the New Left. He still believes, "with no qualifications at all," that the protests against the war in Vietnam were necessary and right. "We probably saved a lot of lives. Probably saved a hell of a lot of lives." As for the movement as a whole, he insists that "the visions and the dreams will always be part of my life. I have the same dreams when it comes to the universal ones like peace and the ending of racism. You know that Elvis Costello song, 'What's So Funny About Peace, Love, and Understanding?' The feeling behind the song, and the beautiful things that are being said, and the intense, almost angry drive toward those things because you want them so bad 'cause they seem so wonderful—I still feel all of that." There is no question that Rubin remembers why he was in the streets of Isla Vista in 1970. Although his leftist radicalism may have faded, that memory is still vivid.

Finally, when we asked him four years ago if he was involved in any political activity, Rubin, like Weston and McNaughton, suggested that the way he lived his daily life was the way he expressed his politics.

"I'm not [involved in] organized political activity. But make sure you put that word *organized* in there, because I consider all the stuff I do political activity. These articles I'm writing are political activity. I mean, everything we do is political. Every stance—the way we treat each other, the way we treat our family, the way we interact with fellow workers, and, as a journalist, the position I take—is by definition political." By presenting his argument in terms drawn from the New Left vision of "personal politics," Rubin once again reveals the extent to which his life continues to be shaped by that vision. The difference, of course, is that the politics themselves have been partially recast.

There have been some changes in Rubin's life since that 1984 interview. His marriage broke up a year or so later, and his writing career has continued to develop into a full-time occupation (he has published over one hundred articles or essays, including work he has done as a stringer for a news organization), but his political stance, particularly his commitment to libertarian values, remains the same.

THE FATE OF SIXTIES COMMITMENT: TAKE FOUR

In telling Steve Rubin's story, we have once again tried to raise questions about the adequacy of certain assumptions concerning the fate of sixties activists. Rubin's is only one case. There are, no doubt, cases where former student activists have become wealthy stockbrokers, corporate lawyers, born-again supporters of the Moral Majority, or even soldier-of-fortune mercenaries fighting communism in Latin America. The fact that there are no cases like this in our sample does not mean that they do not exist. And elements of a turn to the Right and a rejection of New Left orientations are observable in the story of another nonpersister, Sarah Glenn. Recall that Glenn left her radical feminist community in 1980 and moved to New England. She soon took a job as a reporter for a state-wide newspaper. Within two years she had advanced to city editor and had ambitions of becoming an executive in the national management structure of the chain that owned the paper. Her views on economic issues changed as she became more successful, and by the mid-1980s she was supporting some of the Reagan administration's supply-side strategies. "I want a beautiful house, and a great car, and nice clothes," she told us. She felt she deserved them, after years of self-denial. But there were signs of continued commitment to values embodied in the New Left and feminist movements. Glenn initiated and supervised a series of feature stories on her city's gay and lesbian community, stories that were designed to challenge and overcome the prejudice and discrimination against homosexuals. Further, Glenn's use of journalism to address social issues has links to the strategy she employed while working on the "alternative" *Santa Barbara News and Review* and *El Gaucho*.

We are most certainly not trying to argue, then, that there is no evidence for a shift among former activists toward more conservative views; instead, we suggest that such shifts involve fealty to, as well as rejection of, movement principles and perspectives. Steve Rubin, like others who have changed or disengaged politically, holds to the belief that he has not fundamentally changed, that he remains committed to values that were embodied in the sixties youth revolt. Indeed, our respondents see themselves as essentially the kind of people their youthful selves would have wanted them to be.

In Chapter 4, we sketched the process by which this belief in one's own persistence has been sustained. We argued that the intertwined but opposing orientations of movement and counterculture—toward social responsibility and personal liberation—provide material for "ideological work," for maintaining a sense of moral consistency. In the stories presented in this chapter, we can see efforts to seek self-fulfillment interpreted as a living out of the sixties quest for free self-expression, compensating for the loss of commitment to "making history." Joyce Weston, once a youthful idealist who thought she "could change it all," now puts those ideals into practice on an individual level, feeling that "you don't have to be political to be radical." And Steve Rubin, a former Radical Union leader and now a writer, seeks freedom in daily life but is disenchanted with the socialist vision, his pursuit of personal liberty so intense that he has adopted a libertarian-anarchist perspective. All of our former activists, even those most politically disengaged, continue to see themselves as standing outside society's established structures of authority; all continue to resist conventional frameworks for livelihood and everyday life. One might well argue that in a culture that stresses individualism and liberty as central values, it is easier to remain true to those elements of sixties sentiment that emphasized self-expression than it is to build a life primarily in terms of an ethic of social responsibility.

THE NONACTIVISTS: MOVING UP AND MOVING RIGHT

In our collective portrait, we sketched out the differences between the activist and nonactivist cohorts in the areas of political beliefs, political involvement, occupation, and lifestyle. We can explore these differences in more detail by focusing on the lives of several individuals. As in previous sections, cases discussed at length were chosen for their representativeness and for their ability to dramatize important analytic themes. Where relevant, the stories of other respondents will be touched on, expanding on issues that have been raised or questions that need to be addressed. Finally, although this cohort contains no distinct subgroups based on political philosophy or involvement, these men and women are certainly not of one mind; their stories reveal variations in political perspective that allow us to complete the picture.

"What I've Done Is What I Was Supposed to Do"

Clark Jeffries now works as a manufacturer's representative (an independent salesman who represents several different firms) in San Diego County, California, selling packaging materials to soft-drink companies. Recall that Jeffries, upon graduating from college, first went to work as a computer programmer for the Bank of America. He held that job for three years, then moved to Southern California to take his present position, initially in partnership with his father. Since his father's stroke three years ago, Jeffries has maintained the business alone. He is married and has two young daughters. His average annual income is in the $75,000–85,000 range. He owns a large, four-bedroom home in a newly built suburban community. He is an avid runner, and on weekends he can be found chalking the lines and setting up the goal nets for his daughters' soccer games. Reflecting on the life he leads today, Jeffries concludes, "I assume that I ended up just the way I was supposed to. What I've done is what I was supposed to do. I think I ended up basically that way: your really average middle-class person."

When Jeffries speaks about his political beliefs, the legacy of Vietnam —the war itself, the protests against it, the national debate over "what went wrong"—is evident, but it manifests itself in a manner quite different from that observed among the former "bank burners." The problem with Vietnam, Jeffries believes, is that America was not ruthless enough.

He is ready to support another intervention. "I'm of the opinion now that if we ever go do it again, I would back doing it. But only go over and do it. I mean, if you want to go over and win the war, win the damn thing, don't screw around like they did [in Vietnam]." We can learn a lot about "doing it right," he feels, by studying Israel's approach to these matters. "I kind of draw a parallel to the situation going on now over in Lebanon. I don't agree with what the Israeli government does, but I gotta take my hat off to them. It may not be right, and I'm no expert on Lebanon, so I don't know all the aspects of it, but I mean . . . they say they're gonna do something, and they go do it. You know, maybe they blow up a hundred thousand people they weren't supposed to blow up, but at least they went in and did it. They didn't stand back there and maybe blow up a few here and a few there, and that's the impression I get of what we were doing over in Vietnam."

Jeffries' ideas about "doing it right" in Vietnam do not include specific tactics or strategies. "I don't know if that means dropping an atomic bomb, or if that means sending over the heavy artillery to wipe out all the bad guys. I mean you're in a situation with the terrain and the people, that to sit there and try to fight a hand-to-hand combat war, you know, Christ—the thing could have gone on forever. Do it like the Israelis do. It may not be right, but they've set their minds to it and they're gonna go do it."

Jeffries' assessment of foreign policy starts with a general assertion that a tougher stand toward the Soviet Union is necessary. This is the deeper lesson of Vietnam. "I look at it from the standpoint that if you look at the whole world, I think we have to do something to fight off— if you want to call them the bad guys or the Communists—I think there is a need to stand up to those guys. You know, they say they're invited into Poland or invited into Afghanistan, well, they're gonna do it." He does not see any alternative to confrontation. "I think Carter was a very good example of that [failure to be tough] when he made his famous statement that the Russians had lied to him. How could he be so foolish or stupid to think that he could sit there and say that he trusted them, tell them that 'If we don't make any more bombs, promise you won't make any more bombs'?" Here Jeffries laughs at the absurdity of it all. "I honestly don't think that you could sit here and be a total pacifist and say we're gonna throw away all our nuclear weapons, and then we expect the Russians to do the same. I think we'd all be speaking Russian in thirty years. Backing down from them isn't gonna do any good, because if you back down, they'll turn around and go somewhere else. They'll move into Lebanon; they'll move into Israel; they'll move in here. They'll move in there and, before you know it, we'll all be speaking Russian."

Jeffries is less bellicose when it comes to the arms race, however. Although he is opposed to a nuclear freeze—believing that the Russians cannot be trusted—he thinks that the government spends too much money on defense. "I think that you could probably stand up to them and have enough capability to deter them far short of what the hell they're doing [with defense spending]. I think they've gotta have a certain amount of [weapons], but a trillion dollars worth? That seems illogical. There isn't enough money around to pay for all those damn things. It seems to me the ideal thing would be to cut the defense budget in half and you wouldn't have a problem. You know, it only takes one bomb to blow them up. We don't need a hundred thousand of them [to] blow everybody up ten times." Even though he supports the Reagan administration's generally aggressive posture toward the Soviet Union (he voted for Reagan in 1980 and 1984 in part because of the candidate's stand on this issue), he also thinks that Reagan has at times "overdone it." The recently signed Intermediate Nuclear Forces treaty is, he feels, a hopeful sign in this regard.

Clark Jeffries represents one pole of opinion on Vietnam and foreign policy among the nonactivists. Others have drawn different lessons from the Vietnam experience. Jeffries' views on domestic issues, however, are those most often voiced by nonactivists. Like the majority in that cohort, he identifies himself as a conservative Republican and is critical of "the liberals' big spending and handouts" for the undeserving. His comment on this subject could have been spoken by almost any nonactivist: "I think liberals are more inclined to give everything away to you, rather than have you work for it. And I think conservatives, on the other hand, are gonna make you go out and work for what you get. And I'm more of a believer in that. I think that giving everything away to everybody is not the right way to do it, 'cause I don't know how the hell they're gonna pay for it. You know, every time I hear one of the politicians get up and say they're gonna start a billion-dollar jobs program that's gonna put these people back to work for six months—that's not gonna do anybody any good. And who's gonna pay for it?" He is similarly critical of social programs, particularly welfare, and supports the Reagan administration's efforts to cut back federal spending in those areas.

Many of the nonactivists expressed anger over apparent abuses in the distribution of welfare; it seemed to be a source of special irritation for them. Carl Rohrback, for instance, who earns $72,000 a year as an executive for the same large utility company that he joined after graduating from UCSB, harshly appraised the welfare system and its recipients. "It bothers me that you can make more on welfare than you can getting a job. If we are providing that type of incentive, then where is the incentive to go out and try and get a job? It bothers me that we are providing incentives for a divorced mother to have more kids because they get another two hundred on welfare if they have more babies. So they have more babies and more babies and the next thing you know you have a tenement house with a bunch of people with absent fathers or who don't know who their fathers are. We don't seem to have the initiative, the drive, the ambition, in a lot of our people today who are on welfare. We don't seem to have a lot of self-reliance right now. We got more and more takers and fewer and fewer givers. What bugs me is that some of these people on welfare are just irate that some of their funds may be cut or slashed. They haven't given anything, yet they want it all. I think that is a disease in our country—take, take, take. I think it was better when people came over to Ellis Island on a boat from Europe and had a lot of pride in their ethnic background or came to America to start something. I think a lot of people come to America today to get something."

Harry Stevens, now a thirty-nine-year-old retired home builder and the owner of a condominium complex in the Reno, Nevada, area (he earns enough from his property holdings that he does not have to work), made similar comments. "One thing about our country today that really bothers me [are] the handouts we give people. You know, the welfare, and this and that. I believe the kids today are growing up so spoiled. Well, I think the people of America are really spoiled people. They expect things handed to them. They will not go out and work, and it just really rubs me the wrong way, it really does. That's why I think our government is in as bad shape as it is. We've just too many handouts." In some cases, anger over "handouts" is fueled by racial prejudices and is expressed as opposition to assistance to certain racial or ethnic groups. Rhonda Miller, divorced in 1982 and working as an executive secretary at a Southern California race track, opposes efforts to aid the Spanish-speaking residents of the state. "Why do we have to have ballots printed in English and Spanish? We speak English in America, and if you can't cut the mustard, then get out. Why do we have to give it to them? We're saying, 'That's okay, you don't have to work, you don't have to learn how to speak English, you can just kind of mucky-muck along, and we'll make it okay for you.' We didn't used to do that for anybody, why do we have to do that now?"

Miller also feels that the special "privileges" being given black Americans nurture their "different values." "I was raised that you shouldn't be prejudiced against blacks. I thought they were just the same as we are, and they should be given opportunities, and 'why did we discriminate against them?' because they're just people too; their skin is just a different color. I don't think that way anymore. I think there are those who are intelligent, and if they are equally intelligent and equally qualified, they should be given as much consideration as the next guy for a job. But I don't think they all are. I think that they're raised differently. Their motivations are different; they have different values. Not all of them [think] that you have to work for a living. And like, when you go to Hollywood Park, you drive through Inglewood, you gotta turn your rings around, you gotta lock your doors. If you get in an accident you don't get out of your car, because all those black people live there. How could you live like pigs? Those areas are terrible. But before, I just didn't see that. That didn't exist in my mind. I assumed they were there because they're being discriminated against. And maybe they're there now because they're being discriminated against, but I think if they wanted to do something about it, they could; and I don't think they do."

Every nonactivist states that he or she has become more conservative with respect to social programs and the welfare state since graduating from college, and many are very explicit about this change in their thinking. They invariably define their current values in terms of the need to defend what they have worked for and achieved over the years. They see the changes as based on the "realism" and the material acquisitions that come with "maturity."

Miller, for example, justifies her opposition to bilingual and affirmative action programs in terms of her perceptions about the attitudes and behavior of Hispanics, and is especially angry that her taxes are helping to support such programs. Other nonactivists also felt that their hard-earned income was being given away. "I was more sympathetic to poor people and minorities [during the time of the riots]," one woman told us. "Now, having worked twelve years and paid a lot of taxes, I'm sick of welfare. I like to work for myself, not for all the lazy people." And another person: "I think they take too much money from my paycheck to pay for these programs." And still another nonactivist: "I'd say I was much more liberal when I was in my twenties, and I'm becoming real conservative. I just don't feel that we need to give all these people handouts. As you get older and work harder and maybe you feel that work is good for you, you may feel that that is what is wrong with them, because they aren't working."

Such views cannot be attributed simply to the insensitivity of whites who have always enjoyed the benefits of status and a nine-to-five job. For close to six years, Harry Stevens worked sixteen hours a day, weekends included, dealing cards in a casino all night and building houses most of the day. "I almost had a physical breakdown from it," he recalls, "because I did it for so long, and I just completely wore out. All my friends around me were partying, especially working at the club, 'cause those were party people. And when they'd get off work they'd sit and drink a couple of hours at the bar, and mess around and do some gambling and then go home. And these people, after those six years, did not have a dime more than when they started there. But that wasn't for me. If they want to live that way, that's fine, but I don't want to hear them complain about not having anything." Stevens had a different vision. "That was just not the way I wanted to live my life, to work all that time until I'm sixty-five. I said to myself, 'Why not retire when you're thirty and you've got all that life you can live and do the things you want to do?'" He would later sell these houses at a handsome profit and put the proceeds into further construction. Now he owns twelve condominiums and has to work only a few hours each month doing basic repairs and collecting rents. Having made sacrifices, Stevens has little patience for those who seem unwilling to make similar sacrifices; he resents people who "expect to have everything handed to them" and resolutely defends what he has worked to achieve.

Some nonactivists who expressed similar feelings proposed alternative ways of dealing with what they agreed were serious social ills in the United States. Many supported the concept of "corporate responsibility": the business community should take a more active role and government should provide tax incentives for corporations to do so. Some also asserted that the government spends too much on defense and that the size of government was responsible for high taxes. Carl Rohrback, for example: "I think the military build-up [during the Reagan administra-

tion] was a waste. We have too many other problems we should be dealing with—our cities, mass transit, unemployment, you can list twenty
social issues that I think ought to be dealt with before we worry about
building more Trident submarines. We spend a tremendous amount on
our military and there is a lot of waste there. At some point in time
I think we've got to talk about dealing with that monster. I think our
military-industrial complex is a monster. It feeds itself. So the only thing
that's gonna work is that we need to cut the cost of government." In sum,
their fiscal conservativism was not always rooted in hostility toward a
"social responsibility ethic"; they just did not want to see others getting
something for nothing, living off their financial contributions. People on
welfare, Rohrback says, have not "put much into the till."

This process of increasing conservativism can also be observed in the
nonactivists' changing attitudes toward business-labor and business-
government relations. Those who have risen to positions of status or
authority in the business world have become less likely to advocate
workers' rights or governmental regulation. "I probably would have
been in favor of more governmental control back then," one man said.
Now, however, "I worry more about more government control, welfare,
et cetera." "I'm a big believer in less government, not more!" emphasizes
another former Delt who is now a business executive. He then inveighs
against "[Senator Edward] Kennedy's stupid minimum wage bill" and
proposed national health insurance program. "That would be a form of
socialism," he warns.

Carl Rohrback reached similar conclusions. While he once "would
have agreed that labor unions and rights of individual workers need a
greater voice and would have stated that business has too strong a role
in political, social, and economic issues," he now feels, as a business
executive, that business has a much more important role to play "in
shaping the society in which we live." Even Mark Reiss, a nonactivist
who regularly votes Democratic, says he "hates Reagan," and considers
himself a liberal with regard to most political issues, offers comments
along these same lines, criticizing American labor unions for what are,
to him, excessive wage demands, corruption, and lack of commitment
to production quality. These beliefs facilitate his own financial success:
he is the controlling owner of a large company whose workers are not
unionized and, he trusts, never will be. Frank Morrow, still working as
an executive in the steel industry, also considers himself liberal on social

issues and is quite critical of the established political parties (he was a strong supporter in 1980 of John Anderson's independent campaign for president), but takes a similar position on labor unions. Perhaps George Dawes (presently living in Caracas as the head of the South American audit division of a large U.S. bank) put it best: "I think I've come back to being more conservative as I have more things to be conservative about."

In our exploration of the present lives of former "bank burners," we observed continuing efforts to "live out" the cultural and political ideals of the New Left. In what ways are the nonactivists seeking to expand and enhance their lives? What are their goals? Again, Clark Jeffries helps us to address this issue.

For the past several years, Jeffries reports, he has been "trying to branch off into another business, [trying] to buy another manufacturing business." While he "likes being independent" as a salesman and "likes the income," some aspects of his present situation concern him. "The thing I lack now is manufacturing control," he explains. "I don't control what I sell. And the people who I represent could decide one day that they don't need my services anymore, and I'd be gone. So the only way for me to have a little control on the future is to control what I'm selling." More broadly, "control on the future" means financial independence—to be in a position where I wouldn't have to worry where my next paycheck is coming from; to have enough money in the bank or an investment where, if I wanted to, I could pack up and go fishing for the rest of my life, and be able to support my family in, say, your average kind of lifestyle."

Jeffries' "plan of attack" is to find a company that is for sale, "one that's been in business for a while, where a lot of the problems would be solved and all you'd have to do is take it over," and then "merge it with something else, expand it in some way until it gets to be doing ten million dollars in sales and then sell it to somebody else. And then go do another one." Aside from the financial gains, Jeffries notes, "it [would be] a lot of fun. The challenge of it, I think, would make me want to just move on to the next deal, and try another one. That is my plan for the future."

Several nonactivists echoed this concern for financial success and yearning for increased entrepreneurial opportunities when speaking of their goals or their desires for enhancing their lives. Larry Goodwin infuses these concerns with a passion that equals the political fervor in the activists' interviews, and his story raises additional points of comparison between the two cohorts.

"I Want to Make Money"

After graduating from UCSB in 1970, Larry Goodwin, as we have seen, went on to graduate school in business, intending to go into international management. While in school, however, he decided to pursue a career in advertising. He was at first drawn by "the creative aspect of it, more than anything else—the ability to influence consumers' understanding of a product, his likes and dislikes." Then, a professor in graduate school convinced him that advertising would be a way to get "multicompany exposure"—the experience of working with executives from different firms, thus being exposed to many different ways of thinking rather than being confined to one company's approach. "Your experience base is broadened," Goodwin notes, "and you can make better decisions." It seemed like a good choice for an ambitious young man who was just starting out.

Goodwin was very successful in the advertising business. He went to work for a major agency in New York, moving up to an executive position in account management, "the account handling part of the business, the direct interface with the client," as he puts it. His salary in 1983 was $110,000. Excited about his work, he expressed none of the cynicism or moral critique that we heard in Joyce Weston's account. In our 1982 interview, he recounted his initial feelings about the business. "I really fell in love with it. Advertising is intense. As a service, you're always at the mercy of clients, and you're in between the service groups of the agency, those people who are fulfilling the plan, who design the ads, and the copywriters, and the people who design how you're going to spend your dollars, and the people who monitor how you spend your dollars, and the people who research and tell you where you should be spending your dollars. You're the focal point. What we do is, we're the strategists."

After eleven years in advertising, however, Goodwin came to feel that the rewards were no longer there. "I thoroughly enjoyed it until I got exposed to all the bullshit. I'm the kind of person that can bend over and bend over and take a lot of things, but when I found myself entering [meetings] bent over with my cheeks spread, I said, 'It's time to get out!' " What Goodwin felt he was being asked to "take" was a situation where innovation and initiative were being discouraged, and where both his clients and his fellow executives lacked the courage and flexibility to change their traditional ways of doing things. "I got tired of having what I thought were bloody good ideas being bounced off people who had the incapability or unwillingness to listen and, more importantly, make a decision." Since Goodwin's clients represented the top echelon of corporate America, he attributes these failings to American business as a whole. "The incredible lack of decision-making capability within American industry," he says, "especially with the clients I was working with, just drove me crazy."

The ideas that Goodwin was excited about had to do with two types of new technology: computers and telecommunications, particularly cable television. Speaking of the historical significance of these technological innovations in our 1984 interview, Goodwin became almost evangelical: "I'm telling you, technology is gonna blow tradition right straight off the face of the earth. Talk about the industrial revolution as having an impact, and television as having an impact—those will pale in comparison to what computerization and the world of telecommunication and the like is gonna do. There's nothing in history like it." He started studying these two technologies while still at the ad agency and wanted to develop ways to use them as marketing tools, rather than simply as administrative or entertainment tools.

Goodwin believes that growth is a fundamental problem of contemporary American business. Too large and unmanageable, major companies can neither make decisions nor exploit new technological developments (such as the ones he presented). Goodwin's solution was to go outside the world of large business organizations, to reclaim America's risk-taking, entrepreneurial spirit. He quit the agency in 1983 and, using his own savings of $65,000 as capital, joined three other men in starting two small companies. One is a consulting firm in the microcomputer industry; the other develops ways to use cable television as a direct marketing device.

Asked to elaborate on his ideas for using new technologies in marketing, Goodwin responded quickly and with great zeal. Here the scope of his thinking becomes clearer, particularly his sense of himself as a pioneer and his view of technology as the fulcrum for social transformation. "From a technological standpoint, the world of computers is so novel and so new that there's a lot of opportunity to expand one's thinking as to their potential, to at least stretch people's imagination as to what this new thing can represent. What it represents plain and simple is power. Believe me, the sheer awesome power it represents is extraordinary. I mean, business is not going to be conducted in the same way. Like, why not develop an interface with people on a one-to-one basis with a [political] cause. You get a letter coming in every day from Ronald Reagan, sooner or later you're gonna look at Ronald Reagan whether you like him or not. And it could be a personal letter. And it could be written because they *know* you. Some people are gonna view this as an invasion of privacy, but it gives somebody else the ability to be able to know you. And, importantly, you the ability to talk to them. You can talk to them through a vote if it's politics, through the purchase or nonpurchase of its products if it's a marketer."

Goodwin acknowledges that this technology opens the way for manipulation of the citizenry by elites, but he is not concerned. "I'm so excited about it that I dumped the traditional world I was in in order to become an active participant in the future—to be a pioneer, to show people what can be done. The basic bottom line is that technology can be a tremendous benefit to the American people. And it's gonna be abused and misused and people are going to get hurt by it and all, but the aggregate, I think, is gonna be tremendously important and tremendously beneficial."

"I'm having the time of my life," he told us in 1984. When asked what his personal goal in life was right now, he replied, "The one that I do acknowledge very clearly is that I want to make money." The amount he had in mind here was large: "Five million in three years, and I know it's gonna happen. And I'd like to see it happen a little faster than it is, but it's gonna happen." Optimistic and unconcerned about the financial risks involved in his enterprises, Goodwin insisted, "I can make money. I can go back to the advertising business and make a hundred thousand dollars again. But I'm not satisfied with doing that. It's gonna work. One of these companies is gonna hit. I don't even need a lot to live on. I need a couple, three thousand dollars a month to live on. The rest of it I'll plow back into making something else happen." It is more important, he emphasized, "[to] be able to get my ideas tried."

After a short period in which he combined his entrepreneurial activities and work in a small but well-known advertising agency, Goodwin moved on. In our most recent conversation (in early 1988), he reported that he had sold his business shares to his partners, making a good profit, and accepted a position as an executive vice-president in charge of marketing for a multibillion-dollar company headquartered on the east coast. Getting his ideas tried is still very important to him. This new position, he feels, will give him the power to implement many of the business innovations and improvements he talked of in our earlier interviews. In advertising, Goodwin explains, you can only advise the client on such matters; in marketing, you are on the inside and can actually bring about these changes. With the money from the sale of his business interests, and with what he terms the "very lucrative," six-figure compensation he receives in his current position, Goodwin is now halfway—in terms of personal net worth—to the five-million-dollar goal he set for himself back in 1984. The work is hard, requires constant travel, and is extremely time-consuming, Goodwin states, but the financial and emotional rewards are considerable.

The enthusiasm with which he describes his current job and his latest ideas is certainly equal to what we heard in earlier interviews. For example, Goodwin thinks sophisticated marketing techniques could improve the Reagan administration's handling of foreign policy, particularly the threat from the Soviet Union. "Our government simply doesn't market the communist threat of world domination well enough. Merchandising ideas is a role of government, and we need a much better strategy than what we now have." The same goes for the Iran-Contra scandal, which he feels became "a stupid fucking media playground," and was consequently "exaggerated in terms of its seriousness, blown way out of proportion. The Europeans are laughing at us," Goodwin says, because they understand that "that [covert action] stuff goes on all the time" and should not be viewed as a serious problem.

Goodwin also brings great enthusiasm to the topic of changes in business-labor relations, "Unions are no longer the answer" to our nation's economic growth, he insists. "The answer rests with American business." If companies make real "community contributions" by "giving workers a piece of the action" and compensating them with stock, then the quality of American products will improve dramatically as workers come to "feel their contribution means something. Right now, they have no pride in their workmanship."

There was more. In one fifteen-minute conversation, Goodwin offered numerous suggestions for dealing with economic and political problems, but the underlying message was the same. Decisive management, resurrecting the spirit of entrepreneurial capitalism, and the use of advanced technology to market its vision offered the only hope for our country's future.

"I Will Always Be a Liberal Because of What Happened in Santa Barbara"

For the most part, our discussions of lifestyles, concerns for personal development, and broader visions of social change have focused on differences between the activists and the nonactivists. In a few cases, however, the contrasts are not so stark; some nonactivists have been drawn to the ideals of their activist contemporaries and attribute their convictions to their experiences as students during the sixties. In these cases, then, the "liberalizing" influence of the university and the events of that time have not faded. Such influence is strongly evident in Lucy Lizotte's story.

Lizotte lives in the Santa Barbara area, in a spacious ranch house that is set well back from a winding, tree-lined lane. Her husband, Bob, works in county government as a high-level administrator. She quit her teaching job when her second child was born, but has recently returned to it. Lizotte appears to be living the same kind of comfortable middle-class life as other members of the nonactivist cohort, but she differentiates herself from them in several ways.

"I met my husband after graduating," she begins. Lizotte received her teaching credentials in her "fifth year" at UCSB and was starting to look for a job, but when she met Bob at the beginning of the summer of 1971, the two of them "took off around the western United States and Canada camping. My parents thought it was awful that I wasn't job hunting all summer," she recalls. "We ended up roaming around and camping, smoking dope, taking mescaline." She laughs at the memory of it, and at the contrast with her life today. "Bob had just gotten out of the navy, and he let his hair grow for a full year. He looked like Jesus Christ. We really loved that time. Total freedom and total fun."

The "total freedom" only lasted the summer, however. As Lizotte tells it: "Then we decided that we would get Establishment. I got a teaching job in L.A. the week that school was starting. Bob started working for a bank there. Just bizarre! He bought his three-piece suit, and away we went on our journey into middle-class America." Lizotte laughs again, gesturing at her backyard patio, and advances the story some dozen years: "Here we are! I think we are basically middle-class America, into the same middle-class ideals that our parents' generation had. At the same time I didn't want to believe that. I didn't want to believe that I was ever going to settle down, because I wanted my freedom. Then we did get good jobs, we did make good money—but we gave up a lot."

Their efforts to hold on to a little bit of that freedom stand out as a central theme in her story. "We did have freedom still in our life, even when we were getting caught up in the middle-class lifestyle. Even when we were both working, I would take off a week at school and we would go to Mexico. Bob quit the bank, and we went to Europe for a summer after I taught for a couple of years. We sold both our cars to pay for the trip." But that was their last hurrah: "Then we came back, and that's when we made our commitment to work here in Santa Barbara and sell out to the mighty buck."

A lot of information and reflection is packed into that last statement. Two and a half years in Los Angeles had convinced Lizotte and her husband that it was time to relocate. "We were sick of the freeways, and we were both commuting an hour in each direction," she explains. "And that's when we sat down and made a priority list of about twenty things to do in our lives and the highest priority was where we lived. We both decided Santa Barbara was a nice place, so we moved here. We kind of winged it for jobs and had a real hard time for the first year or two, but we did all right and bought a house" in a new housing tract in Goleta, then a rapidly growing suburb of Santa Barbara.

Children came next, with all the attendant responsibilities. "Even deciding to go to work and owning a house and all that, that still wasn't the commitment to children, which Bob and I feel is a lot more commitment than anything we've ever done in our life. That has drastically changed our outlook. We kind of entered into this life the back way. It wasn't like we set out to become the perfect little couple with two kids, living in Santa Barbara. It just sort of happened. Now we are here and we are happy."

Lizotte's comments, presented in this ironic manner, suggest more guilt about the trajectory of her life since college than we heard in our other nonactivist interviews. Her story also hints at a heightened awareness of how the taking on of conventional adult commitments and responsibilities can shape personal development, constraining youthful impulses and desires while providing stability and security and thus opportunities for a particular kind of fulfillment unavailable to those who seek to sustain the romantic existence—the "total freedom"—of youth. But her wistful thinking about that time, and the self-effacing comments she frequently offers when comparing it with her present life, convey an attachment to her past that is uncharacteristic of the nonactivists. More than any other member of her cohort, she bears the imprint of that moment.

"I really became socially aware in college," Lizotte says, "aware of the problems that were happening in our society. Because of that, I continue to be socially aware of what's going on around me, an awareness that I didn't have [before] I went away to school. My freshman year, I remember taking a sociology class. The teacher went on and on about ivory towers and how we were all into partying and surfing and going to the beach, and 'it's too damn bad that you kids aren't socially conscious of what's going on in our society.' We did become aware. And by my senior year, we were very much involved. I can't say I was. I mean, I wasn't burning the bank or rioting in the streets, but the school in general became very involved with what was going on in the real world. We weren't ivory tower types the way we were."

Unlike other nonactivists who have undergone a conservative retrenchment, Lizotte sees a clear and positive connection between her convictions and her experiences in Isla Vista. "I didn't think for myself in high school. I pretty much had conservative views. My father, who was a construction contractor, was extremely conservative in his beliefs, and I basically went away to college with dad's views and I came away exactly opposite of his views. I will always be a liberal because of what happened in Santa Barbara. It's not just the riots but the whole peace movement. It had an effect on our generation, to the point where we became cynical about the government, cynical about the way our country does things. I think I'll always be cynical. I don't think I will ever trust what a president does, and I'll always know that they have the power to do whatever they damn well please. I think the whole thing about Vietnam came at an impressionable age for me. It will affect me forever."

Vietnam was a crucial issue for several other nonactivists as well, but the war did not change their political and social views generally. Carl

Rohrback, for example, attributes his view of the Reagan administration's military build-up as a "waste" to the influence of Vietnam. "It was a bad war, a bad scene for everybody there. I think the net sum of that [experience] changed my political perspective on the use of force and military goals versus maybe better ways to get things accomplished." And Larry Goodwin expresses criticism of U.S. policy in Central America today in terms of his judgments about Vietnam: "It's another reaction to the 'red horror.' I don't believe we can combat it at every front. I think it can be combated in ways other than the military way. I don't think the United States can be the savior of the world." The Vietnam experience moved the foreign policy views of some of the nonactivists at least slightly to the left, and appears to have had a lasting influence in this regard. Moreover, many of the nonactivists reacted to the Iran-Contra affair with disappointment, anger, embarrassment, and frustration over Reagan's "bungling" and his handling of foreign policy in general; several sensed that the president had "lost it." But these views are inconsistent with their generally conservative outlook. These individuals have shifted rightward—and are conscious of having done so—on almost every other issue.

Lucy Lizotte sees herself as "a humanist." "I think I care what's happening in society and what's happening to human beings and what they're doing to each other. It tends to make me more liberal in my social concerns. That's something I don't think my dad has. He went through the Depression and believes that everybody ought to carry their own weight and that the whole problem with government is that people are getting free rides. Well, people shouldn't get free rides, but I feel some people really can't help it and they need help, and a lot of the time the only people that can help them are the government, so I'm basically into social programs. I'm real concerned about the people that are unemployed. I think we are taking a risk in this country. I think we could [have civil war] and destroy our system, just by revolt by people that are just pissed because they don't have anything. Because they're not allowed to work because they haven't had an opportunity. I think that is really a scary thing in our cities. I think that you can only push people so far and then you have problems."

Lizotte is opposed to nuclear power and professes strong environmentalist views. Further, she supported the nuclear freeze initiative in California and has made a number of financial contributions to Mothers for

Peace. She voted for McGovern in 1972, for Carter in 1976 and 1980, and for Mondale in 1984. Finally, she is an active member of the Unitarian Church. It was through the church that Lizotte became interested in the conflict in Central America and developed her opposition to Contra funding. Their pastor has visited Nicaragua, and the church is sending medical aid to the Nicaraguan people.

Lizotte is politically active; in several recent local election campaigns, she worked for the "progressive," liberal candidate. She attributes her recent involvement in large part to the fact that her children are older and require less care. "I've sat back for the past few years not being politically involved, just sort of making it through with my babies and just living my life," she told us in 1983. "I'd like to get involved in some sort of program or group with the right kind of backing and the right kind of support. Now, we are building up our arsenal and doing all these horrible things that I think are wrong. We sit around and talk about wondering if we are going to be around ten years from now." Lizotte added that she wanted to help ensure that her children would have a world in which to grow up. She is now working to achieve this. Though she calls herself a cynic, she persists in believing that "the right amount of energy exerted the right way can make a difference. It really can make a difference."

Lizotte is aware of the contradictions in her positions and actions. She notes that her children, because of where their home is located, should be going to Morris School, where there are many poor and Hispanic children. They actually attend another public school, Buena Sierra, where nearly all the students are white and upper-middle-class. "I have a real problem [with that] too. My husband thinks that I'm a real hypocrite in not sending them down to Morris, in sending them [instead] to Buena Sierra, the nice, white school. I agree, that really is hypocritical. I should be sending them down to Morris and exposing them to that. If I was a true liberal, I would, that's true. I believe it. But by the same token, we are all protective of our children." Moreover, in choosing Buena Vista, she rejected private school as an option. Lizotte is uneasy about the tension between middle-class privilege and social responsibility. Similar dilemmas, as we have seen, confront such "real liberals" as Martha Koch and her husband.

Lizotte plans to resolve the school contradiction in a few years. "I will send them to Santa Barbara High [the public high school in Santa Barbara with the largest percentage of students from minority and low-income families]. I will send them when they're older and they've developed to a point where they can make their own decisions. I do think children should be exposed to that. I went to an all-white high school, and I think it was wrong. I don't want my children thinking that everybody has a swimming pool and a Mercedes. I taught in private school, and every single kid had a pool. Every single kid had a pony. They say, 'What do you mean, you don't have a pool? How weird.' That isn't good."

Lizotte's avoidance of a predominantly low-income school is consistent with the defensive stance that we observed in the lives of other nonactivists, but her assessment of it in terms of her ideals links her to the activists. This almost passionate need for "moral accountability" to one's youthful ideals, even where circumstances and personal indecisiveness lead people to act otherwise, is perhaps the most significant legacy of the movement, one that has meaning for some who remained at its periphery.

7

Conclusion: Interpreting
the Legacy of Sixties Protest

As students, members of the sixties generation who had been touched by the movement and the counterculture were fundamentally preoccupied, not only with social change, but with the ways in which their own lives would and could be transformed. Overwhelmingly, they assumed that to become people like their parents would be a defeat. They agreed that the ultimate test of validity for their youthful commitment would be the nature of their later lives. They took it for granted that simply to play out the careers and personal lifeways officially approved by school, church, state, and mass media would be both personally unrewarding and morally wrong. They assumed that each of them had considerable control over whether or not they would live moral and fulfilling lives, and that the nature of one's life was a measure of one's moral worth. To the degree that one went along with conventional roles and standards, one was deserving of moral condemnation as a "sell-out."

The belief that the sixties generation was different, and that the personal development of its members would simultaneously reflect and generate social change, was held not only by members of the generation, but by a considerable number of commentators, critics, and social scientists, who argued—for various reasons—that the youth revolt was a harbinger or symptom of major social or cultural shifts. In such a view, youth is thought to be the first group in a society to anticipate and respond positively to changes; these changes, in turn, are taken up by others as the vanguard generation matures and permeates the society at large and as older, more resistant sectors of the society die off.

In recent years, it has become more fashionable to believe that such views about the sixties were wrong and even silly, that they were largely the work of intellectual publicists touting "new values" as the wave of the future, that whatever "new consciousness" was present among sectors of the sixties generation when they were young has dissipated, that the very belief in a new consciousness was a quirk of the period, and that patterns of rebellion and unconventionality are best understood as expressions of phases in the cycle of personal life and of history, rather than as indicators of more linear development and enduring change.

The sharp contrast we found between the post-sixties development of our group of former activists and that of our group of nonactivists suggests that those who participated in the youth revolt continue to be affected by it. Still, when looking at former activists we are struck by the wide variation in the degree to which they remain politically engaged, and by the many ways in which they have departed from their youthful images of how a correct life should be lived.

In broad outline, the story we have been telling depicts the gradual individuation and conventionalization of people who, in their youth, were wholeheartedly submerged in a collective effort to break free of conventional identity. We have seen that although they appeared to be strongly bonded by revolutionary enthusiasm, movement collectives began to break apart almost as soon as they formed because of their inability to recognize and encompass the personal needs and interests of members. We traced the ways in which visions of revolutionary apocalypse —and the totalistic commitment demanded by such visions—were replaced by a long-range perspective within which members experimented with roles and collective attachments that fostered the linking of personal interest and political commitment. Finally, we recounted the ways in which, in the 1980s and in their thirties, most former activists were seeking more individualized and settled adult roles rather than continuing to operate in self-conscious opposition to the status quo. The fact remains, however, that in many ways the activist and nonactivist groups are as different today as they must have been some twenty years ago. If the former members of conventional student subcultures represent a kind of baseline of upper-middle-class mainstream identity, then—contrary to some popular mythology—former student radicals have hardly joined the mainstream, even if most are leading lives less politicized and experimental than when they were younger.

How can we account for the continuing differences between these

groups? What, after all, has been the fate of movement and countercultural codes and principles in the lives of individual members and in
the society and culture? How do we assess the historical meanings of
the 1960s twenty years later? What can we learn from the experience
of sixties activists about the vicissitudes of political commitment in our
time?

Answers to these questions are often elusive because the questions
are posed too abstractly in popular discourse about the topic. In order
to grasp what has been lasting and what ephemeral about the beliefs
and commitments that characterized the youth revolt, we have to try for
specificity. What do we mean in particular when we ask questions about
commitment and compromise, about whether people have "stayed radical" or "become conservative," about the degree to which "idealism" and
"maturity" are compatible—and all the other, similarly posed puzzles
that are raised in popular media and everyday conversation about the
sixties generation?

Despite the fact that movement participants often evaded careful
thought and discussion about how their commitments might be maintained, it is possible, by reading our interview texts and documents of
the time, by exploring our recollections of talk and mood, and by trying
to discern the underlying logic of prevailing beliefs, to reconstruct the
hypotheses about continuity that were embodied in the youth revolt. What
follows is an effort to do such a reconstruction, to try to capture a sense of
the movement's self-understanding and to specify, more than is usually
done, various dimensions of commitment. By doing this, we hope to be
able to identify precisely which threads have been broken and which remain intact. And by taking seriously the movement's own assumptions
and predictions about the conditions for continuity, and by then comparing these assumptions with subsequent happenings, we may be able
to learn something about why people who thought they would spend
their lives in the vanguard of social and cultural change have come to
accept a rather less prominent role in history.

THE FATE OF SIXTIES COMMITMENT: TAKE FIVE

What student activists in the sixties were likely to mean by commitment,
and what they were likely to believe would be the fate of their own commitment, changed at various times during the era of protest. Because

almost all of our interviewees were in school at the height of revolutionary militancy, they tended at the peak of their own involvement to imagine commitment in totalistic, revolutionary terms. But other, less totalistic meanings of commitment were widely held both before and after the late sixties. Moreover, political commitment as such was only a piece of the identity kits fashioned in the youth revolt. Let us review, then, the various meanings of commitment that were prevalent in movement and countercultural discourse. In each case, we will try to summarize what our own study seems to show about the fate of each kind of commitment, and try to place these findings in the context of other observations that seem to be plausible about the sixties generation. Finally, we will try to reconstruct movement hypotheses about the conditions necessary for such commitment and attempt an assessment about how well these hypotheses actually anticipated the social future.

Revolutionary Commitment

For a relatively brief time, sixties activists defined themselves as revolutionaries and expected that definition to structure the direction and pattern of their lives. In Chapter 3, we argued that revolutionary commitment is, practically by definition, totalistic—that is, it tends to make illegitimate any personal interest, activity, or motive that does not contribute to fundamental historical transformation. Such a commitment entails a very high readiness to accept the disciplines and demands of one's political collective, including demands about how and where and with whom one is going to live. In the climate of the late sixties, commitment to revolution had implications for carrying out virtually every detail of daily life: to be a revolutionary was to dress, eat, make love, and speak in certain ways and not others; to furnish one's abode as well as one's mind with expressions of one's allegiances; to engage in continuous self-monitoring for lingering signs of nonrevolutionary feeling, taste, or inclination. As we have seen, virtually no discussion took place about how one might live within such total engagement for the long haul; instead, such reflection was short-circuited by the belief in the imminence of revolution. Apocalyptic belief justified the mutual enforcement of total involvement; if one was in the early days of revolution, one had to be totally ready to respond.

Movement members often acted as if revolutionary engagement was purely an act of individual will, a test of one's moral fortitude. Indeed, one of the main reasons that members became disaffected in that period was the climate within movement collectives of moral one-upmanship, of hair-trigger readiness to accuse members of counterrevolutionary tendencies. Still, such moral struggle was carried out within the context of assumptions and perceptions about the state of society and the direction of history. In other words, even when movement rhetoric expressed an intensely romantic belief in the capacity and necessity for individual self-transformation, members were also operating with a certain set of hypotheses about the social conditions that would make such transformations necessary and possible. Even though it was morally incumbent on those who identified with the movement to become revolutionary, it was felt at the same time that external forces would compel that choice for more and more people, including many who were not at all politicized.

In the late days of the sixties, activists had come to believe that the society needed revolution because it could not reform itself in ways adequate to the demands and needs of those who were oppressed within it. In particular, urban black communities faced a future of continuing and worsening hardship: growing unemployment, poverty, and squalor coupled with increasing police-state-style control. The society's political and economic elites were so committed to an imperial international role that they would never divert sufficient resources to address the economic problems of the underclass. At the same time, the imperial posture, when confronted with Third World insurgencies, would lead to continuing Vietnam-style military engagement. American youth therefore could look forward to a future in which war and the draft were likely to be constant threats, with the promise of affluence for personal freedom fundamentally contradicted by the reality of militarism. But the sixties were proving that oppressed groups in the United States and the Third World would not resign themselves to oppression. Elite intransigence would breed rising rebellion; this in turn would result in increasing authoritarianism, fascistic mobilization, surveillance. The space for free expression and action would narrow, and political and social polarization and conflict would intensify.

These were the sorts of beliefs that activists in the late sixties, and, to some extent, the very early seventies, had about the future. They were beliefs reinforced by evidence: the use of increasingly violent police tactics to suppress protest, culminating in the killing of students at Kent State and Jackson State in 1970; the escalation of the bombing in Southeast Asia; the rise of politicians like George Wallace, Richard Nixon, Spiro Agnew, and Ronald Reagan whose rhetoric was matched by the preachments of black revolutionaries like Stokely Carmichael, Rap Brown, Eldridge Cleaver, and Huey Newton; the tendency of the mass media to highlight and dramatize the most violent and bizarre expressions of protest, thereby upping the ante on what constituted "real" action.

One key to understanding the fate of sixties commitment is to recognize that the most dire predictions of sixties revolutionaries did not come to pass. The falling away of members from revolutionary totalism and the eventual reevaluation of apocalyptic expectations were not the inevitable result of maturation and the passing of youth; instead, they are more understandable as consequences of the false predictions that derived from and reinforced the ideological currents that dominated the movement in the last years of the decade. Instead of intensifying polarization and hardening repression, the early- to mid-seventies was a time of accommodation and reform, in which space for political dissent widened rather than narrowed. Elite support for the Vietnam war ended, as did, eventually, U.S. involvement. What came to be called a "post-Vietnam syndrome" concerning foreign intervention was widespread among the elite and the general populace. Although economic conditions for the underclass did not materially improve, reforms such as affirmative action opened up opportunities for the college educated. As a result, black communities in both southern and northern cities were able to achieve a greater political voice (including more control over local police), and black leadership turned away from revolutionary and nationalist rhetoric.

Thus, even a brief sketch of some of the changes that actually occurred in American life and policy in the early post-sixties period suggests why revolutionary commitment was becoming politically irrelevant. It is, of course, well to keep in mind that such conclusions were reinforced by government policies that increased the personal dangers of participating in revolutionary activity (and the stories recounted in this book document the sometimes traumatizing consequences for movement participants), but it is notable that many trials of movement militants ended, like the Isla Vista bank-burning trial, in failure to convict. Indeed, government efforts to repress the revolutionary underground spearheaded by the Weathermen were notoriously ineffective; Weather leaders eventually turned themselves in after negotiating their way out of serious criminal penalties. And while the Watergate scandal lifted the lid on Nixon administration efforts and plans to develop a more efficient framework of surveillance and repression, that scandal, and the investigations of government intelligence that followed it, dismantled much of that framework.

By the mid-1970s, sixties revolutionaries felt compelled to reassess their fundamental beliefs about the potential for reform, free expression, and normal politics in the United States, and also found it possible to abandon their revolutionary commitments without fearing persecution for having had them. In this, their experience was quite unlike that of 1930s radicals, who found themselves facing blacklists and witch-hunts years after they had reassessed and modified their political perspectives. For members of the thirties Left, abandonment of commitment to the Communist Party was, in the McCarthy era, perceived as a kind of cowardice; maintaining one's membership was defined by some as a way of resisting repression, even if one harbored doubts about the validity of the party's politics. For many sixties radicals, moving away from revolution, although often a wrenching experience, could be accomplished while preserving one's identity as a radical. Still, there is some evidence in our interviews that those who had most believed in the imminence of revolution were among those most likely to move away from political engagement altogether. To some extent, the retreat of people like Roger Wade and Steve Rubin, who were intensely politicized as students, can be interpreted as the result of disillusionment. Those who had been skeptical from the outset about revolutionary totalism, like Ed Pines, had more political staying power when the apocalypse failed to come.

Commitment to Political Activism

Prior to the late sixties, when New Leftists thought about the nature of their commitment and tried to imagine how that commitment would look in their future lives, they were likely to talk in less totalistic terms than those that prevailed during the movement's revolutionary phase. Movement members generally hoped that they were becoming and would remain political activists: people who believed that they had a responsibility to contribute significantly to processes of social change, who felt the need and the capacity to take political initiative in behalf of the social vision they shared, who would always try to integrate some kind of political leadership role into their lives.

New Left members were by definition activists as students. Their daily lives, their discourse, their central relationships and interests were organized by their desire to participate in the history of their time. Such a description would be apt for virtually all of the people whom we have labeled former student activists (except for Kenneth Essian, who seems not to have had any real activist commitment at the time he was indicted for the burning of the bank). Before the revolutionary fever of the late Sixties, and after it subsided, most who shared this sense of themselves were likely to believe that they would continue to do so over the full course of their lives.

As we pointed out in Chapter 1, the activist identities of student New Leftists were in many cases rooted in their family backgrounds and upbringing. Much research on the social psychology of student activism in the sixties demonstrated that activists typically were raised by parents who encouraged a strong interest in politics, were themselves politically liberal, stressed that conventional middle-class "success" was less important than "contributing to bettering the human race," and were culturally as well as politically likely to distance themselves from mainstream perspectives. Because such parents were typically middle- to upper-middle-class professionals, living comfortably in suburbia, their children were likely to get some mixed messages in their childhood socialization experience. Parents' emphasis on service was usually coupled with a stress on being outstanding, on making a difference, on the special and remarkable qualities of their children. Parents' emphasis on social equality as a very important social good was coupled to the family's own relative material advantage. Young people raised in this climate were therefore likely to be wrestling with a combination of motives: strong ambition to excel or lead, linked with strong guilt over being privileged and special. Activism within the framework of the New Left was a way to reconcile such contradictory motives. It provided a way to make a difference in history in the name of helping others. The New Left, then, expressed the longing of at least some young people for a way to be both significant and socially responsible, to simultaneously act out one's ambition and assuage one's guilt.[1]

If activist identity in the sixties had roots in childhood socialization, it was crystallized, developed, and reinforced by the ideological perspectives that animated the New Left. The idea of "participatory democracy" was that people in general ought to have full access to history, that society should be organized so that people might have a voice in the decisions that affected them. The New Left's vision required that its adherents be self-conscious centers of political initiative, living embodiments of democratic idealism.[2] Accordingly, on both personal and ideological grounds, student activists were very likely to believe that they would always be politically involved in some way, that they would always try to find ways to respond to issues, causes, movements.

The stories of former student activists we have been recounting show overwhelmingly that, once revolutionary romanticism began to fade, virtually all of them devoted considerable energy to finding ways to sustain their political activism. As we have seen, such efforts were, in part, moves away from the totalism of the late sixties; they represented experiments in balancing and integrating the political and the personal, usually by finding ways to make one's vocation politically relevant. A few, notably Terry Lennox, withdrew very early from such efforts; most maintained strong activist involvements for at least several years into the seventies. But by the end of the decade many of them were rather self-consciously avoiding political activity, although even these people (Bill McNaughton, Cynthia Spivak, Steve Rubin, and Roger Wade, for example) continued to follow political events and engage in political discourse and reflection.

On balance, most of the former student activists that we interviewed have continued to maintain some semblance of the activist identities they crystallized in their youth. The intensity and centrality of their activist commitments are quite varied, and indeed, as Terry Lennox's story illustrates, there is no necessarily linear direction in their movement toward or away from political engagement. However, few of our interviewees— and few members of the sixties activist cohort in general—would claim that their political activity in recent years matches their youthful expectations. There is in the generation some distress, even guilt, about this. Many feel that they have failed to fulfill the promise of leadership for change that they seemed fifteen or twenty years ago to be offering to society. Many have been shocked by the prevalence of New Right and neoconservative politics in the eighties, and by the relative conservatism and apathy of students in these years. Such developments lead some to conclude that their historical moment has passed. Many have come to feel that the demands and pressures of ordinary adult roles have compelled them toward political withdrawal and compromise. Just as they, in the sixties, tended to believe that political commitment was a test of personal fortitude and individual moral integrity, so now many blame themselves and their generation for the weakness of the Left and their sense of political impotence and drift.

Such self-blame is, however, too one-sided. Back in the sixties, activists were sometimes aware that activism had to be supported and nurtured by social conditions and was not simply a matter of personal will. For example, in 1967 veterans of the student movement organized a conference with the title "Radicals in the Professions." The point was to confront what was described as "an essentially personal crisis that is widespread among people in the movement: the crisis of remaining radical beyond the college or graduate school years." (Haber and Haber 1969:289). Those who came were young professionals (doctors, lawyers, teachers) or professionals in training, or activists contemplating the possibility of returning to mainstream institutions. It was the first time that members of the New Left seriously engaged in collective examination of how to live politically for the long haul. Although the conference had few concrete results, a report of it by Barbara and Al Haber received rather wide dissemination. Al was the founding father of SDS; Barbara, his wife, an early member. Their report was called *Getting by with a Little Help from Our Friends*. Reading it more than twenty years later, one is struck by the fact that in 1967, before the New Left had crested in popularity, at a time when movement and counterculture were hardly formed, the Habers nevertheless could write:

> Many people described difficulty in finding emotional sustenance for political activism. They felt they were going dry, losing perspective. Political argument was becoming formalistic; conviction was floating away. Taking risks and being a marginal man was losing its reason. Signs of middle age stodginess were overcoming them. . . . Without adequate sources of support the dangers of co-optation are imminent. (Haber and Haber [1967] 1969: 307)

Even in those early days, then, the question of how to maintain commitment beyond one's youth was urgently felt, and worries about the loss of idealism sounded much like those expressed by our former Isla Vista activists many years later.

The Habers' report also provides us with a unique picture of what movement activists of that time believed about their political futures and about how they, as developing professionals and intellectuals, might find strategic roles in social change. The conference debate about these issues revolved around three strategic models. The first was a scenario more or less rooted in classic Marxian analysis. Some New Leftists, like several earlier generations of American radicals, placed their bets on economic breakdown as the trigger for future social transformation. A new depression would compel the reemergence of a revitalized working-class majority force, linking the already-militant underclass with white workers whose relative advantages were being wiped out. In this scenario, the most relevant role for intellectuals would be as organizers of the political cadre and educators of the political consciousness of newly awakened workers.

A second, more widely held perspective represented a self-conscious updating of Marxian class analysis in which professionals were conceived of as members of an emerging "new" working class. Millions of technicians, teachers, public service workers, and other college-educated workers would be the cutting edge of social change because of their collective action and their strategic position in the new, technologically advanced, economy. Economic deprivation and unemployment would not be the main threat to the new working class; instead, its members would organize to gain control of their work, and demands for workers' control would have a revolutionary effect on the society. This scenario, unlike the orthodox Marxian model, provides radical professionals with a strong justification for continuing to be professionals (rather than joining the traditional working class) and also suggests a fairly coherent direction for their political energy: the organization of fellow "new workers."

A third strategic perspective, probably more representative of the feelings of activist intellectuals and professionals than the two others, the Habers called "pluralistic revolution." Instead of imagining a single unfolding logic of social change, adherents believed that social transformation would be the result of a multiplicity of modes of organization, lines of action, and alternative building. Working in many locales, creating models of alternative work and lifestyle, experimenting with efforts to implement a new consciousness, radical professionals and intellectuals could make an ongoing contribution to political and cultural change while finding ways to live and work over the long term. Instead of expecting economic breakdown or a new class struggle, the New Left and its members ought to envision a process of change that would unfold along many paths with few sharp turning points and breakthroughs.

In order to make localized work politically meaningful, conference participants seemed to assume, some kind of national framework or organization needed to be developed and maintained so that radicals in the professions would take the movement (rather than the profession) as their primary reference group, so that the results of their social and political experiments could be shared and criticized and applied in other locales, so that collective vision rather than personal success would remain the barometer of accomplishment.

These scenarios anticipated the political paths taken by many student activists once the "long haul" rather than apocalypse was understood to define their futures. In our sample, only Barney Thompson adopted the strategic perspective of traditional Marxian class analysis, affiliating with a Maoist party that focused its energies on organizing industrial workers —a path followed by many hundreds of others across the country. None of our interviewees became self-conscious organizers within the context of the "new working class," but the hypothesis that such a class would be the key to the development of the Left remains important in understanding the evolution of the sixties generation, as we will try to suggest below.

The most prophetic scenario was the vision of a "pluralist revolution." In the 1970s, New Left activists moved out of the campus enclave and into a myriad of localized frameworks of political activism and a diversity of activist roles. Most of our interviewees were part of that process. As we have seen, they helped organize a variety of collective projects, including a legal collective and an alternative newspaper. Others, of whom Martha Koch and Denise Saal are the best examples, worked systematically to link a full-time professional career to a consciously formulated political strategy—in their cases, using medical training to become a key figure in labor and government programs dealing with occupational health and safety, and legal training to become a cofounder of an important project defending those accused of capital crimes. Still others, such as Ed Pines and Warren Newhouser, became full-time political organizers in a variety of community contexts and for a variety of causes.

It seems safe to conclude that the activism crystallized in the sixties New Left has been carried forward for two decades, particularly by those former student radicals who have been able to fuse their political concerns with some kind of vocational or institutional base. In literally hundreds of American towns and neighborhoods and work settings, such continuing activism has fostered increased grass-roots participation, more equitable policies and practices, and more protection for individual rights and community interests against the depredations of economic and political power.

Such local activism catalyzed a number of new social movements. It is often forgotten that the women's movement, the environmental movement, movements of gays, the handicapped, and other stigmatized groups, movements for community control and neighborhood revitalization, for tenants' rights, and seniors' needs, began to mobilize in the seventies, to a considerable extent the result of efforts by veterans of the sixties to carry forward the identity and vision they had developed as students into the larger society.[3] And even movements focusing on such global issues as the arms race, U.S. involvement in Central America, and world hunger are rooted in community action and education at the local level.

Indeed, one of the more striking things about the American Left in the aftermath of the sixties is that it is almost entirely made up of these sorts of local groups. No national party or organization representing New Left ideology survived the demise of the Students for a Democratic Society, and no national group today attracts the support or allegiance of the majority of activists who identify with American radical traditions. Twenty years ago, those who met at the "Radicals in the Professions" conference expected that such a national organizational framework would eventually undergird their political work. Indeed, veterans of student protest in western Europe were typically able to find such an organizational structure, either by working within established Left parties (like the British Labor Party, the socialist parties of France and Italy, or communist parties in Italy and other countries) or by forming new parties, of which the German Greens are the most successful example. The sense of drift and fragmentation, of failure and irrelevance that many post-sixties activists feel is rooted, not in the withdrawal from politics on their part, but in the absence of national political structures to provide direction, connection and national visibility for local activism.

Moreover, the absence of such a structure has meant that those former activists who now are pursuing individual career paths feel neither the opportunity nor the pressure to devote resources or energy to support of "the Left." It seems plausible that people like Roger Wade and Sheila Barressi, who experience a continuing identification with the Left, would feel themselves to be more politically involved if they had a European-style leftwing party to endorse as they pursued their relatively individualized intellectual and career goals.

Indeed, we have been struck by the fact that almost none of our interviewees seem able to believe that political activity as an ordinary citizen —supporting organizations and causes with dollars, attending rallies, subscribing to leftist periodicals, and otherwise lending personal support to groups one agrees with—represents "real" commitment. Having once defined political identity in totalistic ways, and having few available opportunities for adopting an overtly ideological stance, these people have, it seems, internalized a concept of political engagement that leaves them with a residue of guilt as they have come to lead more individualized lives and also relatively paralyzed when it comes to taking modest steps to implement their values in public ways. While they have lived by the code of noncomplicity defined in Chapter 1, many have, at least for now, failed to find a political role that satisfies them.

The absence of a national Left political structure was not the only problem that the post-sixties Left activists faced in trying to develop a coherent long-term strategy that would give their political work historical impact. As we have shown, many of the experiments in local organizing and institution-building could not be sustained for more than a few years; even those that survived could generally not avoid extensive turnover of full-time participants. Few people were able to work permanently as full-time political activists; instead, organizing and alternative institution-building were, by the late 1970s, defined as temporary roles, steps in the life course that were beneficial for people in their twenties but almost impossible for people past thirty.

In the early days of the New Left, it was frequently assumed that a long-term legacy of the movement would be the creation of a large number of full-time organizers who would spend their lives providing skills to empower the relatively voiceless and disadvantaged. It was an image of vocational possibility that had some roots in the labor movement experience of the thirties and forties, when a considerable number

of young people, including college students, found career avenues in
the growing union structure as organizers, researchers, educators, and
staff. It seemed plausible that parallel forms of work could be developed
within communities as well as workplaces—an idea advanced by the
Chicago-based community organizer Saul Alinsky after World War II,
and exemplified by those working out of his Industrial Areas Foundation in the fifties and sixties (Alinsky [1946] 1969). The initiation of the
Peace Corps and VISTA by the Kennedy administration gave additional
impetus to this notion, suggesting that the government itself might provide resources to make organizing the disadvantaged a vocation. By the
mid-sixties, as the War on Poverty took shape, and as churches and foun-
dations provided further support, it seemed quite likely that community
organization might well become institutionalized as a career outlet for
youthful idealism.

Such hopes seemed naive by 1969–70, when most activists, as we
have seen, doubted the capacity of the system to remain open to reform, let alone sponsor it. They were, however, somewhat revived by
the McGovern candidacy, which seemed to offer hope for a Left political breakthrough, and then, more strongly, by events surrounding the
Watergate scandal. It did not seem farfetched by the mid-seventies to
imagine that a revival of the New Deal coalition, invigorated by increasingly politicized minority communities, by a burgeoning of left-leaning
educated workers, and by the women's movement, could win majority
support for a new era of progressive reform. In such a climate, veterans
of the New Left would have much to offer as dedicated organizers and
policy-making intellectuals. A new liberalism would, in effect, provide
a sponsoring framework for new vocations dedicated to social change.
(For an interesting illustration of this kind of scenario, see Gitlin 1972.)

To a modest degree, the Carter administration provided some of this
sponsorship. The ACTION program, headed by former student activist
Sam Brown and staffed by others who had been involved in the student
antiwar movement, provided training, funding, and field opportunities
for thousands of young people in organizing projects around the country. But the hope for a new era of reform was dashed by the growing fiscal crisis at all levels of government and a growing corporate resistance to
what were perceived as inflationary demands to increase working-class
income and the size of the public sector.

In the sixties, the New Left took it for granted that "corporate liberalism"—that is, a willingness by the corporate elite to accept the welfare state and support improved living standards for the socially disadvantaged—was a permanent feature of American political reality. Indeed, the New Left was much more likely to criticize the welfare state as a bureaucratic threat to democracy than to defend it, since most believed that it was adequately defended by the powerful. Paradoxically, some of the personal hopes of sixties radicals depended not on a closing down of society to reform and dissent but on the progressive widening of opportunities for change. If repression was imagined as necessitating resistance, the liberal state and reform politics were understood as providing opportunities for political vocation. Indeed, in a climate of reform, radical activists would have room for positive experiment and a relatively solid base from which to advance a vision of democratic transformation.

In short, the problems of the post-sixties Left as a collective force, and of Left activists as individuals, had much to do with the fact that neither their dire predictions nor their hopeful anticipations came to pass in the seventies and eighties. Very little in either the experience or the social theories of the sixties generation of activists had prepared them for the stalemates, stagnations, and ambiguities of public life during the last fifteen years. Conditions were not harsh enough to inspire absolute resistance and opposition, nor were they sufficiently promising to inspire dedicated optimism. The political Right grew in strength, but not enough to put a clamp on popular protest and egalitarian impulse. Liberalism practically disintegrated as a coherent framework of policy and action, but not enough to clear ground for a more radical politics. Those who looked to the radical tradition as a basis for a new politics saw only disarray as socialist policies and politics seemed to fall apart even in those societies—such as the Western European countries—where socialism was most popular. In sum, no established ideological framework has been able to encompass the hopes or explain the experiences of our time, and thus, lacking a workable framework for developing their own discourse, New Leftists found themselves at sea in the eighties. As this is written, thousands of sixties veterans remain engaged, but without much visibility or representation in national political debate (except, perhaps, for Jesse Jackson's 1988 campaign for the Democratic presidential nomination). At the same time, predictions about a revival of the Left have begun to appear (see especially Harrington 1986 and Flacks 1988). In the event of a new New Left, at least some of our respondents may find new outlets for their activism.

Countercultural Continuities

For many people, the really interesting question about the fate of the sixties generation has less to do with the maintenance of political commitment than with the degree to which the sensibility and values associated with the counterculture have animated the lives of participants. Identification with the symbols, styles, and stances of the counterculture was far more widespread than support for the New Left among students and youth in the sixties, and its popularity was taken by a variety of commentators to signify the coming of a new age.

Despite the evident difficulty in defining what "counterculture" might have meant to those who participated in it, or in discerning what "participation" in it actually entailed, it seems plausible to say that by the second half of the sixties, large numbers of young people were questioning what they took to be core principles of social and personal organization in American life. Of these, the most important seemed to be the idea that self-worth depended on the degree of one's success in competitive struggles for status in school and career. Countercultural symbols, practices, and discourse overwhelmingly stressed that self-expression, the opening of self to feeling and to immediate experience, ought to take precedence over the postponement and repression of gratification required by striving for success. Exploring the possibilities for pleasure and widening one's realm of experience were more virtuous, as well as more fulfilling, than striving for money or status. Livelihood ought itself to provide gratification, and if this was not possible then it was fine to work so as to have income sufficient to support a free life. Many young people imagined that they could be artists—musicians, singers, poets, craftspersons—and if one could not make a living doing art, one could at least make a living in order to do art and to live artfully. Accordingly, quite a few students by the late sixties believed that they might work in very mundane jobs—driving cabs, waiting tables, even factory labor—provided that the job itself did not beat one down and that it provided enough to live on. What one wanted most of all was time and space to be free: freely feeling, freely mobile, freely expressive.

For many, freedom meant also freedom from material possessions. To live simply, to abandon the idea that one needed things in order to be fulfilled, to get away from consumer society, was a strongly and widely expressed aspiration. One ought to eat simple, natural, inexpensive foods, and dress simply and naturally, avoiding the fashionable and the formal. One ought to live simply, much more simply than one's parents. One did not need all the fancy gadgets and furnishings that typified an upper-middle-class lifestyle—although a good stereo might be important. One should travel light; the van became an important illustration of countercultural values because it seemed a practical, economical way to move freely, facilitating camping out and simple living. One might need marijuana and psychedelics, since these clearly enhanced one's capacity for feeling and pleasure and experience but were a safer, more natural source of chemical stimulation than alcohol and tobacco.

As we have emphasized, countercultural codes emphasized individual freedom and self-expression, but the experience of the time, and many of the practices and symbols adopted by students and youth, also emphasized collectivity and community. The sixties youth culture was hardly unique in celebrating friendship, for such celebration has always been integral to the experience of youth. But the counterculture heightened the moral centrality of sharing one's fate with one's peers and constructed a vision of such community as a long-term possibility. That vision was acted out in vast celebratory assemblies such as Woodstock, in self-consciously communal households, and in the movement of considerable numbers in the late 1960s and early 1970s into full-time communes. There was considerable awareness that individual freedom from established cultural constraints required social support, that a simple lifestyle based on low-wage jobs might require sharing of goods, that the creation of a new way of life might require physical distancing from mainstream society and the establishment of an alternative community.

The implicit hypothesis of the countercultural perspective was that it was possible to create one's freedom in the midst of the established culture, if one had some creativity and the help of one's friends. Many believed that the old culture was dying and that in its weakening condition, more and more cracks would inevitably open for free spirits. But the triumph of the new culture would be inevitable, since it was the property of the young, who would outlive the old while staying true to the new. Moreover, many considered hedonism, love, and self-expression so seductive that the counterculture would subvert the Establishment if its young adherents would just continue to "do it."

Because we were following the lives of people who had been politically engaged students, and because most students who identified to some degree with the counterculture were not political activists, our investigation provides relatively limited materials for interpreting the ways in which the codes and beliefs and sensibilities of the counterculture influenced the personal development of the sixties generation as a whole. Still, the stories of our respondents provide some clues about such influence.

The lives of all of the student radicals were in some significant ways affected by cultural changes traceable to the sixties. First, all of these people have struggled intensely with the issue of vocation, refusing to simply settle down, refusing to accept readily available opportunities for material comfort and privilege. This conclusion is powerfully reinforced when one compares the former protesters with the former nonactivist students. The latter overwhelmingly have followed career trajectories they began when they graduated from college, trajectories aimed at status and money-making as principal goals. What is most interesting about the comparison is not just that the nonactivists are making so much more money than the activists; it is that the latter have all followed such circuitous, experimental, tentative routes, and many do not seem yet to be at their final career destination.

Indeed, quite a few of the activists remain extraordinarily mobile both geographically and vocationally into their late thirties. Simply to describe the career patterns of many of these people is to illustrate how the countercultural aversion to "success" has been lived out: Steve Rubin, after years as a fishing boat captain, is now working as a free-lance journalist; Barney Thompson, after years as a postal clerk, is now working in a radical bookstore; Kristen Van Duinen is living and teaching in Greece; Terry Lennox, after having lived in a rural countercultural community for many years, is now teaching and writing in South Africa; Ed Pines, after years of earning a subsistence wage working in a hunger project and other small-scale, local efforts, is studying for his teaching credentials.

Through most of the seventies, in fact, the former radicals we interviewed were attempting to live within a countercultural context. When we first contacted them, some were still living and working in some kind of communal or collective arrangement, spending a good deal of energy on trying to make such arrangements practical and durable for the long haul. An important part of the collective experience of our sample—and of the members of their generation who have sought social and personal change—was the inability to sustain the commune and the collective as alternatives to the conventional family and workplace.

A growing literature is tracing the fate of these collectivist experiments in an effort to assess the strengths and limits of social arrangements deliberately constructed to overcome the alienation and oppression inherent in established structures. By now it seems obvious enough that counterculturalists were, initially, extraordinarily naive in imagining that long-established cultural principles and social logics—such as those supporting hierarchical authority, role specialization, personal possession and privacy, monogamy, and professional expertise—could be replaced simply because people ardently desired such change. To some extent, these experiments suffered from their participants' lack of experience and training. The inevitable problems in managing and resolving interpersonal tensions, and in managing practical affairs, were frequently exacerbated by the sheer naivete and inexperience of members, and the prevailing disdain for leadership and expertise.

But it was because these experiments were rooted in the larger culture and political economy that they were limited as frameworks for the permanent construction of satisfying personal lives for many participants. As time went on, participants often found conventional lifeways more attractive than they had expected them to be, when compared with the prospects of continuing to live in alternative ways.

Such changes in the cost-benefit ratios associated with alternative lifestyle were the result of a variety of experiences and social developments. First, there were the burdens of managing life in alternative ways and in relative poverty—many of which had been romantically ignored in the discourse of the sixties. Second, mainstream institutions themselves began to open space for reform and innovation in response to countercultural criticism. As interpersonal informality became more and more prevalent in the seventies, as some established firms and institutions provided greater room for employee voice and expression, as established schools adopted some of the principles of the free school movement, and as established churches welcomed countercultural liturgical influences, the rationale for maintaining nonconventional experiments outside the system became blurred.

A third influence was inflation. It became harder to live at a subsistence level, and harder for collectives to support members through marginal jobs as housing costs skyrocketed and the general cost of living escalated. In Isla Vista and Santa Barbara, for example, rents doubled, tripled, and quadrupled between 1970 and 1980, with each ratchet upward forcing another flock of counterculturalists to leave town or to look for "straight" jobs.

Finally, many participants in countercultural experiments experienced a growing disillusionment with the historical meaning of their effort. This was dramatically illustrated in our stories. If they were sacrificing income and security and mainstream recognition, what was the social benefit? Some had come to doubt their own efficacy as historical agents. Others, seeing the decline of mass protest and militancy, wondered whether the political relevance of their own commitment had disintegrated. Radical law collectives, brought into being by the need to defend black revolutionaries, found themselves handling mundane landlord-tenant cases. Radical alternative newspapers, hoping to report and reflect movement actions, found themselves covering restaurant openings and rock concerts. Such experiences again blurred the lines between "alternative" and "mainstream," further shifting the cost-benefit balance against continued commitment to the counterculture.[4]

As in politics, so in culture. After the sixties, sufficient space for self-expression opened up so that large numbers of graduates of the student revolt could reenter mainstream patterns of job and family and lifestyle without feeling that they had fundamentally betrayed their youthful idealism. The dominant culture turned out to be less monolithic and more permeable than many sixties youths had expected. Indeed, no aspect of mainstream life has been untouched by changes in culture and sensibility begun in the sixties. In sexuality and gender relations, in childrearing and household organization, in aesthetic taste and personal morality, in spirituality and psychotherapy—in all these and many other areas of culture, belief and practice have been deeply affected by the ferment of the sixties and experiments in the aftermath. And, as a result, we have all learned how porous mainstream American culture can be—how much can change and yet how much, fundamentally, does not.

THE FATE OF SIXTIES COMMITMENT: TAKE SIX

So far in this chapter we have been trying to reconstruct the movement's self-understanding of its impact on the lives of its members. We have sketched what appear to have been movement members' implicit hypotheses about long-term commitment, and then, reflecting on our case histories and on cultural and personal developments, attempted to draw some conclusions about how well such youthful expectations anticipated what seems actually to have happened. If movement activists imagined that they would be the vanguard of political and cultural revolution, they were certainly wildly romantic. We have suggested that the declining radicalism of sixties veterans was not necessarily due to their own aging; instead, a key problem for activists in the post-movement era has been that political, cultural, and economic conditions have developed in unanticipated ways.

There is no doubt that the insights into human potential and social possibility envisioned in the sixties had considerable practical validity as leads for social and personal change. But what was beyond the youth of the sixties was a theory of American society adequate to its complexity, its ambiguity, its contradictions. Lacking an organizational vehicle that might have enabled such a theory to be formulated and shared, sixties veterans have been required to improvise in small circles and on their own, continuously renegotiating the meaning of their commitments as their own life-situations and their social understandings have evolved. Contrary to popular myth, however, it is not true that they have abandoned their commitments. Many are still working, still changing, still trying to make a difference.

There is one more angle on the historical meaning and personal impact of the sixties that we want to discuss: the diagnoses and predictions made by various commentators and social scientists. A considerable industry of such commentary developed during that period, for it was hard to avoid the supposition that the emergence and growth of the movement and the counterculture carried historical significance, or were symptoms of important changes in society. Out of that period emerged social theorizing of considerable influence, and much of that theorizing involved predictions about how the sensibilities and orientations represented among the young would affect their development and the devel-

opment of society as a whole. An effort to assess how well such predictions have stood the test of time sheds further light on the meaning of
the youth revolt—and on quite a few other matters as well.

Has America Greened?

The most ambitious interpretations of the sixties argued that the revolt
of youth signified the dawning of a new age. The essential point was that
the traditional cultural framework rooted in the Protestant ethic, which
emphasized self-denial, postponement of gratification, and commitment
to work, was being invalidated by technological, organizational, and
economic transformations. The decline of the entrepreneurial role, the
rise of the giant bureaucratic corporation, the replacement of human
labor by machinery, and perhaps above all the emergence of consumption as the driving force for economic growth, required values and motives quite different from those celebrated in capitalism's earlier days.

Some commentators in the fifties had already made these points, most
notably, perhaps, David Reisman in his highly popular book, *The Lonely
Crowd* (1950). But such commentators assumed not that American suc-
cess-oriented individualism would decline with the decline of the Protestant ethic, but that it would be expressed in new ways. Instead of
striving in market competition, Reisman and others argued, achievement was being redefined in terms of social approval and capacities to
manipulate other people, winning position in bureaucratic struggles for
status and power.

Sixties commentators took such notions of cultural transformation a
step further. Most romantic was Charles Reich (1970), who claimed that
Consciousness I (the Protestant ethic) and Consciousness II (the bureaucratic ethic) would be challenged by Consciousness III (the counterculture ethic). Con III disdained striving and success altogether in favor
of being and pleasure and spontaneity. Although Reich himself did not
develop a theory to explain why Con III was emerging and why it
would prevail, a number of leading ideas at the time pointed in similar
directions. For example, it was widely suggested that emphasis on consumption, demanded by the economy's dependence on growth of the
consumer goods industry and propelled by a continually more pene-
trating mass media, was undermining commitment to competitive success. Young people socialized by mass media were encouraged to act

out impulse and desire, to be hedonistic, to live for the now. More-over, increased leisure-time opportunities and discretionary income in middle-class families required and made possible the cultivation of taste and the pursuit of fulfillment. Family childrearing patterns were chang-ing as well. Middle-class parents were less single-mindedly stressing achievement, encouraging consumerism—whether consciously or not.

Added to this was the increasingly mother-centered character of the middle-class family; boys who identified with their mothers (as many probably did) might well be less committed to traditional striving for wealth, status, and power. Moreover, as greater numbers of young peo-ple attended college, more and more would be exposed to values and perspectives critical of established culture and to definitions of the good life that put the spiritual and the intellectual ahead of the material and the aggrandizing. Such trends in the socialization of the young helped explain the appeal of countercultural symbols, values, and practices, since the counterculture was providing the young with an opportunity to express the otherwise inchoate yearnings and alienations that these cultural changes had fostered in them (see Reich 1970; Flacks 1971; Bell 1976).

Such considerations not only served to explain the popular appeal of the counterculture, but provided a prediction about the future—namely, that the new young as they got older would continue to be restlessly unwilling to conform to demands of established work organizations, whether refusing to be absorbed into bureaucracy, trying instead to find livelihood in more autonomous ways, or becoming a relatively undisci-plined and even rebellious work force within established firms and agen-cies. Reich made rather specific predictions about the growing preva-lence of "natural" clothing and food and personal styles, predicting a society in which people would make their own working conditions and work time, and in which all sorts of formal constraints, rules, and bound-aries would be easily seen as artificial barriers to healthy, expressive free-dom. Surely, having tasted freedom through sex, drugs, music, surfing, and celebration, the new youth would not settle for boring, constricting, repressive routines as they went on in life. Moreover, Reich seemed to be arguing, such feelings are very widespread, affecting a whole genera-tion, not just those relatively few who were highly committed to activist roles.

Reading such speculation in the late eighties, one is astonished by its naiveté and incredulous that *The Greening of America* was ever taken seriously (it was even serialized in the *New Yorker*). Obviously, America has not greened in the ways Reich fantasized. Bureaucratic control (which was, in any case, less rigid than he suggested) certainly softened. As we have suggested, there has been enough loosening of authority and relaxation of formality to enable many members of the sixties generation to move comfortably in bureaucratic arenas they had expected to be constricting and deadening. Many of the new tastes and practices that originated in the counterculture entered the mainstream of popular culture and commodity. By the mid-1970s, most of America was wearing blue jeans. Water beds and granola became staples in middle-class suburbia, and Bob Dylan tunes were programmed on supermarket Muzak. The commodification and absorption of countercultural symbols and styles and practices represented, for many, a kind of relief; instead of waging war on the young, the society and culture were integrating them. But what was remarkable was how little such inclusion changed the central logics of market, bureaucracy, state, and media.

Indeed, instead of redefining work and authority relations, members of the sixties generation have tended to follow strategies of accommodation already well developed by previous generations. For Americans, freedom in the era of mass production and consumption has meant freedom in leisure time to pursue private interests, fulfillments, and escapes. It is a freedom bought at the price of unfreedom on the job. The overwhelming value of jobs is to provide the wherewithal, not only to survive, but to have some free time and privacy. Most workers do not believe that it is worth trying to make work freer and more self-expressive.

The college-educated have been far less willing to make such trade-offs. Indeed, a primary motive for attending college is to gain access to careers that are more rewarding and work situations that provide more freedom and self-determination than do working-class jobs. Accordingly, one would have thought that, having been imbued not only with the established sense of entitlement associated with college degrees, but also with the experience of student protest and countercultural freedom, post-sixties college graduates entering the labor force would indeed have been active agents of change. Instead, what has been much more characteristic of them is a readiness to settle for "alienating" jobs and an eager willingness to express self and seek pleasure through an unprecedented elaboration of leisure-time consumerism. Instead of challenging the work-consumption trade-off, many post-sixties workers—whether college educated or not—seem to have learned to take it for granted.

In the seventies, while most of our activists were experimenting with the development of work and living arrangements alternative to those provided by established frameworks, millions of other Americans were also experimenting with new forms of expression. Out of the counterculture spilled new, non-Western religious groupings, and quite a few Americans visited these new shrines (including two of our respondents, although only Kenneth Essian developed long-standing commitment).[5] New forms of healing—both psychological and physical—were widely publicized, and practitioners won many clients. Guide books to self-transformation proliferated, and Americans by the millions learned about the *Joy of Sex* (in several volumes), about the cuisines of every part of the globe, about innumerable regimens for making the body fit and beautiful. Countercultural prophets like Reich had been right— Americans were hungry for (or at least receptive to) practices and ideas that would heighten their sensuality, increase their happiness, make life and self more beautiful. The counterculture in the sixties had turned out to be a breeding and testing ground for such practices and ideas. By the seventies, entrepreneurs, including many with good countercultural credentials, were learning how to package and market these for wide consumption. The result has no doubt been to greatly widen the range of possibility for everyday expression, release, and relief, although after a few years the considerable charlatanry involved led to disillusionment with the notion that special secrets of happiness lurked outside the bounds of Western culture. Moreover, the explosion of cultural innovation in the seventies signified that Americans interested in change were seeking it through individualized leisure-time pursuits rather than through the greening of the main institutional structures of society.

By the eighties, the story of the sixties generation as told and retold in popular culture was that the hippies became yuppies. The yuppie image was that of the driven young professional or businessperson, whose central goal was to make money in order to engage in elaborately refined consumption. Yuppies were not fifties-style organization men in gray flannel suits, beaten into sterile self-denying conformity by the exigencies of bureaucratic career. Instead, they knew how to play the system for personal gain, seeking the wherewithal to buy the accoutrements of personal freedom and pleasure rather than striving for success in the tra-

ditional sense. Despite such fundamental differences in style and motivation, however, the form of accommodation defined by this imagery
remains: live within the rules of the organization and the market, seek
freedom in the time away from work.

This is precisely the division of self that the counterculture hoped
to overcome. If anything, the division may be sharper for the younger
members of the business and professional sector, because they seem to
have less belief than older generations that career advancement can bring
more opportunity for self-expression and fulfillment in work. Whatever
the color of their cynicism, it is not green.

Restructuring the Life Cycle?

A less publicized but far more cogent prediction about the social and
cultural impact of the sixties appeared in the work of Kenneth Keniston (1968, 1971), who had done pioneering studies of "alienated" and
activist students. Keniston argued that the emergence and prolongation
of adolescence in industrial society, which resulted from the extension of
compulsory education, was now being paralleled by the prolongation of
"youth" as a stage of life. Youth is a time of life after adolescence, in
which the person has achieved full physical and cognitive adulthood but
is socially authorized to remain free from adult role commitments (and
thus not expected to organize a family or enter the labor force). The social
function of this postponement of adulthood was obviously to train for
roles requiring extensive technical knowledge and skill as well as capacities for initiative and autonomy. The elaboration of graduate training,
the development of large-scale research enterprises around universities,
the rapidity of social change, and the contradictions of culture all encouraged young people to postpone career and family commitments past college graduation and into their twenties. A continuing quest for vocation
and identity was further encouraged by upper-middle-class socialization: parents telling children that their lives ought to be as "meaningful"
as possible, that their choices were personally and socially consequential, that they ought not and need not settle for simple and convenient
resolutions. Keniston predicted that this transformation of the life-cycle
would be a significant and immediate outcome of the sixties youth ferment.

Unlike commentators such as Reich, Keniston's prediction was not a sweeping generalization about a whole generation, but was meant to apply to a fraction of one (albeit one that was expected to grow). Moreover, Keniston did not short-circuit the connections between the personal changes he anticipated and large-scale social change. What he did expect was that those who postponed adult commitment would have freedom to develop a fuller, more complex, more individuated framework for their lives and would therefore be capable of achieving a degree of social or cultural creativity less readily available to those who settled down at an earlier point in life.

One of our clearest findings is that former student activists postponed adulthood in just the ways that Keniston had anticipated. It is striking that most of them had not yet settled into a long-term career commitment by age thirty, that none were married or had yet had children. Indeed, some now in their late thirties continue to be unsettled in the conventional sense.

How developmentally beneficial their refusal to follow conventional paths and play conventional roles has been is a far more difficult question. Some express regret that they did not arrive at career decisions earlier, feeling disadvantaged in competition with younger people in their fields, looking back on their earlier years as a time of distress. It is hard for us to evaluate these feelings. As researchers it would not be appropriate to try to pass judgment on the choices and character of the people whom we have been interacting with these many years, all of whom lead lives that express considerable individuation and conscious choice. We can say confidently, however, that Keniston identified an important cultural development. In the aftermath of the sixties, the timing and nature of decisions concerning relationship and vocation have changed for considerable numbers of people. A life pattern oriented toward career fluidity rather than stability, toward avoidance—or at least postponement—of marriage and of child bearing and raising, typifies not only the handful of former activists we interviewed but large numbers of their peers.

In the late seventies and eighties, a supposedly more competitive job market for college graduates, along with increasing ambivalence toward sexual freedom (because of AIDS and other sexually transmitted diseases), was leading some to expect that the extended youth pattern characteristic of the sixties cohort would be replaced by a more traditional emphasis on careerism and family stability. Perhaps the sixties generation will be seen as an anomalous one, a blip of unconventionality in a long-term pattern of relatively smooth transition from adolescence to adulthood in the American middle class. Still, the experience of that generation, and the models of experiment, search, and fluidity that have come out of it, are likely to continue to influence the timing and patterning of adult development.

Is There a Sixties Generation?

A major question about the survival and historical impact of the sixties movement has been whether the generational solidarity and protest that members of the cohort experienced would continue to bind people and shape attitudes as the cohort moved into adulthood and maturity. Many years ago, Karl Mannheim, observing a powerful youth movement in Germany, suggested that "generation" could serve, like "class" or "ethnic group," as a basis for membership solidarity, shared perspectives, and collective action. The generational hypothesis predicts a distinctive perspective for a given cohort as it moves through the life cycle when compared with other age groups. Mannheim thought that such a development was likely in the aftermath of a youth movement, or when people shared in their youth a common historical experience such as a war or economic catastrophe (Mannheim [1928] 1972; see also Goertzel 1972; Abrams 1982; DeMartini 1983, 1985; Braungart and Braungart 1986).

How strong is the generational consciousness of people who were young in the sixties? The question has been debated now for twenty years. Even at the height of student protest, there were those who pointed out that large numbers of the young were not involved. Not only were the majority of youths not in college, but many were supporters of rightwing leaders like George Wallace—and even among college students there were wide differences in social location and attitude (Lipset 1967, 1971). Moreover, Mannheim himself recognized that generations would typically divide along these sorts of class and status lines, proposing the term "generation-unit" to designate such subgroups within the larger age cohort.

Still, by the end of the decade, some survey data suggested that youth, whether in college or not, were developing some distinctive perspectives having to do with personal morality, war, race, and "materialism" (Yan-kelovich 1981). Even if the cohort were divided, the shape of attitudes within it was distinctive, and a kind of dominant perspective seemed to bridge class and locational divisions. By the end of the decade, a wave of antiwar, antiauthority feeling was evident within the army as well as on the campus. The draft threatened the freedom of whites as well as blacks, middle- as well as working-class youth. Music and mari-juana brought young people of all backgrounds together in spirit and in the flesh. Advertisers exploited latent generational feelings, appealing to the "Pepsi generation" and the "Dodge Rebellion." Police hassled long-haired hippies and ghetto youths, fueling the sense of common rebellion. By the end of the decade the media image of a worldwide generational upsurge was reinforcing feelings already very widely shared. It was at that time hard to find young people untouched by at least some elements of youth protest. Indeed, recalling the climate of 1969–70 leads one to the inescapable conclusion that our nonactivist respondents, who pro-fessed so little allegiance to the symbols of the time, were rather isolated from the dominant spirit of that moment among their peers.

As members of the cohort moved out beyond the campus, the ghetto street, the military base, and other enclaves of youth, it was to be ex-pected that their feelings of generational solidarity would dissipate. The ending of the draft and removal of U.S. troops from Vietnam, relaxation of police enforcement of marijuana laws, and the entrance of many youth into adult work and family roles all served to undermine the sense of peer identification and shared destiny. However, as we noted in Chap-ter 3, in 1972 it was this cohort (those then eighteen to twenty-five) that alone voted in the majority for George McGovern, while the rest of the electorate went overwhelmingly for Nixon. And Gallup and other poll data at the time showed that this voting pattern reflected a continuing cohort distinctiveness on a range of items.

Some fifteen years later, there continues to be interest in the possi-bility that the sixties cohort shares a potential for collective generational feeling and action. Alongside the myths of lost and betrayed youthful idealism, there is a rather contrary belief—namely, that the people of the sixties are still "different" and continue to feel a bond with their age-mates. Media promoters search for keys to unlock these latent feelings and so do political operators. A recent case in point was George Bush's selection of Dan Quayle as his running mate, hoping to capitalize on Quayle's supposed generational appeal.

Our study can not, in itself, shed much light on the persistence of generational feeling among members of the sixties cohort. Our two interview groups were very different, we assume, when they were young, and the contrasts between the two groups, which our sampling approach was designed to tap, remain sharp. The fact that both the activists and the nonactivists belong to the sixties generation tells us relatively little about what they have in common. We have, on the other hand, presented some evidence that suggests that the nonactivists were, in their youth, likely to have shared at least some of the prevailing attitudes toward the war, the justice system, student rights, and drug use. The majority of them supported McGovern in 1972, for example. Many of them told us that they have become more conservative as the years have gone by, reflecting, they say, the interests and perspectives they have acquired as they have increased their wealth, comfort, and privilege. If these people are any guide (and their small number and lack of representativeness makes it difficult to say), then whatever generational consciousness they may have had has been overwhelmed by a growing sense of class interest.

Meanwhile, although the former activists retain strong identification with their shared past as youth, it is not evident that they feel much common bond with their generation in the present. Indeed, one of the conclusions many drew as they reevaluated the New Left experience was that generational identification was too fragile and limited a basis for building the collective action needed for significant social change. Marx, rather than Mannheim, was their guide on such matters; and, in each case, their activism shifted out of Isla Vista into projects that sought links with other ages and sectors. Martha Koch worked on occupational health in a labor union context; Barney Thompson joined a Maoist party emphasizing organizing among factory workers; Sarah Glenn became active in feminist groups; Cynthia Spivak taught health education classes to poor and working-class women's groups in the community and in prisons; Roger Wade and Sheila Barressi founded an alternative newspaper aimed at a wide community audience. Each of these was consciously breaking out of the generational mold in order to become more politically effective. In doing this, they were participating in a general movement of New Left activists in the seventies, a movement out of the youth revolt and into America at large.

The Rise of the New Working Class?

From the beginning, it was clear that the New Left was not attracting support from all sectors of the student body, that its origins and strongest support came from a particular sector. An early clue was provided by pollster Sam Lubell, who discerned that:

> *Within the new generation, this conflict of economic identification be-*
> *tween those who look to the public purse and those who look to the private*
> *purse seems to be the major political divider.* This has to do with quest
> for careers involved with "working with people" rather than "just
> making money," rooted in the relative affluence of middle-class fami-
> lies giving kids more freedom to pursue wider career choice. (Lubell
> 1968: 52–60; emphasis in original.)

Lubell's impression held up extraordinarily well as an interpretation of the sources of student radicalism. As we have noted, Flacks's research on the family backgrounds of student activists found that, overwhelmingly, their parents derived their income from public or nonprofit institutional frameworks, or from professional careers that were distanced from or bore a critical relation to the private corporate system. These early studies were generally confirmed by large numbers of later ones. Moreover, Lubell's insight was buttressed by many studies indicating that the interests of left-leaning students were indeed directed toward careers in human service and the knowledge industry.

These kinds of findings helped contribute to an analysis that argued that the student movement was a symptom not of general cultural transformation or generational revolt but of the rise of a "new working class" —sometimes also called the "new class" or the "professional-managerial class." New-working-class theorists disagreed on many matters of definition and prediction, but the essence of the argument was that the rising importance of knowledge, and of social control, in the functioning of advanced industrial (or post-industrial) society gave increasing strategic importance to those who produced and distributed knowledge and were professionally involved in the organization, and systematic socialization, of people. These workers, whose position in society depended on advanced education rather than property, were not tied directly to capitalism as such; indeed, their own educational development and their roles predisposed them to be critical of capitalist values, practices, and outcomes. Their numbers were rapidly increasing; and this increase in numerical power, combined with their increasing importance, gave them potential for political impact as an independent force. Because of their critical predispositions, because many had grievances relating to the conditions and terms of their work, and because they were in considerable tension with the established ruling elite, this rising class could represent a major force for change—perhaps replacing the industrial proletariat as the key dynamic opposition to the status quo in the advanced industrial countries.

The student movement provided strong evidence for these ideas. Here was an ostensibly privileged group, in terms of both personal prospects and social origin, that nevertheless was becoming a source of militant protest and opposition, and that had a surprising degree of impact on the society once mobilized. Moreover, the content of student expression was oriented toward social transformations that would, in fact, shift power away from established economic, military, and bureaucratic structures toward communities, work groups, and other grass-roots sectors where intellectuals, teachers, social workers, and professionals would have a chance for active influential voice. "Participatory democracy," although a vision of universal emancipation, could also be seen as a vision of a society in which the sorts of people young New Leftists wanted to be would have a good deal more relevance. Finally, it seemed likely that student protest, demanding more voice in university governance, could well be a harbinger of future struggles for worker control in which former student protesters would now—as journalists, teachers, social workers, scientists, technicians, nurses, and the like—be demanding a voice within the work settings they would be inhabiting. A "long march through the institutions of society" was predicted by German New Leftist Rudi Dutschke. What he meant was that the democratizing impulse expressed by students would spread, and one way it would spread would be through the organization of the "new working class" that the students were preparing to enter.[6]

Insofar as the new working class theories were intended to discern a new revolutionary agency to replace Marx's proletariat, they were, of course, misguided. Moreover, these theories suffer from difficulty in defining the essential character of the "class." None successfully defined the boundaries of the "class," nor is it entirely clear that the concept "class" ought to be applied to whatever is being referred to. The conditions under which members of the categories might mobilize and radi-calize remained poorly worked out. Despite these caveats, however, the perspective seems the most promising lead for interpreting both the ori-gins and the trajectory of the student activists.

In an early effort to develop such an interpretation, Flacks (1971b) called the group the "intelligentsia," defining this category as including all those occupationally engaged in the creation, production, distribu-tion, and inculcation of culture. It is to this sort of work that all of our former student activists felt called from the outset and to which they have been drawn. Even those who took traditional working-class jobs, like Steve Rubin, a fisherman, and Barney Thompson, a postal worker, continued to write, and by the time we concluded our efforts to con-tact them, both had left their original jobs to devote more energy to intellectual or political work.

If many members of the sixties cohort became "yuppies" and entered career lines aimed at upward mobility and high income, probably a larger number became part of the "intelligentsia," doing work with people, symbols, and ideas—work that sustains contact with the issues of soci-etal maintenance and development. The legacy of the sixties movement lives on most fully in the moral outlooks, political orientations, and life-styles of those in the generation who became part of the "intelligen-tsia." We would expect to find, in an analysis of relevant survey data for example, that large numbers of sixties-generation adults who en-tered corporate career frameworks became more conservative and less and less distinctive as they moved up ladders of career, income, and privilege. Where the generational difference would be found would be among those former students who have not moved up in those ways, whose work and daily social relations bring them into continuing routine involvement with cultural production and reproduction. These people are not the vanguard of "revolution" now; in fact, they have, in the eighties, been demobilized and demoralized. Still, they constitute much of the core of the popular Left in the United States and in Europe. They are the prime constituency of the peace movement, of environmental-ism, of feminism, and of the left wing of the Democratic party and the labor movement. But the long-term political evolution of this sector, its possible relation to the more traditional working class, its potential re-sources for effective mobilization and influence—all such topics remain to be debated and analyzed and theorized. For various reasons, the new-working-class hypothesis has been eclipsed, yet it may hold many of the keys to understanding the dynamics of social and cultural change in American society in general, and the legacy of the sixties in particular.

THE FATE OF SIXTIES COMMITMENT: FINAL TAKE

The story of the impact of the sixties on American history and daily life is not finished, if only because the lives of participants continue to evolve. The most striking thing about the lives of former sixties activists as we found them is their fluidity. The life course certainly presents each of us with some inescapable choices and constraints, yet virtually all of our activist respondents have refused to cede control over their lives to forces outside themselves, struggling instead to define for themselves where they ought to be going, trying at each turn to take paths that express meanings and principles and values rather than merely necessity.

We have written as if what these people have become is in large part the product of their participation in the movement. That is the story we are telling and so we have emphasized it, taking as evidence the ways in which our respondents continue to live in terms that seem continuous with the commitments they shared together. But perhaps both their movement participation and their subsequent lives were determined by still-earlier dispositions and traits. Perhaps their inability to "settle down" and "grow up" rests on a neurotic propensity that also attracted them to adolescent rebellion, and that has little to do with a positive value orientation of the kind we have been arguing for.

Obviously, we are not sympathetic to interpretations that define non-conformity as pathological. We could not dismiss out of hand, however, the argument that our respondents are the way they are because of propensities rooted in childhood as well as conscious "values" rooted in their youth. Personal development is inescapably multidetermined; so our effort to trace current states of being to sixties experience offers only a partial understanding of these people as fully developed human beings.

Sixties veterans have tried to sustain control over what they were becoming. We have also found that they have not succeeded in so doing. At every turn, they had to confront unanticipated changes in economic conditions, political climate, and social dynamics that fundamentally affected the structure of opportunities available to them to be and to do what principle and aspiration suggested they ought. The more un-conventional and experimental their choices, the more difficult it was to sustain them. In particular it proved most difficult to formulate life directions rooted in the notion that one could live simply at low income and thereby be free to do good work. A second difficulty was in formulating permanent alternative work and domestic collectives more attractive in the long run than the relatively secure livelihood and comfortable intimacy available within the framework of conventional work and family structures.

Finally, it became increasingly difficult to sustain political activism as the Left became increasingly localized, fragmented, and diffuse. For at least a decade the Left as a force on a global level has been in a demoralized and defensive condition, in large part because Left activists have been unable to control or adequately account for a variety of major social happenings. The economic problems of the Western capitalist countries were rooted in the exhaustion of the vision and program of the social democratic welfare state, giving new life to the right wing. The evident economic stagnation of the state socialist countries and the desire of China and the Soviet Union to accommodate to American power has been a confusing development for Left activists. Revelations of atrocity and failure in Third World revolutionary countries have been painfully demoralizing for many. For all of these reasons, the Left as an organized, coherent movement, as a source of initiative and vision, has been becalmed for the last ten years. For people like our activist respondents, the result has been a need to make one's own political way in one's immediate circle with less and less obvious historical validation of the meaning of one's efforts.

Given the declining opportunities for effective activism, it is perhaps surprising how much our respondents have been able to retain of their commitment to make some difference in the world. Their scale of operation is modest, as are their hopes, but most of them remain at least potential centers of energy for change.

What is surprising about these people—and about the entire generation of veterans of the sixties movement—is how little they think about the possible political implications of their own dilemmas and troubles. We have seen that several theories of the movement anticipated that in their post-student years members would find bases of mobilization around their own shared "class" interests. However, little of this has been evident. For example, a number of years ago, Fred Block, making use of Keniston's notion of the youth stage, proposed a political program in which the personal aspirations of the sixties generation for a continuously developing adulthood would be articulated as a central theme (Block 1978). Such a program would focus on shortening the work-week, on developing opportunities (including financial support) for life-long learning, on guaranteed minimum incomes, and on expanded opportunities for people to work in community development. Block argued that the movement embodied a social vision that placed self-development at its core, and that political action devoted to freeing people from restraints on growth and promoting developmental adulthood would represent a primary way to fulfill the promise of the sixties.

Such pronouncements were, of course, very rare; instead, people seeking to maintain control over their lives have tried to do so through personal initiative, blaming themselves for failure when such efforts did not succeed, never seeing the sorts of political, collective connections that Block suggested. The opportunity for such a political thrust to emerge remains, but Block's proposal allows us to see more clearly what has been missing from the experience and consciousness of sixties veterans that helps account for their difficulties in sustaining commitment.

A second, related, factor has to do with the new-working-class perspective. Clearly, although the intelligentsia remain leftish, this category has not in the last few years mobilized as a "class for itself," does not possess a distinctive identity, is not evolving a politics expressing its interests. This is true despite the long drought in job opportunities in teaching, academia, and social service, the drying up of the public sector, and the "proletarianization" of work conditions for many educated workers—all conditions predicted to lead to mobilization. Whether one considers the need for child care, or for expanded job opportunities, or for greater voice in the work place, the educated work force has been far less mobilized and New Left veterans far less involved in mobilizing than might have been expected. Public service unionization has continued, but its forms and expressions are parochial rather than class-oriented. And although members of the intelligentsia typically support liberal politicians and advocate social reform, their "long march" has not continued. Instead, again, most have felt pressured into accommodation by the narrowed job market, competing with each other for scarce opportunities rather than banding together to expand them.

The lives we have looked at in this inquiry, then, have been deeply affected by their intertwining with social movement. The flow and ebb of collective action is the primary context within which lives committed to principle are lived. It is not that in ebb times principles are abandoned, for what we have found is quite different. But it is the case that personal conviction is insufficient to make commitment fully meaningful. The spirit of the sixties did not die as its bearers got older, nor did they betray that spirit. Perhaps the spirit waits for a new opportunity that will permit the tide of collective action once more to rise.

Notes

Chapter 1

1. A discussion of media reports on the fate of sixties activists can be found in Whalen 1981 and Whalen 1984.
2. Detailed reviews of these studies can be found in DeMartini 1983 and Whalen 1984. The limited amount of research on the fate of sixties activism is puzzling, given the large number of studies that were done on the sources and dynamics of student protest during the 1960s and 1970s. Moreover, the recent studies of Isserman (1987), Miller (1987), and Gitlin (1987), while providing substantial information and new insights concerning the history of the New Left, do not address its legacy or the post-sixties careers of its members in any systematic fashion. (Isserman deals with the origins of the movement and its relationship to the Old Left; Miller focuses on the 1962–68 period, taking us from the founding of SDS to the "siege of Chicago"; and Gitlin presents an engaging and wide-ranging narrative that covers the entire decade.) In this sense, the study of student activism is a striking example of truncated research: we know a great deal about the interdependent historical and psychosocial roots of the movement and the political socialization of its participants, but relatively little about the continued personal development of those who were or still are involved in New Left activities.
3. Life-history materials are especially suited to the investigation of change over time. As Becker (1970: 424–25) points out: "The life history, more than any other technique except perhaps participant observation, can give meaning to the overworked notion of *process*. Sociologists like to speak of 'ongoing processes' and the like, but their methods usually prevent them from seeing the processes they talk about so glibly. . . . We can . . . give people a questionnaire at two periods in their life and infer an underlying process of change from the difference in their answers. But our interpretation has significance only if our imagery of the underlying process is accurate. And this accuracy of imagery . . . can be partially achieved by the use of life history documents."

4. For more details concerning the procedures used, see Whalen 1984. We also want to emphasize that in building our own story around these stories, we are not asserting that this is the past as it really was; instead, this is how it is remembered as having been (see Fraser 1979: 31–32). This does not create any insurmountable problems in terms of the validity or trustworthiness of the personal narratives, however. We are not primarily concerned with writing a definitive account of protest in Isla Vista or of the history of the New Left but rather with investigating how people responded to the protest and its aftermath: what they felt was happening in their lives and in their society at different points in time and how their views influenced both their personal development and the development of their movement. Where differences of interpretation emerge in these stories, the problem is not so much one of determining which version is "correct" as of understanding what factors might account for the differences.

5. For a detailed elaboration of the history/daily life dynamic and an effort to interpret the American Left in its terms, see Flacks 1988. For an earlier interpretation of New Left aspirations and motivations that makes use of this framework, see Flacks 1976.

6. There is, of course, a sizable literature that deals with this puzzle. Flacks' early research traced the liberation of upper-middle-class activists from conventional status anxieties to specific family and subcultural socialization experiences. This finding was embedded in a broader analysis, arguing that changes in family relations and economic organization, coupled with the experience of growing up in suburban affluence, had seriously eroded the Protestant ethic and undercut established motivations and incentives for competitive achievement and self-discipline (Flacks 1971a; Keniston 1968). We will be evaluating these suppositions in some detail in later pages.

7. From 1960 to 1965, the heroic and saintly image of the organizer was typified by active membership in the Student Non-Violent Coordinating Committee. For a detailed description of the organizer's life in SNCC (especially focusing on white participants), see Mary King's *Freedom Song* (1986).

8. Our choice of this style of presentation recognizes, as historian Carl Schorske (quoted in Henretta 1979: 1314) has emphasized, the close relationship between a book's "mental structure . . . its grammar—the way it gives plausibility to the empirical materials and the tightness of its articulation"—and its interpretation. As another historian, Louis O. Mink (quoted in Henretta 1979: 1318), cogently argues, chronologically arranged narratives can provide us with a deeper understanding of the diverse motives, pressures, circumstances, and ambiguities of individual existence that shape human action. Both from narrative history and fiction, Mink suggests, "we learn how to tell and to understand complex stories" and "how it is that stories answer questions." The fate of the Isla Vista "bank burners" is just this kind of complex story, and we are persuaded that it can best be told through a mosaic of life histories, that is, the experience as it was actually lived by our respondents.

This approach directly addresses questions of time, change, and sequence—
chronological concerns that are at the heart of our analysis.

Chapter 2

1. In addition to the published sources cited in this chapter and the interviews
   with our respondents, our account of the Isla Vista riots draws on numerous
   conversations with other participants and witnesses.
2. This was a purely local student organization, and had no ties to larger state
   or national groupings (such as the similarly named Bay Area Radical Union,
   which became the Revolutionary Communist Party in the late 1970s). UCSB's
   RU was a successor to the campus SDS chapter, which was organized in
   1968 and disbanded a year later.
3. Robert Smith's March 1970 student survey provides more detailed information concerning the extent of participation in the February uprising and
   attitudes toward the violence. From our reading of Smith's unpublished results, it appears that 4 to 6 percent of the students took an active part in
   the rioting. This assessment is based on the number of respondents who
   rated their participation as simply "mildly active" or "very active," or who
   specifically admitted that they helped build street blockades; helped supply
   rocks to the protesters; threw rocks at windows, police cars, or policemen;
   helped set trash fires; or threw fire bombs. Additionally, 17 percent of those
   surveyed reported that they "showed disrespect for the police" at some point
   in the four nights of protest, and roughly 40 percent reported that they were
   "inactive spectators."

   When asked their opinions of the protests and the violence, approximately
   18 percent of the 496 respondents expressed approval of the breaking of
   realty office windows, 13 percent approved of the breaking of windows at
   the Bank of America, 14 percent approved of the burning of the patrol car
   on Wednesday night, and nearly 11 percent expressed approval of the bank
   burning itself. (Note that Smith's survey does not include the nonstudent
   population of Isla Vista; the extent of their participation in or support for the
   uprising cannot be fully assessed.) In terms of the level of opposition to or
   disapproval of the rebellion, Smith's survey found that approximately 60 percent of the students surveyed felt that the violence in Isla Vista was "wanton
   and self-defeating" and close to 48 percent agreed that the violence would
   "lead to more oppression" in the community. These responses have to be
   interpreted against the backdrop of some other figures, however. There was
   even greater disapproval of the escalation of punitive police actions during
   the protests (82.5 percent vs. only 7.8 percent approval), and 43 percent felt
   that the police used excessive force during the disturbances. Perhaps even
   more significantly, one-half of those surveyed felt that "legitimate channels
   of protest (petitions and the like) are not effective means for bringing about
   change," while nearly the same number (47 percent) agreed with the state-

ment that "when grievances pile high and most leaders represent established authority, then violence may be the only effective response" (only 36 percent disagreed).

4. Some appreciation of the number of students who actively participated or were caught up in the 1970 events can be gained by examining the data collected by Robert Smith in a campus survey taken one year after the bank burning. (As nearly 23 percent of those surveyed had not been present in Isla Vista during 1970, all of the following figures underrepresent the actual percentages of students from that year who were variously affected by those events.) Fully 20 percent of those surveyed reported that they had been "very" or "mildly" active in the previous year's protests, with 9 percent reporting that they actually fought the police. When you compare this figure with the approximately 5 percent active involvement in Isla Vista I, the expansion of participation between that first riot and the end of Isla Vista III is evident.

Some other interesting figures: one-third of those surveyed said they had been stopped and questioned by the police, 18 percent said they were caught in police sweeps, over 29 percent reported they had been "severely gassed," almost 6 percent said they had been beaten by the police, and almost 8 percent reported they had been shot at by the police.

Chapter 3

1. Students at Kent State were equally caught up by the vision of revolution. Consider for example, these excerpts from an interview with Ruth Gibson, a KSU activist who witnessed the deadly gunfire of that tragic day in May:

"What did you see coming as you looked ahead in the fall of 1969 or early 1970?"

"Oh, the revolution, of course. I was just absolutely sure that within five to ten years the student movement would become a much broader social movement, one that would encompass many elements and would be stronger and more explicitly socialist. I thought that the movement would unite all the dissident elements—blacks, Mexican-Americans, workers, et cetera—and was just going to topple the government. The government could no longer relate to or express the will of the people. It was an oppressor, a tyrant government; how could it stand?"

"What would happen?"

"I thought that there would be an enormous civil war: a class war, a revolution. A Marxist government would come to power in the United States —not a Soviet-type government, but one which would be responsive to the will of the people, one that would direct the ownership of all major industries by the representatives of the people: the nationalization of all industries. The people would take over the factories. . . . Well, this was on my good days, when I was really exuberant, when I was feeling really positive about everything that I saw going on and I wasn't depressed about the repression that was coming down. Then I'd get this vision: *this is how it could be*" (Bills 1982: 84–85).

2. These figures (including the expectations about "revolution") are based on surveys conducted on a random sample of the UCSB student body in the spring of 1971 by Robert Smith. We are greatly indebted to him for making this data available to us.

3. One additional note: Newhouser was not the only person convicted in the bank-burning trial to go underground. Two others also fled from their sentences, leaving Ed Pines the only one of those found guilty on the misdemeanor charges to serve time in jail.

4. The literature documenting student peer group influence is extensive. Newcomb's classic study of Bennington College in the 1930s (Newcomb 1943) was followed by hundreds of studies showing the ways in which attitude change among college students was mediated by primary associations. See Sanford 1962 for a report and bibliography on this topic.

Chapter 5

1. We also have some more specific, survey-type data on the political behavior and beliefs of our respondents from the early 1980s. In 1982–83, we distributed a short "political attitude and activity" questionnaire to all our respondents. Fifteen activists and fourteen nonactivists completed the entire survey (and one activist completed the Political-Economic Conservatism section but did not complete the Political Activity section). We employed Kerpelman's (1972) Political Activity Scale as a quantitative measure of recent political involvement. This subscale consists of twelve five-point bipolar items that refer to various sociopolitcal activities over the prior three years. Behaviors sampled range from reading political books and magazines to participating in a demonstration, so that the overall score reflects a broad definition of political activity. The questionnaire also included Kerpelman's (1972) Political-Economic Conservation Scale, a twelve-item, seven-point measure of political ideology (or, more specifically, of willingness to endorse conservative philosophy).

While the gathering of this kind of quantitative data represented a departure from the qualitative, life-history approach we had followed to that point, we felt it useful to add to our information in this manner. As these measures are the same ones used by Nassi (1981) in her comparative survey of former Free Speech Movement activists, nonactivist students, and officers of student government, gathering this survey data would allow us to draw contrasts between the resiliency of FSM protesters' political convictions and that of Santa Barbara radicals from the late sixties. The results from both our survey and Nassi's research are presented in the following table.

	Political-Economic Conservatism	Political Activity
Berkeley students		
FSM arrestees	29.9 (30)	22.5 (30)
Student government	43.8 (28)	26.4 (38)
Cross-section	52.2 (23)	20.3 (23)
UCSB respondents		
Activists	26.1 (16)	25.3 (15)
Nonactivists	56.1 (14)	19.4 (14)

The first figure shows mean score (possible range for conservatism is 12–84; for political activity, 12–60). The figure in parentheses shows the number of responses.

Examination of the data in this table reveals that the former UCSB activists were much less likely than the nonactivists to embrace conservative views, as measured by the Political-Economic Conservatism Scale: the mean "conservatism" score of those students who were not active in politics during their years at Santa Barbara (56.1) was much higher than that of the activists (26.1). (The range of conservatism scores in the UCSB activist cohort was 12 to 59.) Additionally, the Santa Barbara activists compare favorably, in terms of enduring liberal and radical proclivities, with the Berkeley radicals surveyed by Nassi. While the range of conservatism scores for the nonactivists was about as wide (26 to 75), only one member scored less than 43, with most scores concentrated toward the higher end of the scale. The mean score among the nonactivists in each sample was almost identical.

Differences between activist and nonactivist cohorts are also apparent when we compare the measures of their political involvement: the mean political activity score of the former UCSB activists (25.3) is nearly six points higher than the mean of the Delta Omega and Kappa Phi group (19.4). In addition, the UCSB radicals have a higher level of recent political involvement than do the FSM arrestees. The scores of the activists on the Political Activity Scale ranged from 14 to 49 (two members of the activist cohort had scores above 31).

Chapter 7

1. In addition to the previously cited work of Flacks, Keniston's 1968 life-history study of fourteen nationally active New Leftists provides important data on the relationship between family background, childhood experience, and activism. Scores of other studies supported and amplified Flacks's and Keniston's findings. (See Keniston 1973 for a book-length bibliographic survey of

this research literature.) Many of the activists interviewed in our study had personal histories that fit the portrait painted by Flacks and Keniston. For a detailed discussion of this sample's personal background, see Whalen 1984.

2. Breines (1982) and Miller (1987) both present insightful analyses of the development of New Left ideology and the personal and political meanings of "participatory democracy." Breines's work is particularly important for its recognition of the tension between this vision of politics and more traditional leftist ideas about organizational and ideological discipline.

3. The extent and impact of left activism in American communities in the aftermath of the sixties remains to be systematically documented. Boyte (1980) makes a preliminary but important contribution in this regard.

4. An interesting early depiction of countercultural disillusionment appears in Kunen (1973).

5. Some commentators on the New Left have suggested that activist youths have gravitated in large numbers to "self-examining" religious and therapeutic communities—"from politics to self-examination" is how Lasch (1979: 43) once described the trajectory. This hypothesis has most recently been proposed in reviews of the new historical studies of the movement. For example, when reviewing the work of Isserman (1987) and Miller (1987), neither of whom attempts a systematic analysis of the New Left's demise, historian Alan Brinkley (1987: 16) concludes with his own explanation for its collapse, an explanation focused on political withdrawal motivated by "the search for . . . the 'Dionysian ego,'" personal fulfillment through "narcissism and erotic exuberance": "Disaffection and rebellion that had once led to political commitment were leading instead to the drug culture, the sexual revolution, the cult of Eastern religions, rock music, and the world of 'hippies' and 'dropouts.' Woodstock and Altamont were replacing Port Huron and the Siege of Chicago as the generation's defining moments. . . . Even some of SDS's most committed early leaders drifted away from politics in their search for 'self-actualization'. . . . The real story of the New Left's demise, then, is . . . the story of the gradually fading political commitment of thousands of young radicals who, having embraced the left as a vehicle for self-fulfillment, abandoned it for other, more immediately gratifying means to the same ends."

The survey studies that have done on the fate of sixties activists (cited in Chapter 1), however, contain no evidence that large numbers of New Left veterans have followed such paths. Moreover, both the published accounts of some former activists (for example, Gitlin 1987; see also the personal accounts of Tom Hayden and Sharon Jeffrey, presented in the concluding chapter of Miller 1987) and our life-history data suggest that withdrawal into countercultural religious or therapeutic lifestyles in the days following the collapse of the mass movement was only a temporary resting place for many individuals who eventually resumed political commitments, albeit in less all-consuming forms. Thus, although the New Left's fundamental commitment to individuality and personal liberation may have become intertwined with the counterculture's preoccupation with self-gratification and pleasure, and may thus have helped to drain energy from the political struggle, few activists completely abandoned their concern for social responsibility and took up hedonistic lifestyles as a result. Indeed, our analysis proposes a very different understanding of the counterculture and its legacy.

6. The literature referred to in the discussion of the new working class includes the following key writings: Levitt 1972; Flacks 1972; Gouldner 1979; Walker 1979.

References

Abramowitz, Stephen I., and Alberta J. Nassi. 1981. "Keeping the Faith: Psychosocial Correlates of Activism Persistence into Middle Adulthood." *Journal of Youth and Adolescence* 10:507–23.

Abrams, Philip. 1982. *Historical Sociology*. Ithaca, N.Y.: Cornell University Press.

Alinsky, Saul D. [1946] 1969. *Reveille for Radicals*. New York: Random House.

Altbach, Philip G., and Robert S. Laufer, eds. 1972. *The New Pilgrims: Youth Protest in Transition*. New York: David McKay.

Becker, Howard. 1970. "The Relevance of Life Histories." In *Sociological Methods: A Sourcebook*, edited by Norman K. Denzin, pp. 419–28. Chicago: Aldine.

Bell, Daniel. 1976. *The Cultural Contradictions of Capitalism*. New York: Basic Books.

Berger, Bennett. 1981. *The Survival of a Counterculture: Ideological Work and Everyday Life Among Rural Communards*. Berkeley: University of California Press.

Bills, Scott L. 1982. "After May 4: 'Kent State Haunts You.'" An interview with Ruth Gibson in *Kent State/May 4: Echoes Through a Decade*, edited by Scott L. Bills, pp. 82–91. Kent, Ohio: Kent State University Press.

Block, Fred. 1978. "The New Left Grows Up." *Working Papers for a New Society*, September–October, pp. 41–49.

Boyte, Harry. 1980. *The Backyard Revolution*. Philadelphia: Temple University Press.

Braungart, Richard G., and Margaret M. Braungart. 1980. "Political Career Patterns of Radical Activists in the 1960s and 1970s." *Sociological Focus* 13:237–54.

———. 1986. "Life Course and Generational Politics." *Annual Review of Sociology* 12:205–31.

Breines, Wini. 1982. *Community and Organization in the New Left, 1962–68*. South Hadley, Mass.: Bergin and Garvey.

Brinkley, Alan. 1987. "Great Days of the Left." *New York Review of Books*, 22 October, pp. 10–16.

Case, John, and Rosemary C. R. Taylor. 1979. *Co-ops, Communes and Collectives: Experiments in Social Change in the 1960s and 1970s.* New York: Pantheon.

California Highway Patrolman. 1970. "Santa Barbara Riot." Vol. 34, no. 2: 15.

Dannefer, Dale. 1984. "Adult Development and Social Theory: A Paradigmatic Reappraisal." *American Sociological Review* 49:100–16.

DeMartini, Joseph R. 1983. "Social Movement Participation: Political Socialization, Generational Consciousness, and Lasting Effects." *Youth and Society* 15:195–223.

——. 1985. "Change Agents and Generational Relationships: A Reevaluation of Mannheim's Problem of Generations." *Social Forces* 64:1–16.

Demereth, Nicholas J., III; Gerald Marwell; and Michael T. Aiken. 1971. *Dynamics of Idealism.* San Francisco: Josey-Bass.

Draper, Hal. 1965. *Berkeley: The New Student Revolt.* New York: Grove.

Eisenstadt, S. N. 1956. *From Generation to Generation: Age Groups and Social Structure.* New York: Free Press.

Erikson, Erik. 1968. *Identity: Youth and Crisis.* New York: Norton.

Fendrich, James M. 1974. "Activists Ten Years Later: A Test of Generational Unit Continuity." *Journal of Social Issues* 30, no. 3: 95–118.

——. 1976. "Black and White Activists Ten Years Later: Political Socialization and Adult Left-Wing Politics." *Youth and Society* 8:81–104.

——. 1977. "Keeping the Faith or Pursuing the Good Life: A Study in the Consequences of Participation in the Civil Rights Movement." *American Sociological Review* 42:144–57.

Fendrich, James Max, and Kenneth L. Lovoy. 1988. "Back to the Future: Adult Political Behavior of Former Student Activists." *American Sociological Review* 53:780–84.

Fendrich, James M., and Alison T. Tarleau. 1973. "Marching to a Different Drummer: Occupational and Political Correlates of Former Student Activists." *Social Forces* 52:245–53.

Flacks, Richard. 1967. "The Liberated Generation: An Exploration of the Roots of Student Protest." *Journal of Social Issues* 23:52–75.

——. 1970. "Who Protests: The Social Bases of the Student Movement." In *Protest! Student Activism in America*, edited by Julian Foster and Durward Long, pp. 134–57. New York: William Morrow.

——. 1971a. *Youth and Social Change.* Chicago: Markham.

——. 1971b. "Revolt of the Young Intelligentsia: Revolutionary Class Consciousness in Post-Scarcity America." In *The New American Revolution*, edited by Roderick Aya and Norman Miller, pp. 223–63. New York: Free Press.

——. 1972. "On the New Working Class and Strategies for Social Change." In *The New Pilgrims: Youth Protest in Transition*, edited by Philip G. Altbach and Robert S. Laufer, pp. 85–98. New York: David McKay.

——. 1976. "Making History vs. Making Life: Dilemmas of an American Left." *Sociological Inquiry* 46:263–80.

——. 1988. *Making History: The American Left and the American Mind.* New York: Columbia University Press.

Flacks, Richard, and Milton Mankoff. 1970. "Why They Burned the Bank." *The Nation*, 23 March, pp. 337–40.

Foss, Daniel A., and Ralph Larkin. 1976. "From 'The Gates of Eden' to 'The Day of the Locust': An Analysis of the Dissident Youth Movement of the 1960s and Its Heirs of the Early 1970s—The Post-Movement Groups." *Theory and Society* 3:45–64.

———. 1979. "Roar of the Lemming: Youth, Post-Movement Groups and the Life-Construction Crisis." *Sociological Inquiry* 49:264–89.

Fraser, Ronald. 1979. *Blood of Spain: An Oral History of the Spanish Civil War*. New York: Pantheon.

Gitlin, Todd. 1972. "The Future of an Effusion: How Young Activists Will Get to 1984." In *1984 Revisited*, edited by Robert Paul Wolfe. New York: Knopf.

———. 1980. *The Whole World Is Watching: Mass Media in the Making and Unmaking of the New Left*. Berkeley: University of California Press.

———. 1987. *The Sixties: Years of Hope, Days of Rage*. New York: Bantam.

Gitlin, Todd, and Michael Kazin. 1988. "Second Thoughts." *Tikkun* 3, no. 1:49–52.

Goertzel, Ted George. 1972. "Generational Revolt and Social Change." *Youth and Society* 3:327–52.

Gouldner, Alvin W. 1979. *The Future of Intellectuals and the Rise of the New Class*. New York: Seabury Press.

Haber, Barbara, and Allen Haber. [1967] 1969. "Getting by with a Little Help from Our Friends." In *The New Left: A Collection of Essays*, edited by Priscilla Long, pp. 289–309. Boston: Porter Sargent.

Harrington, Michael. 1986. *The Next Left*. New York: Henry Holt.

Henretta, James. 1979. "Social History as Lived and Written." *American Historical Review* 84:1293–1322.

Hoge, Dean R., and Teresa L. Ankney. 1982. "Occupations and Attitudes of Former Student Activists Ten Years Later." *Journal of Youth and Adolescence* 11:355–71.

Hurst, John. 1980. "Isla Vista—Ten Years as a Symbol of a Violent Era." *Los Angeles Times*, 25 February.

Isserman, Maurice. 1987. *If I Had a Hammer . . . The Death of the Old Left and the Birth of the New Left*. New York: Basic Books.

Jacobs, Harold. 1978. "The Personal and the Political: A Study of the Decline of the New Left." Ph.D. dissertation, University of California, Berkeley.

Jennings, M. Kent. 1987. "Residues of a Movement: The Aging of the American Protest Generation." *American Political Science Review* 81:367–82.

Johnston, David. 1982. " 'Flower Child' Era Survivor Perseveres." *Los Angeles Times*, 14 November.

Kanter, Rosabeth, ed. 1973. *Communes: Creating and Managing the Collective Life*. New York: Harper and Row.

Keniston, Kenneth. 1968. *Young Radicals: Notes on Committed Youth*. New York: Harcourt Brace Jovanovich.

———. 1971. *Youth and Dissent: The Rise of a New Opposition*. New York: Harcourt Brace Jovanovich.

————. 1973. *Radicals and Militants: An Annotated Bibliography*. Lexington, Mass.: Lexington Books.

Kerpelman, Lawrence C. 1972. *Activists and Nonactivists: A Psychological Study of American College Students*. New York: Behavioral Publications.

King, Mary. 1986. *Freedom Song: A Personal Story of the Nineteen-Sixty's Civil Rights Movement*. New York: Morrow.

Kunen, James. 1973. "The Rebels of '70." *New York Times Magazine*, 28 October, p. 22.

Lasch, Christopher. 1979. *The Culture of Narcissism: American Life in an Age of Diminishing Expectations*. New York: Norton.

Laufer, Robert S. 1976. "Institutionalization of Radical Movements and the Maintenance of Radical Identity in the Life Cycle." *Youth and Society* 7:367–98.

Levitt, Cyrill. 1972. *Children of Privilege*. Toronto: University of Toronto Press.

Lipset, Seymour Martin, ed. 1967. *Student Politics*. New York: Basic Books.

————. 1971. *Rebellion in the University*. Chicago: University of Chicago Press.

Loomis, Edward. 1970. *Bank Burning: A Documentary Novel*. Santa Barbara: Capricorn Press.

Lubell, Samuel. 1968. "That 'Generation Gap.'" *Public Interest* 13:52–60.

Mankoff, Milton, and Richard Flacks. 1972. "The Changing Social Base of the American Student Movement." In *The New Pilgrims: Youth Protest in Transition*, edited by Philip G. Altbach and Robert S. Laufer, pp. 46–62. New York: David McKay.

Mannheim, Karl. [1928] 1972. "The Problem of Generations." In *The New Pilgrims: Youth Protest in Transition*, edited by Philip G. Altbach and Robert S. Laufer, pp. 101–38. New York: David McKay.

Mansbridge, Jane J. 1980. *Beyond Adversary Democracy*. Chicago: University of Chicago Press.

Marwell, Gerald; Michael T. Aiken; and Nicholas J. Demereth III. 1987. "The Persistence of Political Attitudes Among 1960s Civil Rights Activists." *Public Opinion Quarterly* 51:359–75.

Matza, David. 1961. "Subterranean Traditions of Youth." *Annals of the American Academy of Political and Social Science* 338 (November): 102–18.

Miller, James. 1987. *"Democracy Is in the Streets": From Port Huron to the Siege of Chicago*. New York: Simon and Schuster.

Nassi, Alberta J. 1981. "Survivors of the Sixties: Comparative Psychosocial and Political Development of Former Berkeley Student Activists." *American Psychologist* 36:753–61.

Nassi, Alberta J., and Stephen I. Abramowitz. 1979. "Transition or Transformation? Personal and Political Development of Former Berkeley Free Speech Movement Activists." *Journal of Youth and Adolescence* 8:21–35.

Newcomb, Theodore M. 1943. *Personality and Social Change*. New York: Dryden.

O'Brien, Jim. 1978. "American Leninism in the 1970s." *Radical America* 11, no. 6: 27–62.

Potter, Robert A., and James J. Sullivan. 1970. *The Campus by the Sea Where the*

Bank Burned Down: A Report on the Disturbances at UCSB and Isla Vista, 1968–70. Santa Barbara: Faculty and Clergy Observers Program.

President's Commission on Campus Unrest. 1970. *The Report of the President's Commission on Campus Unrest.* Washington, D.C.: U.S. Government Printing Office.

Ramparts. 1970. "Editorial." Vol. 8, no. 11 (May): 4.

Reich, Charles. 1970. *The Greening of America.* New York: Random House.

Reisman, David. 1950. *The Lonely Crowd.* New Haven: Yale University Press.

Rothschild, Joyce, and Allen J. Whitt. 1986. *The Cooperative Workplace.* Cambridge: Cambridge University Press.

Rozsak, Theodore. 1969. *The Making of a Counterculture.* Garden City, N.Y.: Doubleday.

Sale, Kirkpatrick. 1974. *SDS.* New York: Vintage Books.

Sanford, Nevitt. 1962. *The American College.* New York: Wiley.

Santa Barbara Citizens' Commission on Civil Disorder. 1970. *Report of the Santa Barbara Citizens' Commission on Civil Disorder.* Santa Barbara: Santa Barbara Citizens' Commission on Civil Disorder.

Smith, Robert B. 1971. "The Vietnam War and Student Militancy." *Social Science Quarterly* 52:133–56.

———. 1980. "Why the Bank Burned: Grievances, Delegitimacy, and Political Alienation." Manuscript.

Stickney, John. 1971. "The Burning of America." *Fusion* 63 (October): 14–20.

Strategic Hamlet. 1970. 14–28 October.

Thompson, William Irwin. 1967. *The Imagination of an Insurrection: Dublin, Easter 1916.* New York: Harper and Row.

Walker, Pat, ed. 1979. *Between Labor and Capital.* Boston: South End Press.

Weider, Larry, and Don H. Zimmerman. 1976. "Becoming a Freak: Pathways into the Counter-Culture." *Youth and Society* 7:311–44.

Whalen, Jack. 1981. "Understanding the Aftermath of Rebellion: Some Observations on Sixties Student Protest." Paper presented at the annual meeting of the American Sociological Association, Toronto, August.

———. 1984. "Echoes of Rebellion: The New Left Grows Up." Ph.D. dissertation, University of California, Santa Barbara.

Whalen, Jack, and Richard Flacks. 1980. "The Isla Vista 'Bank Burners' Ten Years Later: Notes on the Fate of Student Activists." *Sociological Focus* 13:215–36.

———. 1982. "Sixties Student Activists Face the Eighties." *Radical Teacher* 21:4–7.

———. 1984. "Echoes of Rebellion: The Liberated Generation Grows Up." *Journal of Political and Military Sociology* 12:61–78.

Yankelovich, Daniel. 1981. *New Rules: Searching for Self-Fulfillment in a World Turned Upside Down.* New York: Random House.

Index